Theological
Reflections

Theological Reflections

Essays on Related Themes

by

Henry Stob

William B. Eerdmans Publishing Company
Grand Rapids, Michigan

Copyright © 1981 by Wm. B. Eerdmans Publishing Co.
255 Jefferson Ave. SE, Grand Rapids, Mich. 49503

Library of Congress Cataloging in Publication Data

Stob, Henry, 1908–
  Theological reflections.

  1. Theology—Addresses, essays, lectures.
I. Title.
BR85.S79   230′.57   81-1472
ISBN 0-8028-1881-1   AACR2

To
Amy and Elizabeth Van Dyk
and
Rebecca and Paul Stob

We gratefully acknowledge permission to reprint the articles listed below.

For Part I:

"Christianity and the Rise of Modern Science" from *Christianity Today*, October 22, 1965. Copyright © 1965.

"Faith and Science," an essay first appearing as a series of articles in the April, May, July, August, and September issues of *The Reformed Journal*, 1965.

"Miracles," an essay first appearing in *Christianity Today*, July 3, 1961, copyright © 1961; later used as Chapter 13 in *Basic Christian Doctrines*, ed. C. F. H. Henry (New York: Holt and Rinehart, 1962).

For Part II:

"Some Issues in Philosophy" from *The Reformed Journal*, September 1965.

"Notes on the Philosophy of St. Augustine" from the *Calvin Theological Journal*, Vol. 8, No. 2, November 1973.

"On Taking Too Much Philosophy" from *The Reformed Journal*, January and February 1953.

For Part III:

"The Death-of-God Theology," an essay first appearing as a series of articles in the March, September, and November issues of *The Reformed Journal*, 1966.

"Calvin and Aquinas" from *The Reformed Journal*, May–June 1974.

"A Note to Young Seminarians" from *The Calvin Forum*, January 1950.

For Part IV:

"Jesus and the Old Testament" from *The Reformed Journal*, January 1955.

"The Doctrine of Revelation in St. Paul" from the *Calvin Theological Journal*, November 1966.

"Philosophy and the Bible," an essay first appearing as Chapter IV in *The Word of God and the Reformed Faith*, edited by C. Bouma. Copyright © 1943 by Baker Book House.

For Part V:

"The Mind of the Church" from *The Reformed Journal*, March 1957.

"The Mind of Safety" from *The Reformed Journal*, April 1957.

"The Militant Mind," an essay first appearing as a series of articles in the June, July–August, and October issues of *The Reformed Journal*, 1957.

"The Positive Mind" from *The Reformed Journal*, March 1961.

"On Church Leadership" from *The Reformed Journal*, March 1951.

"Tradition and the Church" from *The Reformed Journal*, December 1951.

For Part VI:

"Note to a College Freshman" from *The Reformed Journal*, September 1952; the response to its criticism appeared in the April 1953 issue.

"Academic Freedom at a Christian College" from *The Reformed Journal*, August 1952.

"Moral Education" from *The Reformed Journal*, September 1962.

"Catechesis: On Using and Revising the Compendium" from *The Reformed Journal*, January and May 1952.

Contents

Preface   ix

Part I
Science

1 Christianity and the Rise of Modern Science   3
2 Faith and Science   9
3 Miracles   23

Part II
Philosophy

4 What Is Philosophy?   31
5 Some Issues in Philosophy   35
6 Notes on the Philosophy of St. Augustine   43
7 Personality, Human and Divine   54
8 On Taking Too Much Philosophy   64

Part III
Theology

9 The Warrant for Theology in a Scientific Age   75

10   Prayer and Providence   84
11   The Death-of-God Theology   94
12   Christianity and Other Religions   116
13   Calvin and Aquinas   126
14   A Note to Young Seminarians   131

Part IV
Revelation

15   Jesus and the Old Testament   139
16   The Doctrine of Revelation in St. Paul   147
17   The Logos Doctrine in John   164
18   Philosophy and the Bible   173

Part V
Church

19   The Mind of the Church   183
20   The Mind of Safety   187
21   The Militant Mind   195
22   The Positive Mind   210
23   On Church Leadership   218
24   Tradition and the Church   222

Part VI
Education

25   Note to a College Freshman   229
26   Academic Freedom at a Christian College   240
27   Moral Education   244
28   Catechesis: On Using and Revising the Compendium   253
29   The Shape of Excellence   263

Preface

THIS VOLUME contains some of the occasional papers and addresses which, in the course of years, were delivered to restricted audiences or published in journals with a limited circulation. At the time of delivery they were not unfavorably received by the well-disposed, and they are now presented to a wider world in the tremulous hope that they will be similarly received by an indulgent public. They are presented not as daring ventures into unexplored regions of inquiry, but as the tracings of a learner's unspectacular journey through accustomed provinces of knowledge.

Although the essays span diverse fields, they are articulated within a uniform perspective and are bound together by a pervasive theological interest and concern, on which account they have been called theological reflections.

The essays are of unequal length and doubtless of unequal quality, but they are left to stand as reflections of longer and shorter walks through valleys as well as plains, through thickets as well as open spaces.

As the dedication indicates, they are offered as a restricted legacy to my grandchildren, and along with them to all who love the appearance of the Lord Jesus Christ or who by these writings may be enticed to enter into his fellowship.

—Henry Stob

Part I

SCIENCE

1

Christianity and the Rise of Modern Science

MODERN NATURAL SCIENCE, which received its charter in the seventeenth century, arose in Christendom during the century which produced the Protestant Reformation. This leads one to ask two important questions: Is modern natural science the offspring of Christianity? and, more particularly, Was it cradled in the Reformation? In answering these questions Christians in general and Protestants in particular must be careful neither to claim nor to disclaim too much.

It is a fact that modern science arose in Europe not before but only after the continent was Christianized, and that it arose independently in no other part of the earth. This suggests that it owes much to Christian principles, which indeed it does. But, of course, it is also in debt to ancient Greece and Rome, as are all things occidental. In its pure form it articulates the Christian mind, but it is not divorced from the Hellenic scientific tradition which culminated in Aristotle, nor is it a stranger to the Latin sense of order which was transmitted to the Middle Ages by the Stoics. Its lineage is complex.

Modern natural science did not arise under pagan auspices, nor did it arise when the Roman Catholic understanding of Christianity was dominant in Europe. This suggests that for its emergence something was needed which neither medieval Christianity nor the revived paganism of the humanistic Renaissance could or did supply. Did the Reformation then supply that which was needed? Did it touch off the scientific explosion? There are indi-

This essay first appeared as "A Firm Foundation for Modern Science" in *Christianity Today*, October 22, 1965.

cations that it did, but Protestants are here obliged to press their claims with care. There is no doubt that certain Christian principles, tending to stimulate men's interest in God's creation but lying dormant or compromised during the Middle Ages, were disclosed and vigorously proclaimed in the Reformation. There is also no doubt that the Reformed teaching tended to draw men into a study of nature, for among the pioneers of the new science were numerous adherents of the evangelical faith. Yet it is a fact that Copernicus, Kepler, Galileo, Descartes, and many other distinguished scientists were loyal sons of the Roman Church. To accommodate this fact it is not necessary, however, to withdraw the Protestant claim. It remains true that the Reformation purged and clarified the biblical conceptions which, when accepted and implemented, worked regeneratively in science. What must be acknowledged, however, is that the new understanding of Christianity thus attained was not absolutely new, nor could it be contained behind ecclesiastical walls; it bore relation to what had previously been confessed, and it worked as a leaven throughout the Christian Church. In view of this, it is perhaps best to say that it was Christianity that supplied the firm foundation for modern natural science, and that the Reformation was used by God so to delineate this foundation as to dispose men to build on it the vast new structure of science.

I shall here make no attempt to set forth, or even to enumerate, all those points of Christian teaching which tended to evoke, and did in fact support, the new science of the sixteenth and seventeenth centuries. But I do propose to consider the three points of doctrine—the teachings concerning God, man, and nature in their interrelations—that appear to impinge most immediately upon the scientific enterprise, and which N. Berdyaev may have had in view when he declared, "I am convinced that Christianity alone made possible both positive science and technics" (*The Meaning of History*, p. 113).

I.

A fundamental affirmation of Christianity is that nature is a revelation of God. This entails at least two further affirmations: nature can be known and nature ought to be known.

A. In Christian teaching God is the all-knowing One who created all things after the counsel of his plan and who has since regulated and disposed them in accordance with his good and all-wise purposes. This means that nature proclaims the "admirable wisdom" of God, a wisdom that is accessible, within the limits of finitude, to those who are created in God's image. It means that nature is shot through with rationality and thus intrinsically intelligible.

The Greeks never attained this conception of nature's intelligibility.

God was for Plato and Aristotle intelligent enough—he was indeed pure thought and perfect rationality; but he was not infinite and omnipotent. Beside him there existed an independent and essentially intractable matter, which could not be completely "formed" or rationalized. A natural thing or process in its empirical concreteness could therefore never be completely known—not even by God: it always retained a residue of irrationality and unintelligibility. This is one of the reasons why a natural science, as distinct from a philosophy of essences, was never developed among the Greeks.

It was only after the Greek notion of material intractability and mathematical inprecision, also in its attenuated medieval form, was abandoned by the Protestant Reformation that the way was opened for natural science to go forward. Science, if it is to proceed with vigor and confidence, must believe that a recognizable pattern is to be found in nature. But modern science is animated by this belief, and it is this even since the promulgation of Planck's Quantum Theory and Heisenberg's Principle of Indeterminacy. And the origin of this belief is plain. As A. E. Taylor says, "The conception of God as perfect and flawless intelligence is manifestly the source of our rooted belief in the presence of intelligible order and system throughout nature: it has created the intellectual temper from which modern science itself has arisen" (*Does God Exist?*, p. 2).

B. But the fact that nature is a revelation of God entails not only that nature can be known but also that it ought to be known. That it ought to be known, and therefore diligently studied, the Reformers never ceased to declare. Nature, they taught, was a book to be read or, more dynamically considered, a discourse to be heard; and no Christian with the requisite talents may absolve himself from attending to it. The traces of God's steps, the patterns of his wisdom, the signs of his power, and the evidences of his glory are in nature, and these are to be carefully observed.

Stimulated and driven forward by this idea, men like Bacon, Boeckman, Boyle, Harvey, Newton, and Ray—men of massive intellect, consuming curiosity, and authentic Christian piety—went out to nature and helped determine the structure and direction of modern science. And men of like mind and similar Christian faith have appeared upon the plane of science in every generation since. In the nineteenth century it was Davey, Faraday, Joule, Kelvin, Maxwell. They were devout Christians all, and it was their religion which enlisted them for science. The power of the Christian idea, accented in the Reformation, that God wants to be heard and read in general as well as in special revelation, forced the Christian scientists of the sixteenth and seventeenth centuries to make the same patient inquiries of nature that the conscientious theologians made of Scripture.

In the course of their investigations theologians and scientists might sometimes arrive at incompatible conclusions, but both sorts of men knew that the message of nature and of Scripture was of one piece, and that where a difference appeared a mistake in reading had been made. What both understood, perhaps better than some of us do today, is that the Bible is not to be interpreted in every place with strict literalness, nor to be regarded as a textbook on science. It would have been impossible for Calvin, for example, to oppose the Copernican theory on the ground that the inspired author of Psalm 96 had declared that "the world is established, it shall never be moved" (vs. 10). He was too astute a student of the Bible to regard it as a purveyor of scientific lore. "He who would learn astronomy and other recondite arts," he said in commenting on Genesis 1:15,16, "let him go elsewhere. . . . The history of the creation . . . is the book of the unlearned."

II.

A second fundamental affirmation of Christianity is that nature is subject to man. The late M. Foster has pointed out a difference between ancient and modern attitudes to nature. "On the ancient view," he says, "man is a part of nature and his true destiny is to conform himself to it, 'to live according to nature'. . . . In modern times science has acquired a different aim, that of mastery over nature" (*Free University Quarterly*, May 1959, p. 126). This is true. Bacon in his *Instauratio* celebrates and recommends the "dominion" of man, and Descartes in his *Discourse on Method* contemplates men as "lords and possessors of nature." As a consequence of this attitude, science has produced in modern times a technical civilization such as antiquity never did or could produce.

The idea that man, through science, is called upon to "control" or "subjugate" nature comes, of course, from the Scriptures, and it was pressed upon the consciousness of men by the Reformers. It roots in the divine mandate: "God said to them, . . . fill the earth and subdue it; and have dominion . . ." (Gen. 1:28). Bacon's conception of the "Kingdom of Man" may seem to some to be indicative of humanistic pride, and it must be acknowledged that the conception readily lends itself to secularization and perversion, but in Bacon's usage it was a simple translation of Psalm 8:5,6: "Thou hast made him little less than God, and dost crown him with glory and honor. Thou hast given him dominion over the works of thy hands; thou hast put all things under his feet."

It must be admitted, and even emphasized, that the aim of science in Christian perspective is not merely "control." The aim, as the Greeks discerned, is also "understanding." And even more importantly, it is "praise." It is significant that Psalm 8, which celebrates the "Kingdom of Man," ends with the words "O Lord, our Lord, how majestic is thy name in all the earth." This indicates that "control" must always be by a man in subjection to God, by a man, that is, who in religious fear stands humbly before his Maker, and who in strict obedience to God's law of love directs his dominion towards the true betterment of man.

Having said this, however, it must be acknowledged that "control of nature" is an authentic biblical idea, and that it is in modern science only because it was first in Christianity. Because it is a Christian idea, the Christian is justified neither in lamenting the existence of technology nor in setting arbitrary limits upon man's jurisdiction. The splitting of the atom, the exploration of space, the colonization of habitable planets, the sowing of clouds to make rain—all this and more is the prerogative of the man who in subjection to God is lord of nature.

III.

A third fundamental affirmation of Christianity is that nature is created. This entails at least two further affirmations: nature has a beginning and nature is contingent.

A. In the view of Greek science, nature (*physis*) was an organism that grows (*phyesthai*), and not a thing or machine that is made. Nature was a self-generating, eternal, divine being that had no beginning. It was the living, throbbing, but impersonal reproductive matrix from which all things—even the gods—arose and into which they were periodically resolved. The consequences of this conception were many and diverse, but one of them was that Greek science put the emphasis not on efficient but on final causes. Not beginnings but ends were in focus. In modern science the opposite is true. Final causes, considered as immanent explanatory principles, have been banished altogether, and explanations are made in terms of efficient causes only.

The reason for this shift is basically a Christian one. It was stated succinctly by Newton in his *Principia*: "This Being (God) governs all things, not as the soul of the world, but as Lord over all" (*Scholium Generale*). What is here said is that nature is not divine, but creaturely; not eternal, but temporal; not self-generating, but made. The events and processes that occur in it are not self-caused, but they occur through the play upon them of a power from without. The ultimate explanation of their behavior is the transcendent God, who in and with time made nature out of nothing.

The banishment from nature of innate final causes was a great gain for science, and it was effected directly by the Christian teaching concerning creation. By the force of that teaching, which was compromised in medieval times by a foreign alliance with Greek modes of thought, the Reformers effected the death of Greek animism. Appetites, natural tendencies, sympathies, and attractions became moribund concepts, and the way was opened for the development of the classical Newtonian physics, and indeed for every later development in modern science.

To Christians, who believe that all things exist for the glory of God, it may appear unfortunate that, under Christian auspices, modern science should banish all final causes and deal only with efficient causes. But as A. F. Smethurst correctly observes, Bacon, Descartes, and Newton "did not suggest that there are no final causes, but only that these are not the concern of natural science. Nor did they mean that there is no purpose in nature, but only that such a purpose cannot be discovered by scientific, experimental, empirical methods" (*Modern Science and Christian Belief*, p. 23). No doubt they were right.

B. Greek science, like Greek thought generally, was rationalistic. The Greek mind supposed it knew beforehand what things were like. This is evident in Greek theology. Whereas the Hebrew knew he had to be told by God himself what He was like, the Greek supposed that he already possessed a pattern of perfection in terms of which he could challenge every claimant to divinity. In science, too, the Greek proceeded apriorily. He supposed he knew, for example, that there cannot be any change in heavenly bodies and that they cannot move except in circles. In the words of Professor Hooykaas, for the Greeks "that which is not comprehensible is hardly real, and what is not logically necessary but contingent is considered a defect in nature, hardly worth to be studied." But, he continues, "the Christian physicists of the seventeenth century—Pascal, Boyle, and Newton—did not recognize an intrinsic necessity of physical events. In their opinion regularity of the sequence of events depends wholly on the will of God" (*Free University Quarterly*, Oct. 1961).

It was when this conception entered fully into the consciousness of men through the mediation of the Reformers that authentic empiricism was born. Modern science is nothing if not empirical, but the origin of this feature is found in Christianity. In the Christian view God is the creator and nature is radically contingent. What happens in it the scientist can learn only through careful observation. What can or cannot happen in it he does not know beforehand, because here as everywhere he must wait upon God's revelatory activity.

2

Faith and Science

IN THIS ESSAY I shall attempt a discussion of a problem that is agitating the mind of not a few of us nowadays—the problem of the relation that Christian faith sustains to scientific activity.

That such a relation exists is generally acknowledged in Protestant circles. Evidence of this acknowledgment is found not only in innumerable writings issuing from the Evangelical Press, but also, quite concretely, in the vast system of Christian schools established by religious people both in this country and abroad. These schools, not the least the schools of higher learning, bear witness to the Christian conviction that a relation does in fact exist between belief and learning, faith and reason, religion and knowledge, Christianity and science.

* * * * *

Yet despite this wide and basic agreement among members of the Christian community, differences come into view whenever an attempt is made to specify more exactly the nature and significance of the acknowledged relation. When such attempts are made, questions arise that indicate that it is not entirely clear to us what it is we are saying when we say that Christianity has scientific or noetic implications. The questions that trouble us are of the following sort:

Just what is the role of the subject or knower in knowledge; and what is the role of the object or thing known? Is the Christian committed to epis-

This essay first appeared in *The Reformed Journal*, April, May, July, August, and September 1955.

temological subjectivism? Must the Christian repudiate scientific "objectiv-ity"?

Is grace creative or restorative? Does it bring into being a wholly new creature or does it merely restore an already existing creature, man, whose essential nature sin did not and cannot destroy?

Does regeneration bring with it new and unique powers of perception and inference? Does it provide a new and different logic? Does it demand employment of a special scientific method?

Does faith so influence observation and reflection that the conclusions arrived at by Christians differ in every respect from those arrived at by non-Christians?

Does faith add a new dimension to a body of knowledge that we hold in common with non-Christians, or does it preclude or destroy all commonness?

Is Christian science continuous or discontinuous with non-Christian science? Or do the two overlap? Or are they in conflict at every point?

Does the antithesis permit or does it forbid cooperation between Chris-tians and non-Christians in scientific research?

Can the unbeliever discover truth? Is the unregenerate's mind all dark-ness, or is there a Light that lighteth every man? Can one who stands in rebellion against God effectually silence the divine witness in his soul and in the world, and thus be ignorant of God and of his world?

Is there a common or neutral stock of information about the world which anyone must embrace regardless of whether he is a Christian or a non-Christian, and regardless of who gathered the information?

Such are the questions—and I have given but a sampling—that remain after it has been agreed that Christian faith has a direct and important bearing on the scientific enterprise.

*   *   *   *   *

I do not presume that I am able to provide a final answer to all of these vexing questions. The final answer, I presume, will not be provided by any one of us, but by all of us together after we have entered into extended conversation with each other. The construction of a Christian philosophy of science requires the cooperation of the entire Christian community.

I shall therefore attempt a smaller, though, I dare say, a not less neces-sary job. I shall attempt to delineate a single problem, and in the process consider some of the differences and agreements that exist among us.

I begin by stating a fact that all of us can immediately and directly verify. The statement of this fact will lead us straight into our problem.

*   *   *   *   *

The fact is that though all of us recognize Christianity as a total com-mitment that embraces the whole of life, there are things which, we believe, cannot properly be qualified as Christian. Whereas we do not hesitate to use the term "Christian" to modify some nouns, we refuse to use the term to modify other nouns.

Thus we do not hesitate to qualify education as Christian and to use the term "Christian education," but we hesitate to speak of "Christian basketball." The term "Christian politics" is quite acceptable to us, but we never speak of a "Christian ballot box" or of a "Christian voting machine." We may speak of "Christian art," but we do not speak of a "Christian brush" or of a "Christian chisel."

The reason for this need not be considered at this juncture. It is enough now to observe the simple fact that we Christians, who are concerned to leave no area of life unclaimed for Christ, nevertheless refuse to speak of certain things as "Christian," and refuse to do so not because these things are in their nature anti-Christian, but because they are simply neutral entities which cannot bear a religious label of any sort whatever.

We recognize, to be sure, that these things can be used for Christ or against him, but we also sense that, in themselves, and as such, these things are neither Christian nor anti-Christian. They simply *are*, being definable in terms of their inherent nature and function, irrespective of who makes, contemplates, or uses them, and to what end.

But now the question comes: Is this also true of certain sciences? Do we make, and are we authorized to make, a distinction among the sciences similar to the distinction we make among other things? Can a man recognize Christianity as a total commitment that embraces the whole of life, and nevertheless believe that certain of the sciences cannot be qualified as Christian? Can the adjective "Christian" be significantly joined to some of the sciences, and less significantly joined, or not joined at all, to others of them? Do some of them stand so close to the central affirmations of the faith that they cannot but take on the color and visage of Christianity; and are some of them, on the other hand, so far removed from these same affirmations as to leave them without any Christian character at all?

To be concrete: Can a formal science or a science of nature be "Christian"? All of us are prepared to acknowledge the existence of a "Christian theology"; are we equally prepared to say that there is or can be a "Christian mathematics"? The meaningfulness of the term "Christian philosophy" we readily concede; but how about "Christian chemistry"? We are sure that there is a "Christian ethics"; do we think there is a "Christian logic"? And what of linguistics? Is, or can there be, a "Christian grammar"?

*　*　*　*　*

Our answer to these questions matters, for these questions are concerned with nothing less than the relation that Christianity bears to our ongoing scientific efforts. The answer we give will disclose how we conceive of that relation, and also how we conceive of Christianity and of science. Involved in our answer, whatever it be, is indeed a whole theology, for every answer will imply some view concerning the role of faith in knowledge, the range and scope of sin's destructive power, and the nature and extent of grace, both special and common.

I shall make no direct attempt to lay all these issues bare. I shall merely review the answers given to the central problem posed, namely: How are we to conceive the relation of Christianity to science—more particularly, to the exact or quantitative sciences?

There are, as I see it, three answers in the field. I do not dare dogmatically to affirm that they exhaust the possibilities, though I suspect they do. In any case all of them are alive in our world, and worth our consideration.

I. DICHOTOMISM

There are those in the Christian church—I call them dichotomists for reasons that will presently appear—who believe that it is absurd to speak of a "Christian mathematics." They deny that faith and grace bear such a *special* relation to the formal and exact sciences as would warrant our calling these sciences "Christian." They think of geometry and chemistry in strict analogy to *things*. They regard the quantitative sciences as being no more amenable to religious qualification than a hammer or a tea-cup. The term "Christian physics," in their view, makes as much and as little sense as the term "Christian automobile." Both terms, they think, are meaningless.

Those who think this way I call *dichotomists*. I call them this because they *cut* the body of science *in two*. They separate the several sciences which constitute the single organism of knowledge into two disparate groups. One group embraces all the sciences that deal with *man*, the other all the sciences that deal with *things* or *relations*. Those in the first group are known as the human or *spiritual* sciences, those in the other as the *natural* and *formal* sciences. The spiritual sciences the dichotomist believes to be modifiable by sin and grace; the natural and formal sciences he believes to be impervious to these. The former are thought to sustain a special relation to Christianity; the latter are thought to sustain no such relation. In this view there is such a thing as a "Christian ethics," but there is no such thing as a "Christian grammar."

*   *   *   *   *

The denial of any *special* relation of Christianity to the exact sciences does not, of course, involve the dichotomist in a denial of the *general* relevance of Christian truth to the scientific enterprise.

As a Christian the dichotomist acknowledges the relevance to all science—including the quantitative sciences—of the Christian doctrine of *creation*. He knows that unless there were God, an intelligible world of nature, and a race of men fitted to explore it, there could be no science at all. But he observes that, were there no Creator and no creation, there would be no hammer, either. He observes, indeed, that were there no Creator there would also be no non-Christian science, since this too is possible only in a God-created and God-sustained universe. The mere fact, therefore, that creation is the precondition of all things human does not entitle us to call the natural sciences "Christian." Were that the case, we would have to call all things without exception "Christian."

Nor does the dichotomist ignore the fact of sin. He acknowledges that its curse lies over all, and he everywhere observes its crippling effects. He holds, however, that sin has not destroyed nature—either physical or human. It has not annihilated physical facts, it has not abrogated nature's laws, it has not robbed man of his ability either to perceive or to think. Thus all men, in spite of sin, can, within the limits of their finitude, know the facts and laws of nature, and it is precisely this knowledge which we call objective science.

Moreover, he observes, there is a grace of God as wide and universal as the fact of sin. This common grace is, or is accompanied by, a general operation of God's Spirit that qualifies *all* men to attain to truths, not indeed about God and the supernatural, but yet about nature and its processes; and it is precisely this knowledge that Christian and non-Christian hold in common within the framework of those sciences that we call natural or exact. It will not do, therefore, to call these sciences "Christian." They are common.

The dichotomist does not wish in all this to deny the existence of the special grace that saves, the importance of a living personal faith, or the significance of both for our knowledge and understanding of the deep and ultimate things of life. He acknowledges that grace and faith radically affect our capacity to attain a total view of the cosmos, and to know its origin and goal. Grace and faith, he recognizes, are the very fashioners of our philosophy. They make their influence felt, too, and that significantly, in all those spiritual and humane studies that deal with norms and values. But they do not affect in this way the sciences of law and fact which are concerned with description and not with appraisal. The natural and formal sciences lie, in their abstractness, tangential to the burning personal center of the Christian faith, and remain in their inner constitution unaffected by it.

Support for this could be found in Professor Brunner's Law of the Closeness of Relation. Says he:

> The nearer anything lies to that center of existence where we are concerned with the whole, that is, with man's relation to God and the being of the person, the greater is the disturbance of rational knowledge by sin; the farther away anything lies from this center, the less is the disturbance felt, and the less difference is there between knowing as a believer or as an unbeliever. The disturbance

reaches its maximum in theology, and its minimum in the exact sciences, and zero in the sphere of the formal. Hence it is meaningless to speak of 'Christian Mathematics';... on the other hand, it is significant and necessary to distinguish the Christian conceptions of freedom, the good, community, and still more the Christian idea of God, from all other conceptions (*Revelation and Reason*, p. 383).

* * * * *

The dichotomist finds support for his view in the well-known fact that in the investigative phases of the formal and natural sciences the Christian student employs the same methods and reaches the same conclusions that the non-Christian does. It is obvious that in philosophy the Christian and the non-Christian are in opposition; they do not hold their ultimate principles of interpretation in common. But it is equally obvious that in mathematics, logic, and physics they are in the most substantial agreement. They agree in acknowledging that two times two equals four, that contradictory propositions cannot both be true, that water is composed of two parts hydrogen and one part oxygen, that one particle of matter attracts another with an accurately specifiable force—and they agree on many hundreds of such propositions besides.

How then, it is asked—how, in the absence of clearly recognizable difference—can anyone seriously speak of "Christian logic," "Christian chemistry," or "Christian mathematics"? Are these sciences not just what they are: instruments with which to articulate rival world views, but in themselves no more affected by these world views than a tool is affected by its employment in the building of a Christian church or a heathen temple?

* * * * *

As has appeared, the dichotomist's denial of any special relation of Christianity to the exact sciences rests not only upon his understanding of Christianity, but also upon his understanding of what science is.

The term "science," he points out, is an abstract generic noun denoting a *collection*—a collection of quite diverse sciences. There is not one science, there are many. And they are different. Some are descriptive, some are normative, some are formal. There are theological sciences, philosophical sciences, social sciences, natural sciences, and mathematical sciences.

Because these are different it is folly, he insists, to treat them as identical, in the manner of those who speak in the singular of "Christian science." The only effective way of treating the problem of Christianity and science is to distinguish, separate, bifurcate, dichotomize. There is a line within the collection of sciences up to which grace and faith do indeed extend, but beyond which they cease to be constitutive. The sciences on yonder side can and should be affected by Christian faith, and they are fitted to articulate that faith. The sciences on this side, being differently situated, cannot do so.

Why not then recognize the fact, he says, and be Christian scientists where we can—in the theological, philosophical, and social sciences. And where we cannot—in the formal and natural sciences—let us, as Christian men, be content simply to be good scientists according to the strict and accepted standards of the occidental scientific tradition.

* * * * *

I have called this view dichotomism. Because the designation is ill-sounding and apparently prejudicial, I feel obliged to say that, in my judgment, the dichotomist has called attention to very significant aspects of the problem we are considering. I think him to be in error, however, precisely at the point that suggested to me the term of disapprobation I have employed. He draws too sharply, too absolutistically, the line that separates the descriptive from the normative sciences and from philosophy. The sciences are many, no doubt, and each is unique, but they are not windowless; they are not insulated against each other, nor divorced from faith, in the simplistic way they are here represented to be. Knowledge is various, no doubt, and there are certainly different levels of truth, but knowledge and truth are also in a real sense one. And this the dichotomist does not sufficiently take into account.

It is the oneness of science and the unity of scientific truth that is emphasized in the view—called rationalism—that we must now consider.

II. RATIONALISM

The dichotomist thinks that Christian faith does not, or should not, affect in an integral way the elaboration of the sciences called natural or formal. He does not think it proper, or strictly possible, to construct a "Christian physics." Physics, he thinks, is intrinsically a "neutral" science, which requires construction in isolation from all faith-determinants; it is an "objective" science which, like logic or mathematics, can only be sullied and compromised by the intrusion of the religious, the personal, the subjective.

The dichotomist acknowledges that what is true of physics and mathematics is *not* true of philosophy or ethics or esthetics or sociology or any one of the other spiritual or human sciences. These, in his view, are essentially "subjective"; at the very least they have an ineradicable subjective factor in them. They therefore can and do manifest the effects of faith and commitment, whether Christian or non-Christian. Unlike physics, these sciences by their very nature articulate basic religious beliefs.

The dichotomist, it will be observed, cuts the single organism of science into two parts. The one part he carefully insulates against the influence of faith; the other he deliberately and approvingly exposes to this influence. He believes that the intrusion of faith compromises the scientific standing of physics; he does not believe that an ethics based on faith is similarly compromised. He will allow the possibility, even the desirability, of a "Christian ethics": he will *not* allow the possibility or propriety of a "Christian physics."

*   *   *   *   *

The dichotomist finds himself opposed by those who insist that a division of the sciences, such as he makes, is without warrant in theory or in practice. Science, they hold, is one, and the various disciplines that make up the single body of science are either open to faith in their entirety, or closed to faith in their entirety. What is true of one department of science is true of all. It is not so that some scientific disciplines are properly amenable to religious determination while others are not. Either all of them are thus amenable or none of them is. If a "Christian ethics" is possible, so is a "Christian physics"; there is no line or border at which faith can be made to halt. On the other hand, if a "Christian physics" is *not* possible, neither is a "Christian ethics"; if faith must be excluded from science at one point, then it must be excluded at every other point.

On this the two chief opponents of the dichotomist are agreed. Both the fideist, who assigns to faith a determinative role in every branch of science, and the rationalist, who assigns to faith a role in none, think that the dichotomist is inconsistent and his position quite untenable. Both deplore his compromising attitude. Both want him to universalize his admissions concerning one of the two sets of sciences he discriminates. The fideist wants him to extend to physics the insight he has into the nature of ethics and philosophy. The rationalist wants him to extend to philosophy and the other human sciences the insight he has into the nature of physics. Neither is satisfied with his partial concessions.

Both the fideist and the rationalist demand attention, but since the rationalist has in modern times been the more vocal of the two, I shall undertake to discuss him first.—What precisely does the rationalist say, and what is the rationalism on which he builds?

*   *   *   *   *

Rationalism is the view that in science sense-observation and rational thought are the only instruments of knowledge. It will be observed that rationalism as thus defined is not opposed to empiricism. It includes this. What it is opposed to is fideism, its strongest and most resolute enemy, with which it vies for the mind of the dichotomist.

Rationalism has never been wholly absent from the Christian church, and it is found within it today. It is given shelter there because it is not wholly intolerant of religion, and is not inconsistent with a certain kind of respect both for the supernatural and for faith. It is not directly opposed to religion and belief; it is merely concerned to assign them to a modest and restricted place, and to provide for science and reason an independent place beside them.

Rationalism holds that science and religion, reason and faith, are two quite different magnitudes, and that there exists no internal relation between them. They co-exist indeed in the same world, where they make characteristic contributions to that world's treasury, but they exercise, or ought to exercise, no influence upon each other. Reason may not allow itself to be governed by the insights of faith; science may not bind itself to the pronouncements of religion. Science must proceed independently and autonomously.

Not only the natural sciences must do this, as the dichotomist contends, but every other science as well. Science is one. There are different departments, to be sure, but basically and structurally all the sciences are alike. They all live by the exclusion of religion from their precincts.

This means concretely that the rationalist cannot recognize the existence of a "Christian physics." But it also means that he cannot admit the possibility of a "Christian philosophy." A faith-philosophy is to him as much a contradiction in terms as a religious-chemistry. When the rationalist, therefore, notices that the dichotomist repudiates the notion of a "Christian physics," he applauds him. But he bids the dichotomist at the same time to forsake the halfway house he occupies and repudiate, too, the notion of a "Christian ethics."

The rationalist says to the dichotomist, in effect: Learn to make a clean break between the natural and the supernatural. Acknowledge the supernatural if you choose, but keep it out of science. You may believe in religious truths, but remember that these are never known by reason or observation, and have no place in science. Remember, too, that scientific truths, if they be truly scientific, are known independently of faith, which may never be allowed to predetermine and prejudge the deliverances of reason or experience.

*   *   *   *   *

The rationalist, it is plain, wants to keep science pure—free of all pre-theoretical, pre-rational commitments. He wants to come to the object of his investigation without any prepossessions or presuppositions. He wants to exclude the variables that the subject is constantly tempted to bring to the object. He bids himself and every investigator to break attachment to everything save the object. He counsels the investigator to divorce himself from every judgment not dictated by the investigation itself. The investigator must come clean—without bias, without prejudice, without preconceptions.

This counsel is, of course, not wholly bad. There are individual, local, provincial, racial, and national biases which impede sound inquiry, and which should therefore be resolutely banned. This is so true that even theological preconceptions must, as most Christian exegetes allow, be set aside when the Bible is investigated. Biblical studies are conducted not in an effort to verify theological conclusions previously arrived at, but simply to hear the pure Word of God. By the same token, in the investigation of any object whatever, subjective prejudices and biases must be set aside in order to permit the object to reveal itself as it really is.

When this is said, however—and it needs saying lest science lose all objectivity and the facts lose their power to constrain—it remains true that the rationalist's demand for a basically presuppositionless science is an impossible demand. The evidence for this will be supplied when the fideist presents his case.

III. FIDEISM

When a man asks how religious faith is related to science, how belief in God affects knowledge of created things, he is apt, I have been contending, to get any one of three popular answers to his question.

He may be told—by a dichotomist—that religious faith is significantly related to some sciences (the sciences of man) and related not at all to other sciences (the sciences of things). On the other hand he may be told—this time by a rationalist—that religious faith sustains no justifiable relation to any science whatsoever, since science in the whole of its domain is constituted by nothing else than reason and experience operating apart from any ultimate commitment. Finally he may be told—by a fideist who repudiates both rationalism and dichotomism—that religious faith is related to every one of the various sciences, since all human experience is the experience of a being who is religious at the core, and since all thought is governed by presuppositions of so basic a nature as to be properly denominated "religious."

These, as anyone can see, are very different answers to a single question. The dichotomist believes that *some* of the sciences stand under the influence of religion and *some* of them do not. The rationalist believes that *none* of them do. The fideist believes that *all* of them do. —The dichotomist believes that some sciences articulate the antithesis, and that others, regarded as in their very nature neutral or common, do not. The rationalist believes that every science is neutral and that the antithesis either does not exist or is without significance for reason. The fideist holds that the antithesis runs straight through all the sciences, and that a decision for or against Christ is made even in arithmetic.

* * * * *

The central affirmation of the fideist is one that strikes directly and with maximum force against the rationalist position. It is this: There is no such thing as a "pure," an "uncommitted," an "autonomous" reason. Reason is a servant of the heart. It is always under the governance of some accepted value, or, more deeply, it is always a function of a person who in the depths of his being has made a religious decision—that is, a decision as to what is Ultimate, who is God. Whenever a man thinks theoretically his thinking is "controlled" by answers he has already given to questions—even though unformulated—concerning the origin and unity of the cosmos, and concerning the interrelation of its parts. All thinking is based upon a non-theoretical, a priori commitment, upon a personal evaluation of what in all the universe is most crucially significant. All philosophizing is done within the perspective of some faith that determines the central category in terms of which the world is interpreted and construed, and that defines what each philosopher understands by rationality.

Support for this thesis is found in the biblical teaching that out of the heart are the issues of life, and also in every analysis that goes beyond the superficial aspects of the knowing process. Intimations of the truth of the thesis are found in the differences that may be observed to exist between reasonable and thoughtful men on the more important issues in philosophy. Says Professor Dooyeweerd:

> It is a fact generally known that the student who sets himself to study the history of philosophy finds himself much embarrassed... because he must observe profound disagreement between the different schools even with regard to the most fundamental principles of philosophy. In this situation the most embarrassing point is that the different schools... all profess to be founded on purely theoretical and scientific principles.... Now, if that were true, it seems a little astonishing that they cannot succeed in convincing one another by purely scientific arguments.... That prompts us to raise the question whether theoretical principles are the true starting point of these schools. Is it not possible that the latter is hidden beneath supposedly scientific theses, and that scientific thought has deeper roots...? (*Transcendental Problems of Philosophic Thought*, pp. 16–17).

The answer given by the fideist is that scientific thought does indeed have deeper roots. He stoutly contends that the only way to account for the deep differences between thoughtful men is to recognize that the decisive factor in our thought life is not our exercise of reason but rather what we take and trust as significant for reason, what first and material premise we allow to govern our reason, what definitive apriority controls our reason. The opposition between Christian and non-Christian philosophy, accordingly, is not an opposition between faith and reason, but an opposition between rival faiths controlling reason. As Abraham Kuyper once said,

> Not faith and science... but two scientific systems... are opposed to each other, each having its own faith.... We have to do with two absolute forms of sciences, both of which claim the whole domain of human knowledge, and both of which have a suggestion about the supreme Being of their own as the point of departure for their world-view (*Calvinism*, p. 176).

This insight into the knowledge situation is not limited to Dutch or even to Reformed scholars. It is possessed by thinkers of various schools, and is widely articulated in contemporary philosophical literature. Edward Ramsdell declares: "Only as we recognize the influence of presuppositions of significance upon analyses of mind and value do we find the differences among the historic schools intelligible. Fundamentally those differences are not in method but in perspective" (*The Christian Perspective*, p. 25). Roger Hazelton observes:

> We do our believing, like our seeing, always within perspectives.... Each view of the world to which our believing points is... framed and focused.... What I am able to acknowledge and accept depends decidedly on where I take my stand.... So true is this that we had better frankly recognize and confess our perspectives, rather than pretend to some impartial, neutral viewpoint which none of us can possibly possess (*Renewing the Mind*, p. 56).

Alan Richardson says, "It is becoming clearer nowadays that without the introduction of a 'faith-principle' no metaphysical system... can be constructed.... Every philosophical system must employ a principle of selection, a value-judgment.... An act of faith is prior to the construction of a metaphysic or to the acceptance of a philosophy of life" (*Christian Apologetics*, pp. 35–36). John Baillie states, "The determining factor in the formation of philosophical systems has again and again been the initial presence or absence of religious faith in the philosopher's heart" (*The Interpretation of Religion*, p. 38). And Reinhold Niebuhr declares:

> Bertrand Russell's indictment of metaphysics as covert theology remains true even if the modern metaphysician seeks to dispense with religious presuppositions and to act as a coordinator of the sciences. He cannot relate all the detailed facts revealed by science into a total scheme of coherence without presuppositions which are not suggested by the scientific description of the facts, but which are consciously or unconsciously introduced by a religiously grounded world-view (*An Interpretation of Christian Ethics*, p. 13).

With these sentiments I agree. I think that the fideist is right when he affirms that all conceiving, judging, and reasoning is done within a framework determined by an a priori choice of perspective; that a world view is necessarily taken from some *point*, which point is *chosen* before the philosophical task begins; that there is an inescapable "subjective" factor in every theoretical construction; that "a person's interpretation of the facts, so far as their ultimate meaning is concerned, does not depend upon his mere looking at them ... [but] ... rather upon the point of view from which he looks at them" (Ramsdell, *The Christian Perspective*, p. 23); and that there are, deep down, but two kinds of men, regenerate and unregenerate, who "face the cosmos from different points of view and are impelled by different impulses," occasioning of necessity "the fact of two kinds of human life and consciousness of life, and of two kinds of science" (A. Kuyper, *Encyclopedia*, p. 154).

* * * * *

If the fideist is right in his central affirmation, if behind every exercise of reason is a commitment for or against God as he is revealed in Christ, is the problem we have been considering not thereby solved? We have been asking whether we can properly speak of a Christian physics, a Christian mathematics, a Christian logic. If we grant, as we must, that all thought is faith-conditioned, and that basically there are but two kinds of faith, Christian and non-Christian, is there any escaping the conclusion that there is or can be a Christian physics, mathematics, logic?

The answer to this question must be carefully qualified. Qualifications are necessary because without them the fideist is likely either to be grossly misunderstood or to be betrayed by his own thesis into talking veritable nonsense.

It is of the utmost importance to observe, for example, that narrowly scientific thought—thought in the realm of the natural and formal sciences—is never directly influenced but always and only indirectly influenced by the religious commitment of the heart. It is influenced only through philosophy, which is the true and "proper" locus of the antithesis in the realm of theoretical activity. This is to say that a natural or formal science, or indeed any particular science, can be Christian (or non-Christian) only in so far as, within it, decisions have to be made on matters of philosophic import. Such decisions have to be made, it is true, within all the particular sciences, but, since these decisions are invariably made at the deepest level of the science, at the point where it borders or impinges on philosophy itself, the effects of these decisions are not immediately, nor always clearly, registered on the surface of these sciences. We find, in consequence, that Christian sciences—particularly Christian natural and formal sciences—do not differ perceptibly on the surface from the sciences elaborated by non-Christians.

There are additional or allied reasons for this. The first is that decisions made within the particular science on matters of philosophical import do not, as such, alter or affect the data with which the science has to deal. There are no Christian or non-Christian *facts*. In mathematics, for example, the number system, the order and the value of the digits, the relations that exist between them, and the ways in which they can be manipulated can be determined by any investigator in the field regardless of his religious commitment, and, when determined, can be held in common by each and all. There is no Christian (or non-Christian) multiplication table.

The second reason why Christian natural sciences frequently differ so little from those elaborated by non-Christians lies in the fact that even when questions of philosophic import arise within these sciences, the distinctively Christian answer to these questions is very hard to determine. Consider mathematics again. It is plain that a Christian mathematician, working on the deeper levels of his science, will have to raise and answer the sort of questions on which Hilbert, Brouwer, Lobachevsky, Dedekind, Whitehead, Russell, and others are divided. He will have to answer questions such as Professor Dooyeweerd formulated in these words:

> Is it permissible (with Dedekind) to include the original spatial continuity-moments and dimensionality-moments in our concept of Number? Is Mathematics simply axiomatical symbolic logic? Does the 'transfinite number' really possess numerical meaning? Is it justified to conceive of space as a continuum of points? (*A New Critique of Theoretical Thought*, I, 549).

In the measure that the mathematician can supply *Christian* answers to these and similar questions, answers dictated by an authentically Christian philosophy, in that measure he may no doubt be said to have elaborated a Christian mathematics. But it is obvious that the Christian answers to these questions are not easy to determine and that, when determined, their truly Christian character would be hard to verify and establish.

* * * * *

It appears, then, that a Christian formal science, or a Christian science of nature, is theoretically possible, and that it is a mistake to deny, as the dichotomist does, that faith, through philosophy, can penetrate the sciences of things and relations. On the other hand, it is no less a mistake to suppose that a Christian mathematics or a Christian physics is something perfectly intelligible and identifiable. It is only as one moves up the scale of the sciences and gets into those concerned with man and his values that the Christian meaning clearly and unequivocally appears.

3

Miracles

THE GOD Christians believe in is the Lord of all. He is the Creator of the world, and also its Sustainer. What he once made he now controls and continuously renews. He gives existence to every being, energy to all that moves, and life to every living thing. He does not do this once and for all and then depart; he does this incessantly. All things are constantly upheld and energized by his present power.

People who believe in this God are not much troubled about miracles, for they see the effects of supernatural power in everything around them. They see each thing, not as a mere part or product of some greater thing called nature, which God once fashioned and then left to run "on its own" according to its immanent constitution; they see each thing as God's *present* work, reflecting his uninterrupted agency (Job 26:7–14). Everything is for them a "sign" of God, one of his "mighty deeds." Each is therefore marvelous in their eyes, a "wonder," fit to evoke astonishment and praise.

In this perspective—the perspective of religion—the usual distinction between the miraculous and the non-miraculous all but vanishes. What we call miracles are in the New Testament called "signs" (*semeia*), "mighty works" (*dunameis*), and "wonders" (*terata*). But what we call non-miraculous or natural events are in the Bible also viewed as signs and mighty works and wonders. In the biblical view, God is behind *everything*, the usual and the

This essay first appeared in *Christianity Today,* July 3, 1961, and as Chapter 13 in *Basic Christian Doctrines,* ed. C. F. H. Henry (New York: Holt and Rinehart, 1962).

unusual, the common and the strange; and he is behind them equally. According to the psalmists and the prophets, the rain is God's doing, and also the drought. So is the snowflake and the wind. So, too, are the movements of the planets and the tides. God "performs" all these, and more. Nothing is outside his jurisdiction; nothing moves except at his command. In everything that has being he witnesses to himself and to his power. Each is a "sign" he leaves of his presence and concern. All indicate that he "doeth great things and unsearchable; marvelous things without number" (Job 5:9).

*   *   *   *   *

It would be premature to conclude from this that in the Christian view "all is miracle," but it would be right to say that in this view nature is no stranger to God's hand. Nature feels God's impulses constantly. It is always suffering his "invasions." Its processes but trace the contours of his will. Nature has no defenses against God; it is pliable in his hands. Miracle is always possible.

The reason is, of course, that God is sovereign. He is Lord, and he is free—also with respect to nature. He is bound by no external rules and he is accountable to no one but himself. He traces his own paths through all that he has made; indeed, these tracings *constitute* what we call nature's "rule." The "laws of nature" that we formulate are nothing but our transcripts of God's "customary ways." They are not prior to, but after, God; they record his habits. They "hold" because God is wont to travel the same way; but they do not bind him. God is free to plant his steps precisely where he will, and sometimes he plants them on unaccustomed ways. He does this, we may be sure, to serve some holy purpose. Perhaps he does it on occasion just to testify that he is free, and so "reveal his glory."

However this may be, he traces his own path always. Sometimes these paths seem very strange to us, as when he causes iron to float, or a virgin to give birth, or bread to multiply. With all our science we could never have predicted he would take these courses; and after he took them we can find no sufficient reason in the preceding causal nexus for his doing so. Strange events of this sort are beyond our science; they are miracles. Yet in another sense they are not so strange. In them God merely celebrates the freedom that is always his but that in "ordinary" events is obscured by their scientific comprehensibility—i.e., by their amenableness to the explanatory techniques we have developed precisely *in response* to events of like ordinariness.

Science builds itself up on observed constancies. In terms of this discussion this is but to say that it grows by observing and recording the general pattern of divine behavior, by noting God's "custom." This custom gives science its stability and worth, and its predictive usefulness. It is quite unwarranted to suppose, however, that science can now turn about and *demand* that things behave in certain ways—i.e., that God keep to the accustomed paths and act only according to the scientist's prescription. Science has no authority to prescribe. It does its work well only when it remains descriptive, when it follows after God, as a reporter. Empiricism in science is therefore eminently Christian, if for no other reason than that it leaves God free, free to do great things which transcend our little systems and transgress the limits of our proud apriorities.

*   *   *   *   *

Because Christianity both allows and professes miracles, it repudiates all rationalistic *naturalisms* that, denying God, think that nature is "the all," and that miracle is impossible. This Christian rejection of monistic atheism is obvious and requires no elaboration here. Not quite so obvious, especially in view of the foregoing emphasis on God's immanence, is Christianity's rejection of the more religious forms of monism: primitivism and pantheism, in both of which the miraculous seems to be given prominence.

In primitive religion or *animism* there are many gods or spirits, and they have power (*mana*) that they exercise in unpredictable ways. These gods are present everywhere, and they disturb and modify all things in accordance with their whims. The animistic world is therefore full of mystery and apparent miracle; almost anything can happen at any moment. Under these circumstances a rational science is quite impossible, for the gods upset even the soberest of human calculations.—There is, of course, no real affinity between this view of things and that of Christianity. Animism is basically a monistic naturalism; the gods are nature spirits. Nature suffers no control here from outside itself; it is "on its own." There is no supernatural; hence there are no real miracles, but only chaos. There is no non-natural principle of order; hence there is no science, but only magic. This interconnection is worth observing. Miracles are possible only in a determinate universe, the kind of universe that makes science possible. Conversely, science is possible only in a universe that is under the control of an intelligent creator, the kind of universe in which miracle is possible.

Extremes always meet, and that is why when "everything is God," as in *pantheism*, we have a universe quite like that in which "everything is nature." There is no real supernatural in either case. It is not surprising, therefore, that sophisticated *pantheism* exhibits the same ambiguity in respect to miracles that primitive animism does. On the one hand, there can be no miracles, for, since everything is God, there is no nature in which the miracle can occur; without nature, the miracle simply cannot be domiciled. On the other hand, there can be nothing but miracle, for, since everything is God, all agency is, not merely ultimately, but immediately and pervasively, divine; all is miracle. Here miracle is either non-existent or only the religious name for "event," and thus all-encompassing. But if miracles are everywhere, they have lost all meaning. Since there is nothing with which to contrast them, no determinate properties can be assigned to them; they lack all character and amount to nothing. The two assertions of pantheism reduce therefore to the same thing: there are no miracles. What underlies this negation is the inability of pantheism to discriminate. In the grey twilight of this and every other monism, all real distinctions have evaporated, including the one at the very heart of Christianity: the distinction between the Creator and the creation. In consequence of this, all talk of miracles becomes meaningless.

*   *   *   *   *

The emphasis in all of the foregoing has been on God—on the true God of biblical revelation and on the spurious gods of primitivism and pantheism. But the universe contains more than God. There is besides him another thing called *nature*, and no account of miracle can be acceptable which does not give this second thing its due.

On the existence of *nature* the scientist quite understandably insists. A wise scientist will acknowledge God, and if he is also Christian he will acknowledge miracle, but he will not therefore part with nature; it is for him a datum, the very precondition of his vocation. He will, moreover, want to keep a certain kind of nature, the kind that is consonant with the scientific methods his success has vindicated. He will demand an impersonal, objectively existing nature with stable characteristics, open to observation, amenable to analysis, and operating in ways susceptible of mathematical formulation.

Because *deism*, without denying a transcendent God, supplies just such a nature, some Christians have been tempted to embrace this metaphysic. In its highest forms it seems to satisfy both the religious and the scientific needs of man. On the one hand there is God, eternal and all-wise, who is the Maker and Sustainer of a world which by its order and design points unceasingly to its intelligent creator. On the other hand there is nature, possessing a fixed constitution and operating according to immanent and unalterable laws open to discovery and utilization. It would appear that within this scheme both the worshipper and the investigator can find room. It is not so, however. Here, as in monism, what is lacking is, precisely, the miracle. It is excluded by an excess of dualism. Except at the point of origin, nature is isolated from God. Even when divine sustenance is acknowledged, it is conceived as merely general and external; providence never penetrates the world. Nature is constitutionally invulnerable; it can suffer no invasion. All that happens in it is exhaustively interpretable in terms of its own fixed properties.

Because of its intolerance of miracles, deism has not been able to win the allegiance of biblically informed Christians. Yet, some Christians, when they posited miracles, thought of them as modifications of a nature deistically conceived. They conceived of nature as a vast interlocked system of things and events ruled by increated laws. Into this nature God sometimes entered to do miracles, but he did so only by "breaking" the laws he had once posited and by "disrupting" the order he had once established. This *semi-deistic* view of things is hardly Christian. Deism is a false synthesis of naturalism and Christianity; this view is a false synthesis of Christianity and deism. It has not fully broken with an essentially pagan necessitarianism.

Of this even its advocates seem to be aware, for when Heisenberg enunciated the Principle of Indeterminacy many of them hailed the discovery with profound relief. It appears that before this time they were ill at ease with their implied suggestion that God sometimes repented of the cosmic arrangements he had made; they did not like to think that God by miracles disrupted the natural order he had once deliberately fixed. Now, however, there seemed to open up an avenue of escape from their distress. With Heisenberg a new "looseness," a kind of "lawlessness," was discovered in micro-nature, and this seemed to provide God with unobstructed access to macro-nature. A "god of the gaps" was accordingly conceived, a god whose miraculous power could be ushered into the world through the interstices of the atom. Passing through the lawless regions between sub-atomic particles, God's power became available for the performance of "mighty deeds," and yet it left every law unbroken, and his original arrangements quite intact.

Apart from the question whether Heisenberg's principle really posits "objective lawlessness" within the atom, it is highly precarious to base a Christian apologetic upon an isolated, even if important, "scientific" discovery. What is required is a view of God and nature framed in positive dependence on the Bible and elaborated in organic relation to the total scientific enterprise as this appears in the perspective of Christian theism.

* * * * *

There was sketched in the opening paragraphs of this essay a view of miracles which claimed to be *theistic*. It was the barest possible sketch, and it was traced with God primarily in view. Yet now that we are considering *nature*, no alteration is proposed, and little needs to be added to what already has been said.

Nature is often likened to a book, even in Christian creeds. The figure is not meaningless, but it is misleading. Nature is hardly a completed manuscript in which each word is statically interlocked with every other, a manuscript to which the scientist goes simply in order to parse unalterable sentences. Nature is rather a dynamic process resembling a discourse now being spoken, and revealing at every turn the meanings and intentions of a living speaker. What the speaker says is not dictated by some necessity from outside; he speaks freely. No doubt his discourse is self-consistent, on which account nature may be contemplated as a harmonious whole. But the concept of the whole is not some lever man can manipulate to exclude supposedly inconsistent things like miracles. Miracles, in the Christian view, are *in* the whole called nature, and they help to constitute it. They are parts of the total discourse. They do not rupture nature; they complete and perfect it.

This becomes very evident when it is observed that nature is but a part of a still larger whole—the grand divine plan for all the cosmos. It pleased God to effect in nature some deeds which are crucial in this plan—the miracles of the Incarnation and the Resurrection—that all other miracles only anticipate or reflect. To suppose that these "destroy" nature is utterly to misconceive them. They "save" nature because they redeem the whole of which nature is a part. They are not illusory events; nor are they real by accident only; they are the very clues to nature as to all else; they state the theme of the grand discourse of which nature is a chapter otherwise unintelligible.

As far as natural *things* go, there is no disposition in Christianity to deny that they are there, that they have recognizable qualities, and that a record of their behavior can be set down and utilized for prediction. Christianity insists only that these things were made by God, that they are still available to him, and that all they are and do reflects his sovereign purposes. As Calvin says,

> . . . respecting things inanimate, . . . though they are naturally endued with their peculiar properties, yet they exert not their power any further than as they are directed by the present hand of God. They are, therefore, no other than instruments into which God infuses as much efficacy as he pleases, bending and turning them to any action, according to his will (*Institutes*, I, xvi, 2).

*   *   *   *   *

To acknowledge the miracle, and to appreciate science, nothing is required but to believe in the God of Scripture and to accept the nature he has made and ceaselessly controls.

Part II

PHILOSOPHY

4

What Is Philosophy?

I N THIS BRIEF STATEMENT I shall do no more than indicate, in a skeletal way, how I conceive philosophy to be distinguished from, and related to, certain other magnitudes existing in its neighborhood.

I.

Philosophy is a distinct and legitimate scientific discipline, distinguishable alike from (1) common sense, (2) the sciences of nature and spirit, (3) theology, and (4) religion.

A. *The commonsense attitude* towards life and reality is one of immediacy and concreteness. It doesn't deal consciously in abstractions. It views and experiences things and events not as complex wholes but as simple unities, and regards reality as an uninterrupted continuum. When recognizing diversities it does so implicitly, and does not distinguish and relate them. It has, in short, no theoretical construction and systematic interpretation of the various aspects of reality. Philosophy, on the other hand, is theoretical. It approaches reality with analytical solvents, carefully distinguishes its various aspects, interprets and relates them, and by way of abstraction returns at last to the inclusive synthesis which is the goal as well as the starting point of all philosophic endeavor. Philosophy, being critical, may be said on that account to supersede common sense, which is always more or less naive. In philosophical reflection the deliverances of common sense are tested, clarified, modified, repudiated, or validated.

B. The special sciences agree with philosophy in being theoretical, but differ from it in being particular, not cosmic. Science deals with abstractions, not ultimate syntheses; parts, not complete wholes. This is why science is many. Each of the many sciences isolates a fragment of reality and limits its investigations strictly to it, employing methods peculiarly its own. Science qua science is thus by definition incapable of a synoptic view. The moment it stands outside itself to include itself within its view it ceases to be science and becomes philosophy. Philosophy is a general science that, as such, seeks to attain an all-inclusive synthesis of knowledge on the basis of a critical appraisal of each particular science's specific contributions. This means that philosophy, in terms of a well-articulated cosmology, assigns to every science its particular field and function, and, in terms of a reflectively constructed epistemology and ontology, evaluates the methods and assumptions of the same.

C. Theology is a particular science. As particular, it treats but a single aspect of cosmic reality (not God, but the historical revelation of God), while philosophy, being the general and coordinating science, treats that entire structure of reality within which the particular sciences have their seat. As science, theology employs concepts, categories, reasonings, and assumptions open to philosophical scrutiny and appraisal.

D. Religion is a matter of the heart, and may be defined as an immediate relationship of the self to God. It is vital and affective, and non-theoretical. As such it lies beyond the philosophical, although its expressions in cultus, theology, etc., are subject to philosophic evaluation.

II.

Philosophy, though distinguishable from them, is yet dependent on (1) common sense, (2) the sciences of nature and spirit, (3) theology, and (4) religion.

A. Common sense is part of the givens (data) of philosophy. It is part of the material with which the thinker works. He may clarify it, deepen it, mold it, but he may never deny it. To neglect it is to impoverish philosophy, and to interpret it away is to do violence to reality. The philosopher does not live on Olympus, but in the everyday world of common sense, and it is to the experience of that world that he must do justice. The philosopher seeks to make explicit the ground and reason of the intuitions, perceptions, and experiences of common sense. This, and not the annihilation of naive experience, is his function.

This has not always been emphasized. Common sense and philosophy have often been thought to be incompatible. This opinion has a long history. It started with the pre-Socratic distinction between sense and reason, and the almost immediate separation of the two. Sense was the instrument of the common man; reason, that of the philosopher. The former lived in a fictional world; the latter, in a real world. One dealt with temporal and insignificant, not to say deceptive, appearances; the other, with eternal realities. One saw but the accidents on the surface of things; the other saw the essences beyond. The rationalistic-idealistic movement never broke with this tradition. Plato's doctrine of ideas helped to form it, and even Kant remained true to it. The empirico-inductive renaissance constituted indeed an incipiently wholesome reaction, but it grew very soon into an empiricistic positivism that on the one hand denied the existence of permanent structures and universally valid forms and, on the other, led, by way of the theoretical abstractions of modern physics, to conceptions as distant from experience as the Platonic ideas themselves.

I think the Christian philosopher, in deference to the sound intuitions of common sense, is bound to break with this two-forked tradition—that of rationalism and positivism. He is not to look with the rationalists (whether of the materialistic or idealistic schools) for intra-cosmic realities behind appearances. He is bound to repudiate the notion of intra-cosmic substances or essences out of which the actual proceeds and in terms of which everything must be interpreted. He tends rather to appeal from bare and abstract principles to the rich and inexhaustible diversities of the actual. On the other hand, he is called upon to oppose the positivistic attempt to rob the actual of its order and stability. The cosmos is a manifold, but the manifold is a cosmos, too. There is change, but the change is intelligible only because there are unchanging structures.

This conception brings philosophy into vital relation with real and throbbing experience. It hauls it down from the cold, thin air of speculation, from whence no fructifying influences can proceed, into the busy arena of warm life, and brings it up from the level of mere description to that of interpretation and guidance.

B. Science. Philosophy is closely related to science, too. Science and philosophy are interactive. Science derives from philosophy its regulative principles, its more or less fixed boundaries, and its generic methods. Philosophy derives from science most of its factual data. This data it combines and synthesizes, building in this way the structure of knowledge into a compact and harmonious whole.

C. Theology. A Christian philosophy is related in much the same way to a Christian theology. The two are interactive. A philosophy is Christian to the degree that it accords to Christ a central place in the universe and to the extent that it bows before the revelation of God in the Bible. To the extent that a theology does the same, it will provide philosophy with all-important data with which to construct an all-inclusive synthesis. But the philosophy will not be based on the theology. Both will be based on the Bible, which may, of course, never be confused with a theoretical and fallible construction of it—i.e., theology.

D. Religion. Philosophy is, finally, related to religion. By religion I do not mean a cultus or a theology, but rather an elemental affection of the heart, a fundamental movement of the soul, a basic attitude of the self. In this sense all men are religious. They are religious because God lives, is all-pervasive and cannot be escaped. One stands, willy-nilly, in relation to him. That relation grounds religion, and the character of that relation determines the character of one's religion. There are only two alternatives here: one either loves, is reconciled to, believes in—or one hates, is unreconciled to, disbelieves in God. And these fundamental attitudes are not determined by reasonings or independent volitions; they determine all reasonings and volitions.

A philosophy based on an ultimate loyalty to Christ will be a Christian philosophy. The only alternative is an unchristian philosophy. The choice between them is never a posteriori. The choice, in the case of the Christian, is divinely and miraculously conditioned. The Christian is constrained by a divine compulsion and committed to obedient thinking. That means, quite practically, thinking in reliance on the revealed God, the incarnate and inscriptured Logos.

5

Some Issues in Philosophy

THERE ARE a great many issues in philosophy that are of concern to the Christian student, and that bear upon the life and doctrine of the Christian church. It is my purpose in this essay to consider three of these. Although there is something arbitrary in the selection of just these three, I judge that each of those selected is directly related to the Christian frame of reference, and that in combination they can serve to trace the outlines of a Christian philosophical perspective. I shall consider in succession the question of *Unity and Diversity*, the issue of *Idealism and Materialism*, and the problem of *Faith and Reason*.

UNITY AND DIVERSITY

There have always been and there probably will always continue to be thinkers and observers who are deeply impressed by the presence of diversity in the world. Some of these may upon reflection be led so far as to deny to the world any unity, plan, order, or structure, and be tempted accordingly to reduce the world to a chaos of unrelated parts. Such men could make a case for themselves by appealing to the admitted individuality of all existing things. They could then conclude that only the particular exists and that the whole is but a convenient human construct—a name, or perhaps a concept.

This essay first appeared in *The Reformed Journal*, September 1965.

Real existence, they might conclude, is nothing but a quantity of discrete unorganized entities, a chaos that becomes a world only after the intervention of an ordering human mind. Such a view would represent, in most general terms, the doctrine called nominalism. It is this view that was the stepping stone to Heraclitus' metaphysics of radical change; it was represented, in different form, in the medieval logic of Roscellin, Scotus, and Occam; and it underlies the greater part of modern scientific empiricism. Kant's epistemological doctrine of unordered sensations and formative categories, James' notion of a world in the making, and Dewey's biological instrumentalism stand to a greater or lesser degree in the same philosophical tradition.

Opposed to diversity is the notion of unity. Men have always sought it and, I think, on good and adequate grounds. Not only is there an irresistible urge in thought towards synthesis and coherence, but the world itself tends to validate the urge. It not only turns many faces towards the observer but suggests that these faces are *its own*. It reveals parts, but reveals them as *its* parts—that is, as elements in a larger whole. It is in consequence of this that our common experience is shot through with a sense of one-ness. We quite instinctively feel that all of life's manifestations belong to one life and world. We are constantly noting the interrelation and interaction of things.

To do that deliberately and systematically, in terms of a unifying and interpretative principle, has been regarded by at least one group of influential thinkers as the specific philosophic task. In undertaking it, representatives of this group begin by positing wholes and patterns. For them the multiverse is basically a universe, the apparent chaos a real and ordered cosmos. This insight is doubtless sound and is wholly consonant with Christian thought. The Christian believes in the unity and order of the world. He regards the world as a creation. That means, among other things, that he believes it to embody a purpose and a plan and by that token a fixed and certain character. It is not a loose and sprawling jumble but a uniquely fashioned whole, revealing in its form and structure the firm hand and persistent will of the Creator. It is, in short, a cosmos. Here Christian and the bulk of non-Christian thought would seem to be in substantial accord.

But what of the *principle* of unity? What is its character? What is it in terms of which the unity of the world is to be conceived? The answers to these questions have been exceedingly diverse. The earliest Greek thinkers sought a solution in the conception of a primeval stuff, from and out of which all things were supposed to originate. This stuff was variously conceived. Some thought of it as water, others as air, still others as fire. Later, when the philosophic mind had perceptibly matured, more abstract and spiritual principles were appealed to. The universe was then construed in terms of mind or will or similar higher functions. But however much men differed in their description of the fundamental principle, all agreed that it was to be found immanent in the world. The world was supposed by all to be self-interpretative. On this view the philosophic task consisted in interviewing the cosmos, coaxing it to yield its secret, and inducing it to reveal what is eternal and unifying in it, whereby it was assumed that the cosmos has something eternal and unifying to reveal.

This assumption the Christian repudiates. It is this assumption, he believes, that accounts for the spurious dualisms that arise to divide our lives. If it be true that the cosmos is a creation and by that token completely enveloped in time, it can yield nothing *in itself* eternal. If it be true that it is a creation and by that token dependent, it cannot itself account for even its existence, much less for its property of wholeness. Though possessing subordinate principles of unity, it can yield no *final* unifying principle. Every *final* question addressed to it is therefore a misdirected question. And because the question is misdirected, the answer it induces is always inexhaustive. This has one invariable consequence. From some other quarter an answer is suggested which proposes to do justice to that aspect of the truth just ignored or minimized. Only, it too is partial, and provocative in its turn of a competing answer. The result is a constant recurrence of rival "isms." Let one take one's stand on thought, and feeling will put in its word; the rationalist makes the mystic vocal. Choose to interpret things in terms of physics, and biology will protest; vitalism lives by mechanism and vice versa. Exalt mind, and things will obtrude; be an idealist, and the realist has a reason for existence. This, if anything, is the message of philosophy's history. Start with a monism that recognizes no extra-cosmic principle, and there is no way of avoiding intra-cosmic dualisms and divisive antitheses.

IDEALISM AND MATERIALISM

There is, for example, the antithesis idealism-materialism. The rival theories designated by these terms agree in regarding the world as a unity. They also agree in supposing that the ultimate principle of unity is intra-cosmic. They differ in their description of that principle. The one believes it to be spiritual, the other believes it to be material. Basic to both opinions is the circumstance that the cosmos does, as a matter of fact, present aspects some of which we classify as spiritual and call mind, and others of which we classify as material and call matter. This classification, however, cannot, according to the theories in question, be regarded as final. The unity of the world demands that one of the phenomena concerned must be regarded as real, and the other as only apparent. That which is mere appearance, says the materialist, is mind; that which is mere appearance, says the idealist, is matter. For the one, soul is a function of body; for the other, body is a function of soul.

This quarrel is milleniums old, has had the most widespread repercussions, and is still engaged in recruiting combatants. I know of no reason, however, why the Christian should take sides. He has a quarrel neither with matter nor with mind. He recognizes both and is not interested either in reducing or in subordinating the one to the other. He is content to let them stand side by side as equally real and legitimate aspects of the cosmos. They are related to each other in various ways, but the relation that holds between them is not one of unilateral domination, but one of mutual dependence and co-operation. Both are created and neither is absolute. Each is correlative to the other. It is only by recognizing this, and not by exalting one at the expense of the other, that the true unity of the cosmos is seen. That unity lies not in the lordship of one cosmic aspect over another, but in the lordship of God over all, and in that divinely ordained structure in which each finds its peculiar place and function.

The antithesis idealism-materialism is therefore not one to recommend itself to the Christian mind. This does not mean that the Christian cannot learn from it. Both parties to the quarrel have a message for him, although he cannot truly benefit from either until he has transcended both. The tendency in Christian circles has been to lend a sympathetic ear to idealistic protestations. This is understandable. Idealism has always emphasized the importance of spirit and the reality of its values. Yet this emphasis was by no means an unmixed good, for it was an over-emphasis that erred in two directions. On the one hand idealism identified spirit with the divine and substituted the transcendental for the transcendent, and on the other, it grossly disqualified the physical. On both counts it stands condemned. True religion is not a human quest and God is not the other-me, nor is the body a mere non-ego and extension an idea. Materialism, on the other hand, was wrong in denying the uniqueness of the spiritual functions although it was right in discarding the fiction of "pure" reason and in invalidating the ascetic disdain of body. The Christian therefore ought to allow neither side to blind him to the importance of both matter and spirit. Both are creations of God and are as real and significant as his handiwork. Both, however, are as relative and dependent as creatures must necessarily be. Neither is a key to the universe, and the antitheses based on the supposition that the one or the other of them is such must be rejected as mistaken.

Conscious rejection of it will be significant, I think, for both theory and practice. It will enable us to fit into our system all those biological and physical facts which indicate the intimate connection that exists between mental and physiological phenomena, and will permit us to acknowledge with less anxiety than has sometimes been the case the relation that our spiritual life sustains to the genetic and environmental. It will enable us, for example, to do justice to the partial and distorted truths of pragmatism and behaviorism without either committing ourselves to the errors in these systems or high-handedly condemning the systems as a whole; for, if matter and spirit, body and soul, are distinct though interrelated aspects of one divinely ordained cosmic structure, a significant connection between them is precisely what we should expect. This will also mean, of course, that we shall be able to give due recognition to the legitimate insights of idealism without succumbing to its deceptive charms. Its emphasis on the uniqueness of the spiritual functions we shall respect, but all emphasis upon spirit on the basis of that spirit's divinity or matter's unreality we shall resolutely reject. In practice this will involve a profounder appreciation of the correlation between body and soul with all that implies for educational methods and techniques.

FAITH AND REASON

Another antithesis that divides our life is that of faith and reason. This antithesis arises from the circumstance that life does present two distinguishable spiritual functions and that these do seem to trace two divergent paths to truth. The antithesis is consummated when unity is sought by affirming the one at the expense of the other, or when the two are left in external juxtaposition. This gives rise to three theories, the last of which it is my purpose to discuss. According to the first of these theories, reason is the only avenue of truth, and faith is to be completely banned from any participation in its quest. This theory has, I think, no conscious adherents in the Christian church and need not thus be here considered. According to a second theory, faith is the only instrument of knowledge, and reason is a sham and a snare. This theory, which may be called the scepticism of the right, has never enjoyed much vogue and may accordingly be dismissed with this reference to it. There is a third theory that enjoys a very considerable following and demands a closer scrutiny. Adherents of this view posit two avenues to truth and distinguish correspondingly different types of knowledge. There are natural truths and supernatural truths. Supernatural truths are never known by reason and natural truths are known independently of faith. The first constitute the deliverances of religion, the second the deliverances of science. Religious truths are non-demonstrable, for they are accessible to faith alone, and faith, being personal, individual, and irrational, cannot be expected to fulfill the logical demands of evidence. Scientific truths, however, are demonstrable, which means that, when presented to the mind, they *must* be acknowledged if that mind's integrity is to be preserved. Scientific truths are therefore public, while religious truths are private. The source of all the disputes between science and religion (the theory goes on) lies in the denial of this fact and the consequent violations of each other's territorial rights. Reason may not invade religion and criticize the evaluations and allegiances of faith. Faith, on the other hand, may not invade science and predetermine and pre-judge the deliverances of reason. Each must honor the sovereignty of the other, and each must allow the other to pursue its independent way. If this is done, then, when on any specific question they are found to be in agreement, it will be found to be due not to any influence exerted by the one upon the other, but solely to the fact that each by its own route arrived at truth's wide gate. Their agreement will be the agreement of truth with truth, and the truth so arrived at will be the more certain for being the precipitate of two independent processes.

What are we to say to this? No one may speak here with finality. The problem of the faith-reason relation is too old, too profound, and too perplexing for that. Yet one may perhaps presume to criticize proposed solutions in terms of certain general theses. I shall undertake no more than that.

*   *   *   *   *

What does it mean, then, when one separates faith from reason in the manner just described? It means that religion is denied all theoretical expression other than that involved in value judgments, and that science is denied the wide and absolute perspectives of religion. But it means more than that. It means that, strictly speaking, the Christian student, save perhaps the theologian, is a myth. For the demarcation line that severs science from religion also severs the religious from the scientific. That means, of course, that no single individual can be both at once. In his religious moods he exercises faith, and accepts, on evidence unsatisfactory to the accepted scientific logic, transcendent mysteries that lie beyond the power of reason to attain or comprehend. In his scientific moods he holds all that in strict abeyance, and investigates the cosmos without benefit of supernatural aid. He is forbidden, indeed, to assume that there is a supernatural at all. He must play the game. One of its rules is that nothing save the very minimum—such as, for example, the validity of thought—may be legitimately assumed, and that beyond this all faiths and hopes, all wishes and aspirations are to be resolutely banned. They are too apt to prejudice the issue. He must come to his scientific studies uninformed, or at least *as if* he were uninformed. He may believe when in church or when upon his knees that Christ is seated now at God's right hand, from whence He guides the destinies of individuals and nations, but he may not use the fact to interpret the events of history, for it is a "religious" fact, not a "scientific" one, and there can be no intercourse between these two. Genesis may be significant on Sunday, but on Monday geology supersedes. In other words, a man must cut himself asunder and posit an antithesis within himself. In the privacy of his chamber he may distinguish himself from his fellows by belief in the skandalon of the cross; in the lecture room and laboratory he must be like his fellows in exercising a supposedly neutral and impersonal reason. He must own a private and a public self, and must sedulously avoid confusing the two. Christ may rule his heart, but He may not rule his head. Christ may be regarded as significant for religion, but He cannot be regarded as having an equal significance for science. It is meaningful enough to speak of a Christian religion and even of a Christian theology and ethics; it is unmeaningful to speak of a Christian philosophy, to say nothing of a Christian science.

Against such a view the Christian is bound to protest in the name of life's inviolable wholeness. It is doubtless true that, after a manner of speaking, there is no "Christian" but only a "human" reason; yet it is merely true in the general sense in which there is no "Christian," but only a "human" faith. It is beyond dispute: faith and reason are natural functions, common to all men, and integral to their native constitution. Man is a reasoning and believing animal. But "Man" and "Reason" and "Faith" are, from the point of view of any individual, obvious abstractions, and abstractions are never more than indirectly relevant to life. Life's interest, and ours, is not in Man, but in *this* man, and in this man's *use* of faith and reason. It is on the level of particularity that adjectives become significant. On this level it becomes apparent, for example, that, though there be no Christian faith as such, there is a Christian exercise of faith. Faith, as exercised by the Christian, is not a new function, but an old one with a new direction. It is characterized by a new allegiance. It attaches not to false and dimly apprehended gods but to the one true God revealed by Christ, and to the Christ who is his revelation. This gives it its distinctiveness—this and the fact that it is an expression not of Man, but of a particular kind of man. Now this distinctiveness is no less definitive of reason. We sometimes speak of reason as if it dwelt in splendid isolation. Of course, it does nothing of the kind. It dwells in man, of whom it is a function. More than that, it dwells in individual men and in specific kinds of men, and is, in consequence, always specific in reference, and personal in character. It is like faith in being the expression of the man. If the man be Christian, the expression will be Christian; there will be a Christian exercise of reason. This means that reason will be exercised not only in conformity with the laws of thought as a form of obeisance to the immanent Logos, but also, and that unflinchingly, in subjection to the incarnate Logos, which is the Christ, and the inscriptured Logos, which is his Word. Christian reason, like Christian faith, will be childlike, humble, obedient. It will not mark out an area in which revelation may not speak; it will not devise a science in which Christ is not Lord. Christian thinking will be conditioned thinking, thinking conditioned by the character and nature of the thinker, and by that thinker's basic loyalties. It will not be something separate from faith, but rather something joined to faith in the deeper unity of selfhood. It will not be neutral, in the sense in which that word has become a kind of shibboleth, but will be colored and controlled and "biased" by the immediate apprehension of that truth which, though not perceived apart from thought, is never the deliverance of thought, but always a miracle and a gift. It will be a thinking in the shadow of Christ and of his cross; or, to put it somewhat differently, a thinking "prejudiced" in favor of The Truth.

A science built on thinking of this kind will be a Christian science. How, and in what degree it will differ in its further methods and in its more particular conclusions from a science that refuses the assistance of a super-natural revelation and represents some other datum as the final truth, it is not my purpose to discuss. I think it will differ in significant respects, though the difference will perhaps be most apparent in the sciences of spirit, and especially in philosophy. In what respects a religiously orientated metaphysics will, in its turn, affect one's theoretical constructions in the natural sciences, it is difficult to say, though there is obviously no warrant for regarding the difficulty as an indication that there will be no effect at all. Much depends on what we mean by "science," "fact," "interpretation," "system," and similar indefinite concepts. The investigation of the question, it would seem, will have to be conducted by the thinking Christian community, and it is doubtless time that on this point we frankly shared our partial insights.

One thing would seem to be quite certain: that we cannot and may not insulate our scientific moods from our religious attitudes. We cannot with impunity compartmentalize our lives. We may not introduce the kind of antithesis that separates the student in us from the Christian, so destroying our essential unity. That will only make us lame and ineffectual both in our religion and in our science. More than that, we may not violate the sovereignty of Christ, excluding from his jurisdiction the largest tracts of our existence and withholding from him the allegiance that is there his due. Christ is this world's king and he is ours. This lays on us an awful obligation: to be engaged, as the apostle says, in "casting down imaginations and every high thing that is exalted against the knowledge of God, and in bringing every thought into captivity to the obedience of Christ."

6

Notes on the Philosophy of St. Augustine

I N WHAT FOLLOWS nothing more is attempted than a general characterization of St. Augustine's philosophy. What is here set forth must therefore be taken, not as a contribution to patristic scholarship, but simply as a possible aid to those who are either meeting St. Augustine for the first time or are wishing to renew an almost forgotten acquaintance with him. My notes on his philosophy will call attention, first, to its fragmentary character, and then, in due order, to its religious, its inward, and its platonic character.

ITS FRAGMENTARY CHARACTER

Augustine's philosophical doctrines lie scattered throughout his writings. Only his earliest writings—*Contra Academicos, Soliloquia, De Magistro, De Vita Beata, De Ordine, De Immortalitate Animae*—are predominantly philosophical in the usual sense of the term, and they are far from being the most significant of his works. They are brief and relatively fugitive monographs (most of them are transcripts of conversations held at Cassiciacum); they address themselves to questions of limited scope; they reflect to a much greater degree than his later writings a Neoplatonic spirit and emphasis; and they lack the profundity of his maturer thought. His later writings, on the other hand, are predominantly theological, ecclesiastical, polemical,

This essay first appeared in the *Calvin Theological Journal*, Vol. 8, No. 2, November 1973.

and devotional, and they constitute no sustained and systematic address to philosophical questions. They are indeed full of philosophical insights, but their articulation is usually incidental to some other purpose and thus never absolute and final. In consequence of this, the student of Augustine's philosophy is required, first, to cull from various sources the scattered remnants of his thought, and second, to impose upon them an order which Augustine does not himself provide. It may be noted here that of his later writings his *De Civitate Dei, De Trinitate, De Doctrina Christiana,* and *Enchiridion* are of special philosophical importance.

Augustine's philosophy is not only scattered; it is incomplete, unfinished. It does not come full circle. Someone has correctly observed that Augustine's philosophy, "though not a mere aggregate of discrete and incompatible insights, is nevertheless more a temper, approach, and spirit, than a finished system." It may be added that whatever of character, determinateness, and stability it has (and it has much of this) is owing more to its establishment of certain key positions than to its fixing of external boundaries. The openness, the absence of rigidity that characterize Augustinian thought are reminiscent of Plato. The Platonic dialogues do not so much settle questions once and for all`as give the mind direction and open up new and stimulating vistas. So, too, the writings of Augustine. The charm and power of Augustinianism lies at least as much in its tone and method as in its several conclusions. (The contrast between the open systems of Plato and Augustine and the closed systems of Aristotle and Aquinas is worth noting). The openness of Augustine's system accounts for the fact that thinkers of very diverse opinions have in spite of their differences counted themselves Augustinians. Anselm, Calvin, and Pascal are examples.

ITS RELIGIOUS CHARACTER

God is the chief theme of St. Augustine's philosophy, and its central principle. This means that Augustine's philosophy is predominantly metaphysical, as opposed to practical or physical. But the metaphysical object or principle is Personal. It is in fact God—i.e., the personal, infinite, triune creator-God of Christian revelation. From the time of his reading the *Hortensius* of Cicero, God was the chief object of his reflection. His developing God-concept determined his choice and rejection of Manichaeism, his approval of Platonism, and his eventual acceptance of Christianity. Augustine's whole philosophy is one which is God-centered. God is everywhere and always the (personal) principle of interpretation. He is the keystone of the whole building.

> For if he ask whence he is, God created him; whence his wisdom, God enlightened him; whence his happiness, God has given him to enjoy God. As

existent he is fashioned, as spectator he is enlightened, as participant he is gladdened [by God]. . . . In God's eternity he thrives, in God's truth he shines, in God's goodness does he take delight (*De Civitate Dei*, XI, xxiv, 41).

Augustine combines in the closest possible unity the religious and the philosophic quest. His quest for truth is not a disinterested pursuit of knowledge for the sake of knowledge. Philosophy for him is not a merely intellectual enterprise that takes its rise in wonder and curiosity. It is rather a movement of the total man toward the one object that will completely satisfy every truly human longing. It takes its rise in a felt need to be made whole in every part. For Augustine the search for truth and the search for salvation is one and the same. Philosophy and religion are not two ways to God, but one. There is no divorce in Augustine of piety and reflection, worship and inquiry, love and logic. This fusion is owing, of course, to the fact that it is GOD with whom Augustine is dealing. God is an object to be known, but he is also a subject (person, agent) to be loved; and he cannot be known unless he is loved. God is the Truth to be apprehended, but he is also the Light that illumines; and he cannot be apprehended save in the light that is graciously bestowed and thankfully received. Knowledge and praise, truth and love can therefore not be severed. This feature of Augustine's thought is perhaps nowhere more clearly exhibited than in the *Confessions*, where at any time the recital of a psalm may lead to a theoretical disquisition, and where a philosophic argument is as likely as not to be punctuated by a paean of praise.

Because of his religious orientation Augustine does not separate reason from faith, but regards and exercises them in indissoluble unity. Augustine has nothing but praise for reason. He regards it as the highest gift of man, a capacity that distinguishes him from all lower creatures and confers upon him an extraordinary dignity. He believes further that the deliberate exercise of reason is obligatory. He is sure that it is man's duty to think, to judge, to discriminate, to know, to understand—in short, to develop science (Wissenschaft). He recognizes, moreover, that by the exercise of reason non-Christians have discerned many truths, especially concerning the cosmos. He is convinced, however, that in the construction of an all-embracing philosophy of life it is impossible, and illegitimate, to divorce reason from faith. There are at least two considerations that are decisive here. First, it is evident to Augustine that nothing can be adequately known unless it is known in its relation to the ultimate principle of explanation. But this principle of explanation is for him a Person—God. Now precisely because he is a Person, God cannot be known unless he makes a special disclosure of himself. But the special disclosure, for the authenticity of which no logical or empirical evidence is available, must be *believed* if it is to be appropriated at all. Belief or faith is therefore the very precondition of philosophic understanding, the sine qua non of wisdom. It is, secondly, not only the nature of God (the object of knowledge), but also the nature of Man (the subject of knowledge) which militates against the divorce of faith and reason. Man is a unity; his reason is never exercised in isolation from his other faculties, particularly his will. This means that there is no "pure" reason, a reason unaffected by moral choice and religious commitment, a reason unmodified by a basic faith.

It is to be noted, finally, that Augustine makes no clear distinction between philosophy and dogmatic theology. This means that he does not operate with the later (Thomistic) distinction between nature and grace, the natural man and the redeemed man. He declines to do this because he wishes to take man concretely, as redeemed or unredeemed, and not abstractly and unreally as "natural." That is, he wishes to take man in his actual concrete religious context of sin and grace. Accordingly, as a Christian, taking himself for what he concretely is, Augustine is both unable and unwilling to elaborate a "natural" and purely "rational" philosophy. He is concerned rather to acquire and elaborate a Christian wisdom enriched by all the insights provided by faith and revelation. In consequence, like most of the early fathers, he does not bother to differentiate theology and philosophy. He regards "Christian wisdom" as one single whole. He always speaks, or at least intends to speak—and this increasingly as he grows older—from within the Christian (religious) framework. He never ceases to desire to know and understand the content of Christian belief, and he is far from disparaging the reason by which such understanding is attained, but he is progressively determined to have his thinking guided and directed by the presuppositions of the faith, and exercised within the community of believers in obedience to the Scriptures and the Creed. Augustine does not inquire whether the product of such thought is to be called philosophy or theology. He is content to regard it as Christian wisdom.

ITS INWARD CHARACTER

There are in general two ways open to one who, like St. Augustine, is making his way to truth. The one way leads through nature and the senses; the other leads through the mind and reason. Those who follow the one are commonly known as naturalists or empiricists; those who follow the other are commonly known as idealists or rationalists. Augustine is, in general, to be classed with the latter group. For him the way to God lies not through nature but through consciousness, not through sense but through thought, not through the external but through the internal. His reiterated teaching and admonition is: "Go not abroad, return unto thyself, in the inner man dwelleth truth" (*De Vera Religione*, Ch. 39).

From the point of view of the history of philosophy Augustine's preoccupation with the inner and personal is a continuation of the shift in philosophical perspective initiated by Socrates and carried forward by Plato and Plotinus—the shift, in Windelband's words, "from cosmological to ethico-religious interests, from physical to psychological conceptions." Wholly in the spirit of Socrates, Augustine decries the tendency of some to study nature in preference to man: "and men go abroad to admire the heights of mountains, the mighty billows of the sea, the broad tides of rivers, the compass of the ocean, and the circuits of the stars, and pass themselves by" (*Confessions*, X, viii, 15). For Augustine, as for Socrates, self-knowledge is the portal to truth. Appreciation of the importance of the self, both as the interpreter of nature and the gateway to God, came to Augustine through Neoplatonism. Platonic idealism supplanted Manichaean materialism in his thought and supplied him with a spiritual view of the soul which enabled him to assert both his superiority to the physical and his openness to the divine. A direct consciousness of the self's reality—the insight that the existence of the self is affirmed in every doubt and denial—enabled Augustine to extricate himself from the scepticism of the Middle Academy and to establish a sure basis of knowledge. For Augustine, as for Descartes, the soul is better known than the body.

The self constitutes the immanent pole around which Augustine's philosophy revolves. It constitutes the center from which he moves out. It is the point from which he views the whole. The drama of existence is the drama of the soul in tension with the reality above and below it. If this appears to contradict what was said above about the centrality of God, it should be observed that Augustine's philosophy has two centers—God and the soul. His philosophy is, accordingly, elliptical in form. "Deum et animam scire cupio. Nihil ne plus? Nihil omnino" (*Soliloquies*, I, 7). Augustine's whole effort is to get these two together. The descent of God in grace and the ascent of the soul in virtue are calculated in his philosophy to effect a union of the two. Augustine, to be sure, never thinks of the union as a metaphysical fusion. He denies an original identity between the Spirit of God and the spirit of man. Man's soul is a creation out of nothing and not an emission of God's breath or spirit. He accordingly denies the possibility of an eventual absorption of the soul in God. Neither grace nor virtue can bridge the ontological gap separating creature and creator. But he does assert repeatedly that God is the soul's fulfillment and the soul is God's tabernacle, that attainment to God is realization of self, that the true love of self involves the love of God, that knowledge of God is knowledge of self, that, in short, an encounter with the one is an encounter with the other.

It must be acknowledged, however, that the two centers—God and the soul—never quite coalesce in Augustine's philosophy. His thought has two foci, and it remains in tension between them. He never succeeds in effecting a final synthesis between the agape motif of Paul and the eros motif of Plato, between the God-centered philosophy of revelation and the man-centered philosophy of the Greeks. His philosophy never finds a single center of gravity. It is therefore not quite correct to say that his philosophy is completely theocentric. Its theocentrism is compromised by an unresolved egocentrism inherited from the Neoplatonists.

ITS INWARD CHARACTER: THE SOUL'S DESIRE

To fully understand Augustine's inwardness it is necessary to understand his conception of the universe and man's place in it, and also to consider his doctrine of love. The cosmos, according to Augustine, lies midway on the scale of reality between the being who created it and the non-being out of which it was created. It therefore neither wholly is nor wholly is not, being shot through with contingency. "And I beheld the other things below Thee, and I perceived that they neither altogether are, nor altogether are not, for they are, since they are from Thee, but are not, because they are not what Thou art. For that truly is which remains unchangeably" (*Confessions*, VII, xi, 17). Man is part of the cosmos, but he is the highest part. Above him is God, below him is nature. He is linked with nature through the body; he is linked with God through the soul. Nature and the body are next to nothing; the soul is next to God. The soul, therefore, lies midway between God to whom it is subject, and nature over which it is lord. "Let the soul, then, reflecting upon herself, seek her own place in conformity to her nature, under Him to Whom she is to be subjected, above the things over which she is to be placed; under Him by whom she ought to be ruled, above the things which she ought to rule" (*De Trinitate*, I, x, 5).

Because the soul is not God, but a creature, it is not sufficient to itself. Its "good" lies outside itself. That in which it can rest, that which can completely satisfy it, it does not possess. It must seek it. This fact gives the soul its characteristic dynamic; it is restless and full of desire (eros, acquisitive love), desire for that which will complete it, fill it, satiate it. This desire, this love, is the very mark of the soul. Basically, and in general, this desire is for happiness. More particularly this desire is for truth, beauty, goodness, in the possession of which happiness consists. This desire for happiness is natural, universal, simply human. There is no one who does not seek happiness. There is no soul that does not love (desire).

Love, or desire, is neither good nor bad in itself. It becomes good or bad in reference to its more immediate object (its ultimate object remains constant, viz. happiness). As A. Nygren puts it: "That love is right which sets its desire on a right object—that is, on an object which really can satisfy man's needs; that love is wrong which is directed to a wrong object—that is, to an object which is unable, or only apparently able, to satisfy man" (*Agape and Eros*, Pt. II, Vol. II, p. 265). Of objects that can be desired there are ultimately only two:

Behind the manifold things on which love can be set, there is an inescapable Either-Or: love is directed either upwards towards God, the Creator, or downwards towards created things. This gives Augustine his fundamental contrast between *Caritas* and *Cupiditas*. *Caritas* is love directed upwards, *Cupiditas* is love directed downwards. *Caritas* is love of God, *Cupiditas* is love of the world. *Caritas* is love for the eternal, *Cupiditas* is love for the temporal (*ibid.*, p. 265).

Two things must now be observed. First, it is clear to Augustine that the soul cannot find satisfaction in the things below it. The reason for this is that, although the things below the soul are "goods," they are goods of a lower order than the soul itself, and their possession therefore cannot enhance the "being" or the "good" of the soul. They can only drag the soul down to their own level—i.e., closer to the nothingness out of which the cosmos was raised by creation. Secondly, it is nevertheless the case that men normally seek their "good" in that which is below. According to Augustine's own repeated testimony this is precisely what he himself did during his Manichaean days. And it is what the Epicureans did, and do. In doing so he and they sinned. Their cupidity was the measure of their blindness and perverseness. It should here, of course, be added that in those who do not seek their "good" in that which is below the soul, but rather in the soul itself, the blindness is no less great, and the absurdity is greater, since desire for a good beyond itself is the distinguishing mark of the soul.

It is in consideration of the fact that men tend to seek their "good" in the lower levels of reality, below the soul, that Augustine is constantly calling men to return to themselves, not indeed in order that they may rest in themselves, but in order that they may pass beyond themselves to God. He bids them climb the eros ladder and ascend from the goods and beauties of the corporeal world, through the world of the soul, to the eternal. He says to them: "He is within the very heart. . . . Go back into your heart" (*Confessions*, IV, xl, 18). Recalling his own experience he says of himself: "And being thence admonished to return to myself, I entered even into my inward self. . . . And I entered and beheld with the eye of my soul, above the same eye of my soul, above my mind, the Light Unchangeable" (*Confessions*, VII, x, 16). God, then, man's "Good," is found only in and through the soul lifted up above the world of sense, of matter, and of flesh. This is the meaning of Augustine's inwardness.

ITS PLATONIC CHARACTER: GENERAL

Augustine wished to understand what he believed. That is, he wished to discover the deeper meaning and the further implications of the revealed truths he had apprehended and accepted by faith. He wished in particular to know who God and man are, and to understand their interrelations. This understanding he could, of course, acquire only by rational activity; he had to theologize, philosophize. Now, no one ever does this in a vacuum. Every thinker stands in a scientific tradition which supplies him with perspectives in which to make his observations, terms with which to label them, categories with which to classify them, principles with which to interpret them, and frameworks within which to construe them. So, too, Augustine. His times, his tradition, presented him with intellectual tools with which to work in the mine of Scripture and Christian experience. Not only that, but it presented him with already formulated questions: it urged upon him its own problems.

In view of this two ways lay open to Augustine. He could reject the proffered help and go his own independent way by formulating the basic problems differently, and by creating his own intellectual apparatus, and thus arriving at new and highly individual insights and conclusions. Augustine did this to a significant degree. That is why we speak of *Augustinianism*. But it is impossible for even the most original thinker to disengage himself entirely from his tradition and to escape the intellectual climate of his day. And it is quite absurd to suppose that he can dispense with the terms and concepts which constitute the scientific coin of the realm.

The other way open to Augustine, therefore, was either consciously or unconsciously to attach himself to a living philosophical tradition, to become a member of a "school," and in the spirit and with the tools of that school to interpret Christianity. This Augustine did—in part deliberately, in part unwittingly. He attached himself to Neoplatonism. He did not, of course, wish to be a Neoplatonist as such; he wished to be a Christian. He wanted the matter, the content, the substance of his philosophy to be Christian throughout; and he did not from the day of his conversion regard Neoplatonism either as identical with or as a substitute for Christianity. He had in fact deliberately forsaken it in favor of Christianity. But he used Neoplatonism as a glass through which intellectually to apprehend Christian truth. He adopted its general spirit and direction; used many of its distinctions; profited from its analyses; and in general identified himself with its temper and outlook. In Augustine's hand, consequently, Christianity took on a Neoplatonic *form*. His philosophy can thus with considerable justice be called a *Christian Platonism*.

Whether the *matter* of Christianity can be pressed into Platonic or any other "alien" form is, of course, a question of considerable moment, and one not capable of facile solution. On the one hand, it is difficult to see how, in interpreting Christianity, one can entirely avoid the use of existing thought structures. On the other hand, it is patent that Christianity, if it is to retain its uniqueness, must at crucial points burst the bonds of any alien structure imposed upon it. This state of affairs is reflected in Augustine's philosophy. Augustine's fidelity to Scripture, the Christian tradition, and his own spiritual experience leads him at many junctures to rupture the Neoplatonic scheme. On the other hand his general commitment to the scheme leads him at certain junctures to misconstrue Christian teaching and even to import alien matter into it. This importation of alien matter is particularly regrettable. In taking over something of the substance (as distinct from the form) of Neoplatonism, Augustine did the cause of Christian truth no special favor.

I wish at this juncture to be well understood. I am very far from contending that because Augustine's philosophy incorporated certain Neoplatonic insights his philosophy is for that reason alone, and to that precise extent, unchristian. I agree with Emil Brunner when he says: "... the view that everything in Augustine which is Platonist or Neoplatonist is, for that very reason and for no other, unscriptural, is erroneous" (*Man in Revolt*, p. 241). Truth is not foreign to the pagan and the unbeliever, and such truth as he possesses we may appropriate. It may indeed be said that we are bound to do so. Thus Calvin declares,

> If it has pleased the Lord that we should be assisted in physics, logic, mathematics, and other arts and sciences, by the labor and ministry of the impious, let us make use of them; lest, if we neglect to use the blessing therein freely offered to us by God, we suffer the just punishment of our negligence (*Institutes*, II, xi, 16).

This judgment of Calvin accords, as we might expect, with Augustine's own view. Says he: "Let every good and true Christian understand that truth, wherever he finds it, belongs to his Lord" (*De Doct. Christ.*, I, xi, 18). And again: "Whatever those called philosophers, and especially the Platonists, may have said true and conformable to our faith, is not only not to be dreaded, but is to be claimed from them, as unlawful possessers, to our use" (*ibid.*, ch. 40). In this he and Calvin are undoubtedly right.

The question in the present instance, however, does not concern the legitimacy of incorporating stray elements of truth into the Christian scheme. It concerns the legitimacy of "subordinating the distinctive faith principle of Christianity to that of an alien philosophy" (A. Richardson, *Christian Apologetics*, p. 37). Of such subordination Augustine is sometimes guilty. He does not always see that pagan philosophy, too, proceeds from religious presuppositions and articulates a faith, and that what proceeds directly from that faith, which is antithetical to our own, cannot be embraced in a Christian synthesis. He does not always see what Gustav Aulen once observed: "When the Christian faith is incorporated into an... [alien]... world view, the natural result is that the pressure of this view is felt at all points and that it produces a perversion of the central content of faith" (*The Faith of the Christian Church*, p. 96).

ITS PLATONIC CHARACTER: FORM

That Platonism is present in both the form and substance of Augustine's philosophy could be demonstrated at length, but here only a single feature in each category will be cited to illustrate the fact.

On the formal side there may be mentioned the one-sidedly ontological conception of philosophy which Augustine inherited from the Platonists, and which he never abandoned. Whereas the true and proper task of philosophy is the relatively modest one of attaining a totality view of the created cosmos, a task involving patient analysis of the concrete realities of life, Augustine, in typically Platonic fashion, regards philosophy as a contemplative engagement with eternal ideas, issuing at last in mystic flights to non-sensuous realms.

Among the unfortunate by-products of this conception is the view of immortality entertained by St. Augustine. Instead of emphasizing, what indeed he knew, that the ground of the soul's continued existence did not lie either in the simplicity of its nature or the uniqueness of its function, but ultimately in the will of God to preserve it in being, and proximately in the resurrection of Christ from the grave, Augustine finds the witness and the guarantee of the soul's immortality in its capacity to enter into relation with ideal truth. Just as truth is immortal, unchangeable, so that which is able to possess it must also be immortal. This view is indistinguishable from that of Plotinus.

Apart, however, from its by-products the Platonic-Augustinian conception of philosophy fails to do full justice to what in the terminology of that philosophy are called "phenomena," and it fails to appreciate the role in philosophy of naive experience or common sense. Common sense is part of the givens of philosophy, and it is to the experience of that world that he must do justice. The philosopher seeks to make explicit the ground and reason of the intuitions, perceptions, and experiences of common sense. That, and not the annihilation of naive experience, is his function.

ITS PLATONIC CHARACTER: MATTER

On the material side there may be mentioned Augustine's teaching about the scale of being. According to his view the cosmos lies midway on the scale of reality between the being who created it and the non-being out of which it was created (*ex nihilo*). It therefore neither wholly is nor wholly is not. Within the cosmos, which exists between being and non-being, Augustine recognizes a further distinction: that between man and nature, soul and body. Of these two man (soul) occupies the higher rung of the ladder of existence. Nature and body are next to nothing (non-being); man and soul are next to God (Being).

Perhaps this ladder of existence with its four rungs of God, soul, body, and nothing answers to something real in the Christian universe, but it seems much better suited to express a theory of emanation than the fact of creation. The most fundamental distinction a Christian philosopher makes is that between God and the created cosmos. Between them there is a metaphysical gulf fixed. There is no chain of being of which God and the cosmos are links. It is precisely by its doctrine of the ontological discontinuity of God and creature (its doctrine of the non-univocity of Being) that Christian philosophy distinguishes itself from all ancient and modern monisms.

With respect to the nether link in the chain, non-being or nothing, the Christian philosopher is careful to point out that it is not a something which by diminution can be approached, nor a something out of which or into which a world can be or has been projected, but that it is precisely nothing. If there is room for the term "non-being" in a Christian metaphysic at all, it is only as a term to designate the realm of God's possibility.

As for body and soul, which exemplify the two types of cosmical existence, material and spiritual, they cannot be said to have varying amounts or degrees of being, nor can one be closer to God, or closer to nothing, than the other, on the scale of being. An entity possessing the powers of intellection and volition may perhaps be said to be closer to God than one which lacks these powers, but then not in any ontological sense, but only in the spiritual and ethical sense of being able to apprehend and respond to God. The ladder of existence with which Augustine operates here is a structure incapable of expressing the necessary theistic distinctions and is at best a constant temptation to think in monistic and emanational terms.

* * * * *

In spite of these strictures, however, Augustine is and remains a most distinguished teacher of the church, a saint of the first magnitude, and a thinker who cannot be circumvented by anyone who aspires to do philosophy or theology in this or any future age.

7

Personality, Human and Divine

PERSONALITY, both human and divine, was born with Christianity. This is, of course, not to deny the fact that the notion was implicit in all religions prior to the Christian. The Hebrews certainly ascribed to God attributes which we would call personal. But among the Hebrews the term was unknown and the idea it expresses was vague and undifferentiated. It was not otherwise among the Greeks, who of all the ancient peoples made the greatest advance in speculative thinking. Socrates, though substituting man for nature as the subject most worthy of man's contemplation, never passed beyond the purely ethical, and thus never arrived at that fulness of conception in description of which we use the term "personality." Plato seems likewise to have made no advance in this matter on his teacher. The conception of personality attains in Plato to nothing like definiteness, man being conceived not in the individuality and sanctity of his own personality but as an element in the state, his individuality being lost in the milieu of the social organization. And the gods were in no better case. If the eternal ideas excited love in the heart of their beholder, they were unable to return the love. It was the same with Aristotle who, as Spinoza later, conceived of God as incapable of reciprocating affection.

It was in Christianity that personality came into its own. In Christ and in the whole redemptive process, which culminated and became intelligible in him, the *heart* of God became known. The incarnation was an unmistakable evidence of a very real likeness between God and man. From the point of view of the incarnation God becomes intelligible as a person. "I and the

54

Father," said Jesus, "are one; He who hath seen me hath seen the Father." In Jesus there was effected both a dignification of man and a humanization of God, and those who followed Jesus were provided with a conception of personality never before achieved and one which was destined to persist in all subsequent occidental thought.

The conception was given philosophic standing in the Trinitarian controversies. It is a fact, curious in the light of opposition to the ascription of personality to deity, that the notion of personality, as a category of thought, was first developed in the course of speculations—or better, intellectual formulations of beliefs—concerning God. Largely ethical in denotation, it made its debut in ontological discussions. In spite, therefore, of the fact that personality is a human term (we being inevitably shut up to such), we shall best be instructed in its meaning by a reference to the Nicene Creed, where it is raised to the dignity of a philosophic principle.

Whatever, as respects meaning, our notion of personality may or may not owe to the Nicene Creed, it is indisputable that the term itself first emerged in the discussions preceding it. And that circumstance holds out the promise that etymological studies will be rewarding, for the term must have had a signification which recommended it to the minds of thinkers who, if criticized at all, are criticized for being too discriminating about terms. Of the terms that presented themselves as adequate to the expression of the plurality in distinction from the unity of the Godhead, two persisted—*persona* among the Latin thinkers and *hupostasis* among the Greek. The Latin *persona*, originally signifying the mask worn by the actor on the stage, came later to designate the actor himself, and, finally, since actors were always persons, came to stand for persons as persons. It always retained, however, something of its original meaning and conveyed the notion of a person as a "party," a functionary. It suggested a role, or aspect, the significance of which depended on its relation to a greater whole. The Greek *hupostasis* was a corrective for the Latin *persona* and tended to signify real concrete existence as opposed to mere appearance. The first word was, therefore, more Sabellian, abstract, relative; the second, more tritheistic, concrete, absolute. In the church they came to be used as synonyms and thus, modifying one another, maintained a mean.

All of this is significant as affording some explanation of the hesitancy of some thinkers, such as Hegel and Bosanquet, to ascribe personality to God. As Plato before him, Hegel tends to find the essence of personality in relationship, in membership in a society, as being constituted in a real sense by the non-ego, as deriving its meaning from an ethical context, just as an actor is what he is only in so far as he is a participant in a drama. So also Bosanquet, for whom the ethical and legal associations of the Latin *persona* are determinative for his conception of personality. Personality is found only in the sphere of morality (in relation therefore), where there is will, opposition, achievement. And that being what we mean by personality, we cannot predicate it of God.

The corrective of Bosanquet's philosophy would seem to lie in that conception of personality (of which Lotze hazarded an expression) which is characterized by more fidelity to that middle view conceived (though hardly expressed—for want, doubtless, of an adequately descriptive term) by the Nicene Fathers, and which they managed to keep central by supporting it on one side with *persona* and on the other side with *hupostasis*.

* * * * *

However instructive etymological studies may be, we must seek elsewhere for the vital meaning of a term. Knowing that "person," as historically fixed, denotes both an ethical subject and a concrete existence, we have still to ask, What precisely, in life, do we mean by personality? In virtue of what attributes do we call an existence a person?

That a person to be worthy of the name must possess *life* and *consciousness* will be on all sides readily conceded.

To these must be added *rationality*, inasmuch as to be a person one must be not a mere feeling consciousness but a thinking consciousness as well.

A person is, moreover, an *individual*. By this is meant that he distinguishes himself from "things," from other persons, and from his own passing states. It involves likewise his uniqueness, incommunicability, and substantiality. Individuality so defined has been challenged, and perhaps strict analysis does demand the admission that Individuality is never complete in finite personality. Ours is a sort of quasi-individuality, there being a very large common element in us. The self, without content, reduces to almost nothing; for which reason we hesitate to ascribe personality to an infant. Yet the content of self is precisely that "common land of sentiment and cognitive experience which we share with a multitude of other selves." Thus the self, the one, includes relations to the other, and these very relations go largely to constitute it. The non-ego, paradoxically, seems to make the ego; we are, it appears, what we are not.

Self-consciousness is another attribute of a person. It denotes that faculty of a self whereby it can turn back upon itself and observe its own goings on. By it a person becomes, by a unique mental agility, both subject and object at once. Prominence was first given this faculty by St. Augustine. It was given new importance by Descartes, and was vaunted by the non-Humian English empiricists as *the* essence of personality.

Volition, or the possession of a will, is also characteristic of a person. By a person we mean one who has the ability to initiate actions, to be a cause, to choose, to override necessity, to create. Kant, in whom the substantialistic notion of the soul was replaced by the activistic, is especially responsible for the prominence of this aspect of selfhood in current discussions. By him the self, or consciousness, was reduced to something fluid, not fixed; something in process, not in persistent substance. He found the essence of the soul in the creative activity of thought.

Personality is characterized, too, by *permanence, continuity, self-identity.* "Our days are bound each to each by consciousness." Amidst the changing states of consciousness there seems to be an unchanging element with reference to which, indeed, they may alone be declared to be changing. The fact of memory points indubitably to a self or ego that maintains its own identity while containing separate experiences, and the same continuity is implied in thinking and judgment, for obviously all reasoning implies the identity of the subject to whom the successive steps in the inference appear.

A person to deserve the name must also have the capacity for *morality.* He must possess the ability to make moral judgments. A person is conscious of being free to choose either of two proposed courses and is thus constituted an ethical and responsible subject.

A person, therefore, is a consciousness which thinks; which is unique; which distinguishes itself from things, from other persons, and from its own states; which is self-conscious; which acts; which persists; and which is capable of morality.

* * * * *

We must now briefly take up the question of *the reality* of personality as we have described it. Is there a self, a substantial ego, distinguishable from mere "things" or from impersonal organism? Or is there no self, but only a series of mental states not requiring a self in which to inhere? Or is mind but a mode of matter, and mental life intelligible in terms of physiological structure or biological functions? The question is important for theism, since it involves its epistemological groundwork.

The inadequacy of matter as an ultimate principle in the universe has too often been pointed out to need restatement here. All types of idealism have on this front come to the assistance of theism, though Hume, by the acids of his scepticism, dissolved the self along with the extended matter of Locke and the merely perceptual matter of Berkeley.

The reality of the self as an independent vital principle, whether psychologically it is viewed substantialistically or activistically or both in a complex unity, is and must be maintained by theism. In maintaining it it must be remembered that, though the question has intimate psychological bearings, it is, primarily, an epistemological and metaphysical problem. The rejection of the soul in favor of the nervous system as an explanatory principle in experimental psychology does not, obviously, commit one to the acceptance or rejection of selfhood as an ultimate existence. Crass materialists, as Haeckel and others, may indeed correlate the mind and brain, but when they do so they do so as metaphysicians and not as psychologists.

The Humian reduction of selfhood to impressions is done with much cogency, but the psychological setting of his denial is unfortunate. Whether or not the order and regularity in impressions is merely a psychological order, as he maintained, would seem to be impossible of being determined empirically. He and the theist join in confessing that they have never had an impression of the self. Hume adds that he does not introspect the self; the theist insists that he does introspect the self. The question at this point does seem to be left hanging in the air. The validation of one or the other position must be referred to the whole of the philosophy subsequently erected on it.

Theists, in establishing philosophically the foundation of their system, have generally followed St. Augustine in finding in personality or consciousness the one indubitable reality. With their master they have found in selfhood the presupposition of all philosophic inquiry. Augustine, recently out of the New Academy, was in search of certainty, a sure eminence from which he could survey the world. He found in self the fulcrum Archimedes sought. Whatever may be false, conscious being is real. Whatever one may doubt, one may not doubt self-consciousness, for it is implied in the doubt. Wherever one may err, one cannot err in affirming self, for "si fallor sum." This certainty is not limited, either, to the order of being. We have certainty also in the logical order, for we know, if not what the nature of a thing is, at any rate that it must either have or not have an assignable property. In the ethical order we at least recognize that the higher is to be preferred to the lower. Mathematics includes propositions we cannot doubt. Thus in every department of human thinking we have certainty. Our certainty of self as manifested in all these activities is therefore a certainty of personality, which is nothing more nor less than a unity of psychical states. Thus Augustine provided himself with a secure beginning and subsequently made all his ideas center about the principle of the immediate certainty of inner experience. He is followed in this primary faith by all reputable theistic thinkers.

All this is not, with theists, merely a question of knowledge. Personality is not only the thing we know most surely and the principle of all knowing; it is our best approach to reality. Says Herman Bavinck, "The only way by which we can come to reality is that of self-consciousness." And this approach determines our basic category, so intimately is epistemology bound up with ontology. It is from personality in man, the one reliable datum of experience, that, philosophically, we arrive at personality in God. We make the inescapable assumption that reality must be most intelligible in terms of the highest we know, that reality must somehow consist with our best notion of it, that thought, in other words, has ontological validity.

Accepting personality as the ultimate category, our further philosophy will have to be concerned with its justification. This may be done either by showing (with due deference to the new Kantian logic) that personality is the precipitate of an a priori deduction of the categories, valid because it implies all others; or by permitting the adequacy of one's whole philosophy to bear witness to the soundness of one's basic category; neither of which will, of course, be here attempted.

* * * * *

We have finally arrived, by a somewhat circuitous route, at that stage in our inquiry where we may ask the question directly: May we then ascribe personality to Ultimate Reality? Is God personal? Finite personality is, of course, given; we having started out with the immediately realized, the experienced fact of our own existence.

That God is likewise a person is the faith of the theist. He has come to realize that anything outside or beyond his own personality is an abstraction, without meaning save in the personal context, and this fact has sustained his conviction, elsewhere derived, that God, too, is personal. For in no other case would the universe be intelligible.

The inadequacy of the so-called theistic proofs for the existence of a personal God has, since Kant's attack, been generally recognized. God cannot be arrived at as the conclusion of a tight argument. And it is indeed not upon the cogency of these arguments that the conviction of the theist rests, although many are unready to admit that all forms of the ontological argument are invalid. Yet these proofs are as a whole nothing but intellectual formulations of a conviction independently arrived at, attempts to account for and explain something which already exists, and any attempt to make them more must end in embarrassment. For the Christian, God's reality and personality is an experienced fact.

If the formal proofs lack demonstrative power, the argument by implication would seem to be in no better case. Yet idealists and theists have not been so ready to concede its worthlessness. There is in every judgment, as thinkers have often pointed out, a transcendental reference. Consciousness, and its typical functions, demands a greater that sustains it. Our every judgment is in the name of something beyond ourselves. For our thought we need an ultimate validator and for our moral striving we need an ultimate norm. And if these circumstances, independently considered, do not get us God, they constitute an overwhelming presumption in favor of his existence, and combined with the deliverances of religious experience carry for many full conviction.

St. Augustine was the first to recognize the ontological implications of finite selfhood and employed a form of the ontological argument in his attempt to arrive, philosophically, at the certainty of God. By the finite human self which he had established Augustine did not mean an entity that has merely will, intellect, and emotion. Self-consciousness includes besides these, awareness, aspirations, and a nisus towards truth, beauty, and goodness. With Plato he recognized the existence of ultimate standards. Each of our judgments bears a reference to them. Even when we doubt or err we do so in their name or with reference to them. Thus the individual consciousness is attached to something transcendent and universally valid—valid because we are compelled to affirm its validity in denying it. But unlike Plato, Augustine perceived that these universals, since they are incorporeal and abstract, cannot be thought of as self-existent. They must be united in a One. They must be conceived as ideas in God. Hence God must be affirmed as having resident in him truth, beauty, and goodness, which means that we must ascribe to him intelligence and will, which in turn compels us to think of him as a person.

Herman Bavinck in his *Philosophy of Revelation* proceeds similarly. For him, too, the self is primary, but it is not arrived at by a contemplation of the knowledge relation, as in Augustine, but by psychological introspection. According to Bavinck we immediately introspect or intuit the self. It is immediately given in experience. But in introspecting the self we introspect not bare existence but a particular existence, not merely a "that" but a "what," not merely a "zijn" but a "zoo zijn." And the self that we discover is a hampered, finite, dependent self. We introspect ourselves as "dependent, limited, temporal, creaturely." "The core of our self-consciousness," he says, "is the feeling of dependence." If such is the self we intuit, then selfhood presupposes a someone or a somewhat with respect to which it is dependent, and that someone is God. And since finite self-consciousness is known as free and personal, Ultimate Reality (God) must be personal, for the finite cannot exceed the infinite.

But to neither of these arguments can we assign the rank of philosophic proof, it being very doubtful in Bavinck's case, for example, whether the *content* of the self's dependence is intuitively discovered, as he alleges when he says "all men feel themselves dependent upon a Being who is the cause and ground of all that is." This content is rather the deliverance of reflective thinking, the validity of which would have to be demonstrated.

However that may be, the personality of God has a sure and unmistakable witness in the religious consciousness. The core of religion consists in communion with a person both at hand and afar off. The religious concepts of love, forgiveness, and prayer are meaningless except on the supposition of a personal God, and they represent experiences too vital to be meaningless. It was in satisfaction of the deepest instincts of our religious life that Jesus taught us to call God "Father." As William James says,

> The pivot round which the religious life revolves is the interest of the individual in his private, personal, destiny. . . . The Gods believed in—whether by crude savages or by men disciplined intellectually—agree with each other in recognizing personal calls. Religious thought is carried on in terms of Personality, this

being, in the world of religion, the one fundamental fact (*Varieties of Religious Experience*, p. 401).

* * * * *

The notion of divine personality has not lacked dissenters. Ever since Greek satirists dethroned the Olympian gods with their jibes there have been sophisticates who have shunned anthropomorphism as the plague, and have on that account refused to ascribe personality to God. Theists have not denied the charge of anthropomorphism, content to be so designated if the term be understood as signifying a belief in a God having personal qualities. For, it is evident, we must conceive of God somehow if we are not to take a skeptical position, which has major difficulties of its own. And if we do not conceive of him after the analogy of consciousness, we must conceive of him after the analogy of something lower, which, while not avoiding anthropomorphism, is guilty of the irrationality of preferring the lower to the higher. For, as James Martineau says,

> There are but three forms under which it is possible to think of the ultimate or immanent principle of the Universe—Mind, Life, or Matter. . . . Man is equally your point of departure, whether you discern in the cosmos an intellectual, a physiological, or a mechanical system; and the only question is whether you construe it by his highest characteristics, or by the middle attributes which he shares with other organisms, or by the lowest, that are absent from no physical things (*Study of Religion*, I, 336).

Although I do not know of their objections being argued explicitly in a philosophic fashion, there is an observable tendency in scientific circles to reject divine personality as being synonymous with cosmic caprice. Science with its objective and impersonal approach to things is, in any case, unsympathetic to personality, making provision in its calculations for the disruptive "personal equation" in observations, and having no end of trouble with those studies, such as history and psychology, in which the onerous personal element refuses to be downed. In the latter case theism would seem to have little to say save that if personality cannot be contained in laboratories or made to conform to nice formulas, it is so much the worse for science. And as regards caprice, the very laws so highly vaunted by science are most intelligible in terms of a law-giver—i.e., a person.

There are objections of a philosophic nature, rather more formidable, to the effect that since absoluteness and personality are antipodal they cannot be combined in God. On this it may be observed that if absoluteness means "out of all relation, and incapable of entering into relation" it is obviously inconsistent with personality, but then not personality but absoluteness must be denied of God. But that is not what the term means to a theist. He holds to an absoluteness that is neither the unrelated, which would land him in a kind of exaggerated deism; nor the All, which would commit him to pantheism; but one independent ground of all things, a conception broad enough to include both transcendence and immanence.

Weightier objections arise from such analyses of finite personality as I attempted some pages back. If personality actually be what we have provisionally defined it to be, with what justification do we ascribe it to God? Sense experience and unhappy affective experiences are characteristic of selves as we know them. By what logic do we ascribe them to God, who by definition is incorporeal and perfect? Without succession there is no thought or consciousness, as we know it, but succession as implying change cannot be predicated of the absolute and infinite. In reply to the latter of these objections it may be said that while succession is necessary for the cognitive functions of finite personality, it is not so for God, who, eternally unchangeable, must be conceived as always possessing the whole content of his mind simultaneously, a conception, a faint image of which we may find, as respects stored data, in our subliminal consciousness; and, as respects logical procedure, in the ready insight of the seer and thinker as contrasted to the laborious inferences of the plodder.—It may be said in reply to the former of these objections that it is not at all plain that bodies are necessary to personality, the presumption indeed being that such is not at all the case inasmuch as personality is itself an independent spiritual entity, as is evident from its habit of persistently defying all attempts to be interpreted in terms of body; and furthermore seems to be most vigorous there where bodily affections are submerged—as Plato saw.

The really formidable speculative objections to divine personality converge about the subject-object aspect of selfhood, in the discussion of which I shall attempt little more than a restatement of Lotze, who, as the recognized champion of personalism, gave the matter classic treatment in the fourth chapter of the ninth book of his *Microcosmos*. The objection runs like this: "An Ego (or Self) is not thinkable without the contrast of a Non-Ego or Not-Self; hence personal existence cannot be asserted of God without bringing even Him down to that state of limitation, of being conditioned by something not Himself, which is repugnant to Him." There are, Lotze points out, only two intelligible readings of this objection. The first is that the ego has significance only as contrasted with the non-ego, and can be experienced only in such contrast. To this he replies that it is correct that the ego *is thinkable* only in relation to the non-ego, but the ego may be experienced previous to and out of every such relation, and to this is due the possibility of its subsequently becoming thinkable in that relation. That the ego has such independent existence would seem to appear from the circumstance that if its whole being were constituted by the contrast there would be no intelligible reason for calling it an ego in distinction from non-ego.—The second interpretation of the objection is that "the self-existence cannot be produced by an external condition in a being to which it does not belong by nature, yet it could never be developed even in one whose nature is capable of it, without the cooperation and educative influences of an external world." This objection, Lotze makes plain, arises from the failure properly to discriminate between the ego and the non-ego. There is an inner core in the ego which is the living subject of personality. Even in finite being the forms of its activity flow from its own inner nature; the external world, or non-ego, operates only by bringing to the finite mind stimuli which occasion the activity which that mind cannot produce from its own nature. Infinite being, on the other hand, does not need that its life should be called forth by external stimuli, but from the beginning its concept is without the deficiency which seems to us to make such stimuli necessary for the finite being.

*   *   *   *   *

In some such way theistic thinkers have known how to defend infinite personality against objections. As Lotze points out towards the end of his discussion, in doing so they have been compelled, by the exigencies of circumstance, to undertake to demonstrate and defend the proposition that as we possess personality, so does God; while the truth of the matter is that only God is truly personal, and personality in man is only a faint image of its glorious and perfect antitype.

The actuality of this superiority is indubitable to anyone who, honoring Scripture, believes in God as the Creator. Created in the likeness of God, we bear his image, and it is especially in selfhood that that affinity is manifest.

Independent evidence for this notion lies not only in the restrictive and obstructive conditions under which we have seen finite personality to operate, but lies likewise in the developmental and aspirational qualities of such selfhood. It remains a sound principle that the ideal as well as the actual provides data on the basis of which an entity must be judged. You have not said the whole about an acorn when you have described it as a mere acorn. So likewise with the human self: growth is the law of its being. Its potential perpetually outruns its *actus*. It has a transcendental reference. It never is what it may be. It has infinity to traverse and is always on its way.

8

On Taking Too Much Philosophy

A counselor recently advised a Christian college student not to take too much philosophy. Don't take too much of it, he said, for philosophy, being an affair of reason, is likely, when taken in quantity, to weaken your faith. Was the counselor right?

In so far as the counselor was warning against the evil of excess he was right. And in so far as he was warning against the danger of too many courses in philosophy he was also right.

Don't take "too much," the counselor said. Indeed not. Excess is always bad. It is everywhere to be avoided. Too much is simply too much. Of nothing should there be more than there ought to be. In saying this the counselor was clearly right.

Don't take too much "philosophy," he added. Here, too, he was right— if by philosophy he meant "academic courses" in the field. A student can take too many philosophy courses. He can take them in undue quantity, and lose by so doing. A student's life being what it is, too many courses in philosophy means too few courses in history, literature, physics, and the rest, and this is plainly bad. Too many courses in philosophy may also mean too little time for play and prayer, and this, too, is bad. Life and the world is made up of

This essay first appeared in *The Reformed Journal*, January and February 1953.

many things, and preoccupation with any one of them at the expense of any other is bound to hurt a man. In noting this the counselor was clearly right.

* * * * *

If the counselor was right on these two counts he was wrong, I think, on others. A basic misconception underlies his statement. His counsel reveals a misunderstanding of philosophy in both its formal and its material aspects.

Don't take "too much philosophy," he said. By this he meant, don't take philosophy "in quantity." Take a pinch of it if you must, but not a large amount. Get a little of the philosophic mind into you, but not too much.

Now this assumes that, formally considered, philosophy is the kind of thing that a man can have too much of. The assumption, of course, is false. Philosophy, like wisdom and virtue, does not admit of excess. A man can't be too philosophical. He can be too abstract, too rationalistic, overly critical and detached, but he can't be too philosophical.

Consider what philosophy, in its formal aspect, is. It is a persistent attempt to acquire an understanding and appreciation of the cosmos as a whole. It is a passionate endeavor to see the world of men and things as they truly are. It is the untiring effort to disclose the structure and pattern of the world, to discern and apprehend the interrelation of things, to see how part is linked to part, and how all things join to constitute a single and intelligible whole.

This being so, a man can hardly have too much philosophy. He cannot be too much engaged in this absorbing enterprise. The counselor was quite wrong in recommending moderation here. To become philosophical is the business of us all, and we always need more philosophy than we have. Life needs to be seen steadily and seen whole. This is but to say that it needs to be seen in philosophical perspective. The student has no call to dabble in philosophy; he is bound to throw himself into it with every energy of his soul. This does not mean that he must heap up courses in school philosophy. It does mean that he must, in and out of school, love and pursue wisdom and be in never ending quest of cosmic understanding.

* * * * *

If the counselor was wrong in setting limits to the student's engagement in the philosophic enterprise, he was in even greater error when he set forth the grounds for the limitation that he urged.

Don't take too much philosophy, he said, for it is "an affair of reason" and thus likely to shake your faith. The counselor here gives expression to a notion which at this late date is still sometimes found in Christian circles. It is the notion that philosophy is the attempt to attain *by pure reason* an understanding of the world, the attempt to attain by the *unaided intellect* a knowledge of the origin, structure, meaning, and purpose of the cosmos.

That this is what philosophy materially is, is the view, of course, of most, if not all, non-Christian thinkers. Descartes, at the beginning of the modern period, gave classic expression to this view when he declared that the philosopher, if he be truly such, takes nothing for granted. He makes no assumptions. He starts from scratch. He begins with a completely open mind. He does not believe; he thinks. He is guided by no divine word supernaturally communicated: he is guided by reason. He follows no authority; he follows the argument. He questions every presupposition. He makes no commitments; he challenges all commitments. A completely neutral and autonomous reason is, for him, the sole instrument of knowledge and the only judge of what is true and right.

Now some Christians have uncritically accepted this material definition of philosophy. The moment they did, however, they were in trouble, for being Christians still, they knew that faith in a supernatural revelation is the only way to wisdom and understanding. They were left, therefore, with no alternative but to repudiate philosophy. Philosophy became for them an attempt to dethrone God and put intellect in his place. It became for them a "fool-osophy," a vain and impious business, that every devout Christian should be at pains to avoid. —I think that somewhere along the line philosophy became this for the counselor in our story. It became vain. That is why he hesitated to recommend it to the student. He conceived of it as an affair of the reason operating independently of faith and revelation, and thus unworthy.

If this be so, however, the counselor not only misconceived philosophy, he failed in his duty to the student. If this be philosophy then the student had no business philosophizing at all. If this be philosophy then to philosophize is to think without conscious dependence upon God, to subject his Word to our own canons of judgment, to deny Christ's Lordship over our minds, and to regard ourselves as the final interpreters of all existence. And this the Christian may not do, not even in the smallest degree. In all consistency the counselor should not have allowed the student to take even a pinch of philosophy. If philosophy is what he thought it to be, his tolerance was weakness, not to say sin.

Moreover, if philosophy is what he thought it to be, he failed in his duty to the college and the church. He should have urged the removal of all philosophy courses from the curriculum. The primary aim of philosophy courses is not to acquaint the student with the history of thought. Introduction of the student to the philosophical literature, both Christian and non-Christian, is only a means to an end. The primary aim of philosophy courses is to teach students to philosophize, to attain to and mediate a world view.

But if to philosophize is to think in independence of the Christ, how can a Christian college encourage it?

Fortunately, to philosophize does not mean to think in independence of Christ. Descartes was wrong, and the counselor was wrong. Philosophy has a religious root. Its reigning motif is, or is determined by, a basic faith. Thought is never neutral. It is always and inescapably the expression of a commitment that lies deeper than itself. It rests on belief, and is an interpretation of the world in terms of that belief. It springs from dogma, and is the systematic articulation of that dogma. It is rational, but its definition of rationality is determined by religious decision. All philosophy is one in this respect. There is no philosophy that is not religious, that does not have a god it serves.

This is why philosophy can be Christian without ceasing to be philosophy, and why it can be philosophy without ceasing to be Christian. There is nothing in philosophy as such to alienate a man from Christ. There is no enmity between faith and reason, Christ and reflective thought. This is the reason why a Christian college dares to teach philosophy, why it encourages its students to philosophize. It recognizes that philosophy is compatible with worship, consonant with the most complete submission to the Word. It wants no one, therefore, in the name of faith, to impugn the philosophic life. It wants no counselor to cite philosophy as a threat to real devotion.

This is not to deny, of course, that there are philosophies which do oppose the faith, philosophies which are strong in their antagonism to the Christ. On the contrary, all that has been said is to the effect that no philosophy can be neutral with respect to him. Philosophies are either for him or against him. The god a given philosophy serves is either the God of whom Christ is the Revelation or some spurious and fictitious god. A philosophy is either Christian or it is not. But the existence of false philosophies is no reason at all for abandoning or even limiting the philosophic enterprise. It is rather a reason for working harder at the task of bringing every thought into subjection to the Christ, and enlisting every student in the work. The counselor erred when he advised the student not to take too much philosophy.

* * * * *

Now it is possible that I misunderstood the counselor. Perhaps he was concerned to make a point quite other than the one I hit upon. It is quite possible that, were he able now to talk, he would say to me:

"All that you say is true, and I was not concerned to challenge it. I know that all philosophy is religiously oriented. I know that a Christian philosophy is possible and necessary. I know that a Christian student should get as much Christian philosophy into him as he possibly can. But I also know that most philosophy is anti-Christian. Philosophy grew up in the first instance among those who were strangers to the oracles of God. Its development has been almost exclusively in the hands of those who wished to exercise their reason either in independence of special revelation or else in conscious opposition to it. It is only lately, I am told, that a serious and successful attempt has been made to construct a philosophy on Christian suppositions. It is evident, therefore, that only a very small part of philosophical literature is Christian, and that the vast bulk of it is in opposition to the Christ.

"It was this that I had in mind when I counseled the student. I knew that if he took a lot of philosophy he would be tempted to read widely in anti-Christian books. I also knew that in colleges professing to be Christian a student is often invited, sometimes even urged, to read unbelieving literature. This troubled me, and in counseling the student I gave expression to my concern. I voiced the grave doubts I entertain about the wisdom of sending Christian students to pagan authors for light. The simple fact is, I don't believe a Christian student can profit much from reading in secular philosophy. Such reading can do him incalculable harm—and what good can it do?

"I hold, you see, that the philosophy of non-Christian thinkers is falsified by their idolatrous commitment and by their rejection of the living God. I hold that the truth is not in them. I do not regard them as safe guides to wisdom and happiness. I believe that the origin and purpose and meaning of all created things cannot be learned from them, for they are in the dark concerning these. They have substituted lies and vain imaginings for the truth.

"I consider it best, therefore, that a Christian student have the minimum of traffic with them. That is why I counseled the student as I did. Don't take too much philosophy, I said. I meant thereby: Don't read too much in pagan and modernist authors. They cast hardly any light at all upon the philosophical problems which as a Christian student you confront, and they are apt to lead you seriously astray."

* * * * *

Had the counselor been asked to justify his counsel, he might have spoken in some such way as this. And had he spoken in this way he would have placed himself in a new and better light, for there is truth in what he says. But the full bearing of that truth is, in my judgment, not articulated. The counselor discloses important negative implications of the truth he apprehends, but he neglects almost entirely to exhibit its positive features. He is silent about the benefits to be derived from conscientious engagement with the entire body of philosophic literature, non-Christian as well as Christian. He seems either to deny that anything can be learned from unbelievers or to deny that what can be learned is worth the risk. If these denials are mere seeming, there is no quarrel. If they are real, and seriously intended, they wrench the actual situation quite out of focus, as I shall attempt to indicate.

Before I make the attempt, however, I wish to acknowledge the truth that lies in the counselor's remarks. There is a certain force in his position and this deserves due recognition.

* * * * *

Let it be observed, then, that the counselor's advice and warning is perfectly in order when addressed to a boy who, still unformed, adopts as his intellectual companions pagan and unbelieving authors with whom he seeks or finds an inner spiritual accord.

I don't know that it has ever happened, but it is possible for a philosophy student, while browsing in the library, to come upon Thomas Paine's *Age of Reason*, to read it, and to fall in love with it. It is possible, too, that under the spell of this experience he will steep himself in *Man a Machine* by De LaMettrie, and go on from there to court Voltaire, Ingersoll, Bertrand Russell, and others of their kind.

When a boy does this, he needs arresting. He needs our counselor. He needs a man who will say to him: Don't take too much of this philosophy. Don't read too much in these mistaken authors. Stop feeding on them. Change your lean and enervating diet and substitute for it wholesome Christian food. Quit the destructive spiritual regimen which you have so foolishly imposed upon yourself. Leave your intellectual companions and stifle your infatuation for them, for they are corrupting you in mind and soul.

In the situation such counseling is not allowable only; it is mandatory. When a student such as I have described comes to the attention of a Christian teacher, that teacher, if he knows his duty, will put him under surveillance and restraint. He will instruct him, and until he regains his sense, impose on him the strictest fast of pagan meats. The teacher will, in other words, echo the counselor's advice and, under the circumstances, enforce his point even more unqualifiedly.

* * * * *

Consider another matter. —The counselor believes that a student's actual or contemplated study of non-Christian writings should be a matter of concern to Christian teachers. In this the counselor is right. The Christian teacher should be much concerned about the student's reading.

This concern, however, should not, except in rare and passing instances, lead him to impose restraints and prohibitions. Pagan literature does not call for rejection; it calls for appraisal. It demands the critical, not the averted, eye. Its existence obliges the teacher not to publish bans but to provide guides.

What is important to notice is that the literature—its existence and its nature—puts the teacher under obligation. It puts him in debt to his student.

This is, if he be conscientious, what causes him concern. He would remain unconcerned were it possible either to legislate the literature out of the student's life or to allow it free play upon his mind. But neither is possible. The literature can neither be simply ignored nor simply accepted. It must be judged, weighed, and sifted, and there's the rub. For judgment demands a standard, and a standard must be formulated.

Here, then, is the debt he owes. He owes the student an articulated standard, a well-defined set of basic principles. He owes him canons of interpretation, critical tests and solvents. And it is Christian tests he owes him.

Unless he is able to provide these, he cannot in good conscience refer the student to the literature. He may not send him out without giving him his bearings or the means of ascertaining them. He is bound to provide direction.

This is but another way of saying that he must form in the student a Christian mind, apt to judge all things by Christian standards, and to see all things in the perspective of the Faith. Only in the degree that the teacher is engaged in the task of forming in him a Christian mind can he contemplate with equanimity the student's engagement with non-Christian thought.

It is doubtless true that the formation of the Christian mind by education requires the utilization of all the best that has been thought and said, both by non-Christians and by Christians. But the basic principles for the formation of the Christian mind are just as surely derived from the Scriptures and from sanctified reflection on them, and it is these, as I said, that should be in the possession of one who hopes to get Christian profit from the study of non-Christian thought. Only as one carries something to pagan books can one take something of lasting value from them.

There is so much justification, at least, for the counselor's depreciation of unbelieving literature.

*   *   *   *   *

There is one other point that requires comment. —The counselor advised against "taking" philosophy, and we have understood him now to mean philosophy that is not Christian. If we further interpret his word "taking" to mean "adoption of basic principles," then obviously there is no possibility at all of a Christian "taking" non-Christian philosophy. The Christian cannot, without ceasing to be himself, adopt non-Christian principles of explanation.

It is not, then, in order to get these that the Christian studies secular philosophy. He does not want these; and he may not take these. The only basic principles he may take are Christian principles, and since these are antithetical to all others, his taking them commits him to an uncompromising rejection of the others.

So much is plain from what has already been said about the religious root of all philosophy. Never may a Christian, in thought any more than in deed, forsake the Christian foundation on which by grace he is established. This foundation is not taken from philosophy at all, much less from the pagan sort. The Christian finds it laid for him—by Christ—and on this, by God's preserving grace, and in the measure of his own faithfulness, he stands immovably. It is because of this that he owns and is able to claim truth wherever it is found.

Part III

THEOLOGY

9

The Warrant for Theology in a Scientific Age

THE PRESENT CONCERNS of theology are engendered in part by the cultural situation in which it finds itself. Emerging in the Renaissance and gaining strength in the seventeenth, eighteenth, and nineteenth centuries, but come to full bloom today, is an all-pervasive mood and outlook called secularism. Among the many things that characterize secularism is the adoption of the natural sciences as exemplifying the very nature of learning, and the employment of the scientific method of observation and experiment as the only instrument of knowledge. This secularism typically rejects metaphysics, and especially theology. Theology, to it, seems not only unable.to give any clear account of its logical procedures, but has in the past impeded knowledge and obstructed the progress of science. This secularism has typically taken control of the modern thinking man, and the presence of it has put religion and Christianity on the defensive and made theologians nervous and uneasy.

It is not the case that theology has totally surrendered to and adopted the secularist outlook. It continues to assert its own integrity and independence, but it is becoming increasingly concessive, being willing in recent years not only to fabricate a secular version of the gospel but even to proclaim the death of God. The need of the hour, therefore, is for a rehabilitation of theology. Theology, conscious of its anchorage in a transcendent reality, must boldly affirm the existence of God, and explicate the meaning of his being and acts for the entire world. Theology must also reassert its right to be heard by convincing a science-oriented generation that it too is a veritable science, relevant to people of every age, and capable of illumining the totality of existence. The purpose of this essay is to make such a claim for theology, and to indicate that its affirmations are worthy of assent—even the assent of the most critically intelligent.

I begin with a sampling of the more central affirmations that a Christian theology makes, and then go on to inquire whether affirmations of this sort are entitled to be called knowledge—veritable knowledge, bearing significantly upon the condition of modern man.

A. THE CENTRAL AFFIRMATIONS

The central affirmations of the Christian faith may be succinctly stated as follows:

1. God *exists*, is *real*. He is an infinitely good, wise, and powerful personal being, who, lifted above the world in true transcendence, is yet always present to it in grace and judgment.

2. God *created* the world—not out of himself, not out of some co-existing matter, but out of nothing. The real is therefore dual. There is necessary being, and contingent being. There is the Creator, and there is the creature. These two cannot be univocally subsumed under one category, and they are to be neither confused nor separated.

3. *Man* was created in *God's image*, is in unbreakable touch with God, and was made to be—in free responsibility—a member of that enduring fellowship of love and justice called *The Kingdom*, a kingdom which God is historically bringing into being, and of which the Christian *church* is the earnest and the symbol.

4. The human race—contrary to God's will—fell from rectitude into the power of *sin*, with the result that man, while retaining his humanness, exists in alienation from God, self, and neighbor, where in stubborn pride he resists the promptings of God's Spirit and becomes the heir of *death*.

5. God, from the very moment that man fell, out of *pity* for man's isolation and brokenness, has reached out to restore him to self-integration, social cohesion, and transcendent peace.

6. God's nature and purposes are fully and finally revealed in *Jesus Christ*, not only or even primarily in his words, but especially in his person and deeds, and particularly in his death and resurrection.

7. Those who believe in Christ, trusting him for their salvation, are in principle *new creatures*, made privy to the meaning of existence, empowered for self-mastery, commissioned for social service, and destined—in the economy of grace—to enjoy forever the eternal life in which they already now participate.

This is a *sampling* of the central Christian affirmations. Clustered around them are a host of subordinate statements which theology integrates with the central affirmations through the agency of both naive and scientifically-mediated human experience.

The question now arises: Are assertions of this sort to be called true; and may they—taken together—be called a branch of knowledge? My answer to this question is affirmative, although I concede that theology is a *singular* branch of knowledge, a *peculiar* science. No doubt it is for this reason that its status has sometimes been questioned, and its deliverances ignored.

In what follows I hope to present its credentials, and to register its claim upon recognition and acceptance as a science.

B. THE CRITERIA OF SCIENCE

To get some structure into our discussion we do well to ask ourselves what conditions theology, or any other thing, must fulfill in order to be admitted into the community of the sciences. I suggest that, at the very least, it must satisfy the following conditions:

1. It must have a determinate *subject matter*—a specifiable *object*, or a meaningful facet or dimension of experience—which it seeks to depict and understand.

2. It must have warrant for supposing that the object of its study is *real*—a veritable *existent*—and not something merely imagined or wishfully projected.

3. It must rest on a real and established *relation* between the object of knowledge and the inquiring or knowing subject. There must be an intelligible *object*, an intelligent *subject*, and between them an effectual correlation must be set up.

4. It must exhibit fidelity to the elementary *canons of rationality*, namely internal *consistency* and external *coherence*. This means that its component parts must not contradict each other; and the whole must be compatible with what is elsewhere and otherwise known to be true.

5. It must fulfill the rational demand for *evidence*. That is, it must announce and implement creditable procedures for *validating* its assertions.

6. It must *serve* the entire human community by extending and deepening man's understanding of the universe. Its contributions should affect not only the ongoing work in the other sciences, but also the life and practice of society in general.

I propose to structure our discussion around these six conditions or criteria, with the hope that when we are finished we will have come closer to knowing both *what* theology substantively is, and *whether* it does in fact yield rationally grounded and intelligently structured knowledge.

C. THE SUBJECT MATTER OF THEOLOGY

The first requirement of a science is that it have an object to study and that it be able to give an intelligible, even though preliminary, account of it to the uninitiated who may be curious about it. —This requirement is met in different ways, and with varying degrees of clarity, by the several sciences.

1. It is most easily satisfied by *the formal* and *the natural sciences*— presumably because they take their objects (or properties of objects) from the world of sensory experience. So, if you should ask a scientist in this general area what it is he is studying, the arithmetician would say "numbers and their relations"; the geometrician would say "space and its configurations"; the physicist would say "the structure and motions of matter or the oscillations of energy." And so on.

2. The stated requirement is perhaps less easily satisfied by *the human and social sciences*—though in identifying and describing their objects of study practitioners in these fields can appeal to areas of experience recognizably and admittedly shared by the generality of men.

3. It gets relatively more difficult when we come to *philosophy*, not only because the object of philosophic scrutiny lies on a deeper and obscurer level of existence than that of the particular sciences, but also because what the object of philosophy is, is itself a philosophical problem and therefore periodically in dispute. For some, philosophy is merely a non-informational clarifying discipline. For others it is an informing science which deals with boundary-indifferent and omnirelevant questions, and which has as its object, not indeed the whole of reality, but yet reality-as-a-whole—the structure, pattern, or anatomy of the cosmos. In its highest reaches philosophy attains to *metaphysics* or ontology, which is essentially a search for the ultimate, the absolute, or the unconditioned.

4. In a significant sense theology lies close to metaphysics. But there is an important difference. Metaphysics, at least as that has appeared in the speculations of the West, inquires after what in the cosmos is creative of, or the source of, everything else. It typically absolutizes some selected feature of the created world and interprets all else in terms of it. *Theology*, on the other hand, posits or recognizes an object, not in, but beyond, above, and outside the world. Its object is the *supernatural*, the *transcendent*, the independent and eternal principle of existence, the super-cosmic ground or cause of everything other than itself. Its object, in short, is *God*—the "Holy One." It should be added that, though God (better: God in his disclosures) is the object of theology, theological thought is not restricted to God. Theology has to do with the world, too, especially with man, but with both of these only in relation to God.

D. THE REALITY OF GOD IN THEOLOGICAL PERSPECTIVE

A science is required not only to name and give a preliminary account of its object, but also to provide warrant for its reality. In the case of theology, the question is: Is there a real being who embodies the "meanings" which theology has packed into the word "God"? Does the idea of God have its counterpart in reality? In short, *is* there God? Does he *exist*?

This *kind* of question is not acute in the natural and social sciences, whose objects are relatively easy to locate, though this sort of question has arisen in reference to the "essences" and "substances" postulated by some metaphysicians, as well as to the electrons, neutrons, and other entities postulated by the physicists. But the question is acute in theology, because God is by nature and definition invisible. He cannot be grasped or even pointed at.

What warrant, then, does theology provide for its assertion that God, conceived of as supernatural intelligence and will, not only exists, but is Existence itself, and therefore the source and ground of all else that has being? —In theology three ways have been followed. God's existence has rested on either (1) logical inference, or (2) rational insight, or (3) direct, non-inferential awareness.

1. The way of *logical inference* goes by induction from certain features of external reality—such as finitude, motion, adaptiveness, and the like—towards the Unmoved Mover and the Ultimate Designer. The *cosmological* arguments function in this way.

2. The way of *rational insight* goes by analyzing the concept or idea of God and discovering that existence is part of the very meaning of "God." The *ontological* argument functions in this way.

3. The way of *direct non-inferential awareness* exploits man's universal moral sense of obligation, and concludes that the categorical imperative can issue from none other than God, the Ultimate Obliger. It also calls attention to the inexpungible "Sense" of God—the *sensus divinitatis*—which is native to all men, and is the seed of religion. The way of non-inferential immediate awareness is preferred by Augustinians and Calvinists, and is adumbrated by St. Paul in Romans 1 and 2. It appeals for verification of God's existence to the universal sense of his presence which, though subject to repression by human perversity, can never be extinguished.

E. THE GROUND AND SOURCE OF THEOLOGICAL KNOWLEDGE

The third requirement is that a science must rest on a real and established relation between the object of knowledge and the knowing subject.

1. Theology fulfills this demand in its own case by laying a correspondence between God and man in the doctrine of the *image*. Man, though finite, is like God and can enter into cognitive relations with him. Man can know God, as he is known of God, for God made man in his image and likeness. —Theology accounts for the possibility, not only of its own knowl-

edge of God, but also for the possibility of knowledge of anything at all, by its doctrine of *creation*. God made both man and things. The one he made intelligent and the other he made intelligible. God, therefore, is the link between knower and known. Without him all knowledge would vanish. He is the very precondition of science.

2. A very great difference between theology and other sciences must, however, be noted at this juncture—a difference owing to a difference in object. Theology is involved in a cognitive relation with God; other sciences, including philosophy, are involved in a cognitive relation with the world. Because non-theological sciences are in relation to the created cosmos, the *initiative* in knowing is always taken by the knowing subject, man. He locates the object to be known; he grasps it, he masters it, he reduces it to idea. Man in these instances is the discoverer and comprehender, and his tools are observation, experience, and reason. In theology the situation is different. The object of cognition—God—is not properly an object at all, but a subject, an agent. He cannot be sought after, approached, ferreted out, analyzed, mastered, reduced to idea. He cannot be discovered or uncovered. God is a *Person*, and if he is to be known he must take the initiative. To be known he must do the approaching, he must make the disclosure. He must *reveal* himself. Hence in theology it is not discovery and reason, but revelation and faith that are the key words.

3. The *method* of theology, as the method of every other science, is suited to its object or subject matter. But methodological suitability in theology means *receptivity* to the revelation of God, and the name for that receptivity is faith. Revelation and faith do not connote something unscientific. They are strict scientific categories, given the situation in which they figure and function—the God-man encounter.

4. Another point must be made here. —Because it is God who, at his own initiative, is known in theology (and not some creature), the very *shape* of theological knowledge is different from that of other knowledge, the knowledge of merely cosmic realities. God, who is supernatural, absolutely transcendent, is and must remain, even when revealed and "known," the ultimate "*Mystery*." As C. A. Bennett has said, "The mystery, the transcendent, the Unseen is foreign to the native air of our minds. It is opaque to human intelligence. Though grasped, it is not comprehended. It reveals itself but also conceals itself. God is known but he is known in a cloud of unknowing."

5. This is reflected in the nature and function of theological *language*, in what the philosophers have lately been calling "*God-Talk*." In other sciences —those dealing with created things—the terms used in discourse are employed in a univocal sense. In theology this is impossible. If, in calling God "father," the theologian were to be understood in a univocal sense, he could be charged with bringing God down to the level of the creature. What he means when he

calls God "father" is that God is "like," but also "unlike," our earthly fathers. He is not using the term equivocally, but neither is he using it univocally; he is using it *analogically*. And in so doing he is precisely scientific—i.e., he is using language fitted to the object of knowledge with which he is concerned.

F. THE CONSISTENCY AND COHERENCE OF THEOLOGICAL STATEMENTS

It must be noted, in the fourth place, that to deserve the name of science a thing must be characterized by *critical thinking*.

1. This means, quite simply, that technical reason (formal logic) must be stringently followed within the science. Nothing can rightly be called science that is not held together by logical bonds which correlate its parts and exclude all inner *contradictions*. Now, theology in principle fulfills this demand. It aims to be, and presents itself as, a *system*—not a closed system which excludes all accessions and alterations—but nevertheless as a system, in the sense of a concatenated assemblage of harmonious truths, a system from which are banished all internal contradictions. In a responsible theology there are *paradoxes* aplenty, but there are no contradictions, for no mind, least of all one fashioned in the school of God, can embrace at once both A and Non-A, except perhaps *dialectically*—which is another matter altogether.

2. But there is still another logical demand that science must satisfy: it must *cohere* with, be compatible with, every other truth that has been established and acknowledged. To be a science is not to be alone, but to be a member of a community of sciences, and all of these sciences together are in principle required to develop a single unified universe of knowledge. Theology accepts this demand and, while it will not hastily and irresponsibly accommodate itself to every claim made in other departments of learning, it will refuse to assert in theology what has been convincingly refuted elsewhere. It therefore goes on its way with poise; it is confident that whatever has truly been *revealed* will not, and cannot, be in conflict with that which has truly been *discovered*. —Not only that: theology, for its own enrichment, gladly utilizes all relevant materials and insights which other sciences can contribute.

G. THE VALIDATION OF THEOLOGICAL ASSERTIONS

The fifth condition is that science must fulfill the rational demand for *evidence*, that it must *validate* itself. This demand is very closely related to the previously stated condition, that it must obey the logical laws of critical thinking. But the two demands are not identical. In focus here is the question concerning *"proof,"* and this raises a number of issues not directly germane to the question concerning consistency and coherence.

1. The first thing to be observed is that, though sciences of every sort are required to validate their assertions, *no single type* of evidence will suffice for all. This is so even for the non-philosophical particular sciences—natural or social. What is required to prove a mathematical statement is a flawless deductive inference from accepted definitions and fixed axioms. Nothing of this sort may be demanded to establish the truth of an historical, an ethical, or an esthetical judgment. These sorts of judgments are validated in their own ways, in ways appropriate in each case to their subject matters and methods.

2. It may also be here observed that the *tightness of demonstration* achievable in mathematics is not achievable even in physics, let alone ethics and theology. As one moves up the ladder from the formal and quantitative towards the normative sciences "proof" alters its complexion and loses its rigor. But this should disturb no one. It certainly should not tempt one to mathematicize all the sciences, including philosophy, as Descartes proposed to do.

3. If one should now ask, What is the kind of evidence that theology is prepared to present in support of its assertions, then I should reply that it validates itself in much the same way that the great *constructive philosophers* attempted to validate their systems. Plato, Hegel, and others like them, never thought of their systems as being the conclusion of a strict inductive or deductive process. They thought of them as hypotheses, as heuristic proposals, and they presented them for acceptance as illuminators of experience.

4. In like manner it must be said that *theology*—in particular, Christian theology—is not the mere precipitate of ordinary methodological inquiry. It is not a construct based on discovery and erected through the employment of logical procedures upon merely cosmic givens accessible to ordinary experience. Nor is it a mere hypothesis. It is a response to and a systematic articulation of divinely revealed truths. Accordingly, if its assertions are to be critically examined, they may not be rejected because they are not the necessary result of inductive or deductive mental operations. If theology is to be tested at all—as it may and should be—it can only be tested in terms of its *explanatory efficacy*, in terms of its ability to *illumine* and *integrate* consciousness and life. Its truth is vindicated by its power to order and interpret the whole range of human experience, and to disclose the hidden structures and meanings of cosmic reality. Conscientious Christian theologians are always putting their constructions to *the test of reality* in this way, and in the measure that they faithfully depict Scripture they are finding their theologies corroborated and validated by things as they *are*.

5. But of course this is not to *demonstrate* Christianity. It is not to

"prove" it in such a way as to lay an unwilling mind under intellectual constraint. No one was ever forced inwardly to affirm the Gospel. It is only as one wills to do so that a perspective on the world is opened up which brings the whole of reality in support of the choice. It is as one commits oneself to Christianity that corroboration for it is found on every hand. By this it is validated.

H. THE VALUE OF THEOLOGY

Finally, a science worthy of the name will contribute to the universal store of knowledge, and in its own way affect both the economy of the other sciences and the life and practice of the human community.

If all authentic sciences do this, theology is, in this respect, the chief of them. Theology deals with supernatural realities, with extra-cosmic verities. Better: it deals with the eternal and living God, whose engagements with men in grace and judgment undergird and envelop all human endeavors. What theology has to say, therefore, affects all that man thinks and does—in science and without. It does this because nothing can be insulated against the influences of religion, and theology is religion made articulate. I therefore agree with Cardinal Newman when, in his address called "The Idea of a University," he declared, ". . . the omission of Christian theology from the list of recognized sciences is not only indefensible in itself, but prejudicial to all the rest"—and, I may add, is injurious to human society.

10

Prayer and Providence

INTRODUCTION

PRAYER, unuttered or expressed, is an address made to God by a human being on the assumption that communication is possible between the finite and the infinite.

Prayer, as simple *communication*, does not of itself imply *communion* or spiritual fellowship with the Divine. It may, and sometimes does, resemble nothing so much as a desperate call upon a distant stranger whom one hardly knows and does not love, but whom one faintly hopes will—whether gladly or reluctantly, whether whimsically or habitually—attend to a frantic human cry of need and despair. Such a cry or call (often instinctive) is, of course, not the purest kind of prayer, but it is an addressive action implicit in which are a number of propositions—constituting a set of beliefs—that underlie *all* prayer. Among these propositions are the following: (1) God exists; (2) God can hear or take notice; (3) God can help. In the event one or more of these propositions are false, all prayer is groundless. And where these propositions are disbelieved no prayer can consistently be uttered. On the other hand, if these propositions are true, prayer is both warranted and desirable, and even mandatory.

The problem of prayer, therefore, is centrally the problem of God. It impinges directly upon the issue of God's *existence*, his essential *attributes*, and his *relation* to the world. I shall, accordingly, structure my observations about prayer in terms of these three issues.

I. THE EXISTENCE OF GOD

A. There are those—called atheists—who profess to know that God does not exist. And there are others—called agnostics—who, professing ignorance, remain uncommitted, and regard God's existence as an open, and irresolvable, question.

The Christian regards both of these classes of men as mistaken. The Christian can of course not demonstrate the existence of God by either inductive or deductive arguments. There are no theistic proofs that satisfy the canons of strict logic. There is no intellectual stair that leads uninterruptedly from the finite to the infinite.

But the Christian believes—and indeed knows—that a way has been paved from the infinite to the finite. The world, he knows, is full of the signs of God's presence. God's footprints are everywhere upon the sands of time, and his fingerprints are on everything that has been made. In the constitution and design of nature, and in the pulsations of all things living, God's intelligence and power are indelibly registered. It is true that not all men notice these signs and registrations. The significance of nature's constellations and processes does not penetrate the consciousness of all, and thus, at this level some men can plead ignorance of God and others can go so far as to deny his reality altogether. But in the final analysis they can't. For God approaches men not only through the hazy and misty corridors of nature, where his entrance into mind can be barred by inattention and penultimate preoccupations. He enters men's minds *directly*; he evokes their reluctant awareness; and he registers his claims upon their conscience.

The Christian's warrant for making this quite dogmatic statement is in part his own experience of God within his heart and mind; in part the witness of people of all ages, climes, and cultures to the inescapability of a haunting presence before which they could not but tremble or adore; and in part—though most centrally—the apostolic teaching that God is such a one as will not let himself be unknown to any man. God, the Bible declares, does not allow himself to be fenced out of mind. He *does* allow men to *repress* their consciousness of him, and he does allow men to *misconceive* and misconstrue him. But he does *not* allow men to be *ignorant* of him.

By that token he does not allow them to be *irreligious*. Because he is the great Unavoidable, all men must react to him. And all men do. We find them everywhere positing some god—not always the true one; and everywhere practicing religion—not always the right one. The true God, who irresistibly evokes a human awareness of himself, is in the broken and fragmented mind of fallen man refracted into the likeness of a creature, and then worshipped as such. Sometimes, as in most ethnic religions, he is transmuted into such a figure as can be prayed to, and about whom an elaborate ritual can be created. At other times, as in atheistic or agnostic secularism, he is transmuted into an impersonal force, an abstract essence, a beckoning ideal, or an engendering value; and then he is neither prayed to nor hedged about with ceremony. But in each instance the surrogate god to which men attach themselves is a reflection—though a distorted one—of the God of whom they cannot but be aware, and in response to whose presence they must necessarily make some radical commitment.

Perhaps to some this analysis of man's existential status and posture seems forced and unactual. The secularist, by his own profession, is without intimations of deity, and he has no taste or flair for religion. He does not go to church, he sings no hymns, and he does not offer prayers. The universe for him is a flat mundane surface, limited by birth and death, stretched between womb and tomb, without any dimension of depth, with no heaven above, and no immortality beyond. Is it fair—against all his protestations—to plant a god in his head, and—against his earnest disavowals—to make him out to be religious? I can only reiterate that it is. In the Christian understanding God not only exists; he exerts his pressure on every soul; and that pressure cannot but be felt and responded to. Men do have a native and indelible awareness of God—what Calvin called the *sensus divinitatis*—and they are therefore ineluctably compelled either to affirm him or to establish a *substitute* for him. In their brokenness men habitually make substitutions. Avowedly religious people residing outside the realm of grace create a pantheon of spurious gods around which they build a cult. Secularists, who repudiate the gods and eschew all cult, posit some impersonal object of ultimate concern about which they seek to integrate and direct their lives. By this token even the secularist has a "god"—something other than himself in which he trusts, something which evokes his allegiance, something he wills to serve. His religion may be without ceremonial accoutrements, and it may in the usual sense be prayerless, but it is a religion nevertheless, and to this extent it reflects the reality of the one true God revealed in Jesus Christ.

This being the case, prayer, or some imitation of it, is a world-wide phenomenon. It is not confined to the Christian community; it is universal. Of course, the basis of men's prayers, the rationale and shape of them, are not identical. They vary with the form and texture of the religion of which they form a part. But wherever—as in all the ethnic religions—the existence of God is acknowledged, there prayer inevitably follows. For, if God exists, and is in some sense recognized, how can men not call upon him and do him homage? And in all the established religions of the world this is what men regularly do.

What, then, of the radical secularist? Well, we do not discover him at prayer, but we often find him engaging in a *surrogate* for it. We find him meditating. *Meditation* is, of course, not true prayer, and the Christian should not take it for such. It is a *substitute* for prayer, a posture suited to the nature of the substitute "god" that the secularist has posited. Being a caricature, it

has no authentic religious value. This does not mean, however, that meditation and introspection, and similar psychological practices are barren and
devoid of all value. They have considerable mundane value, and they have
this for Christian and secularist alike. For the secularist, who conceives of
God as an abstract ground of being or as an impersonal force pervading the
universe, meditation and reflection can serve to put him into tune with what
he regards as the melody of the spheres, and induce quietude and resignation.
For the Christian, meditation can serve a similar wholesome purpose. The
busy world is often too much with us. It intrudes, obtrudes, and scatters us,
and for our mental and spiritual health we are often obliged to retreat into
solitude, there to reflect and meditate, and in the process to rediscover and
restore ourselves. Only, such meditation must not be confused with a
genuine address to God. It does not soar, it can evoke no divine response, it
can effect no changes in the external arrangements of the world, it cannot
influence the course of historical events, and it can establish no rapport with
God. Meditation is at worst a spurious substitute for prayer, and at best a
mere preparation for it. In any case it lies before the threshold of that
divine-human communion which, in prayer, the Christian seeks both to
attain and to express.

I come now to a second consideration.

II. THE NATURE OF GOD

For prayer to be meaningful it is necessary not only that God should
exist, but also that he should possess a determinate *character*. To justify
prayer, God must not only be thought to *be;* he must be thought to embody
relevant *attributes*. In particular, he must be thought *capable* of hearing
prayers, and thought *willing* to attend to them. The God confessed in the
church is just such a god. He is a god who, though highly exalted and
incomparable in his glory, is yet in some real sense like us (we being made in
his image). He, like us, is both an "individual," separate and distinct from
every other entity; and he is also "social." He participates from all eternity in
the intra-trinitarian community which constitutes his essence, and he participates in time in a creator-creature relation which intends and generates
community. Being so constituted—as individual and societal; being distinct
from, though in relation to mankind; and being, moreover, cognizant both
apriorily and experientially of man's needs and circumstances, he is in empathy with man, and in free grace receptive of man's every address.

A. The first point to notice here is that the Christian God is *able* to hear
prayers. Notice that at this juncture I am not contending that he is able to *do*
anything in response to these prayers. Whether or not he is able to *do* any-

thing depends upon his mastery or non-mastery of the world, and that is a question that we shall consider in the third and final section of this essay. Here we are only asking whether prayers can reach him and register themselves upon his consciousness.

1. The Christian answer to this question is that prayers can reach and register themselves with him because (to begin with) he is, in his very nature, a veritable *person*, a true *self*—and thus intrinsically *addressable*. Were he less or other than this—were he only a supreme essence or an intricate structure—he could become a reference point for human self-improvement; he could even be aspired after and enjoyed; but he could not meaningfully be *addressed*, for he would be unable to hear or notice. But God, in the Christian view, is a centered self possessing all the marks of selfhood—life, intelligence, volition, and affection. He lives, perceives, understands, wills, and feels. He is not merely the super-personal ground of human personality, as Tillich contends. He is in the strictest sense a person. Of course, his personality is infinitely complex (consider his triune nature), and it transcends the limitations that characterize our own (which is only analogous to his). But this means that he is not less, but more, personal than we are—more acute, more aware, more sensitive than we shall ever be. It is this fact that justifies prayer. God is not a mere object, but a subject; not a thing, but a self. And though he has no ears (for he is not corporeal), he is infinite *Spirit*, and this enables him to hear.

2. A second and third reason why God is *able* to hear and understand our prayers is that he is both immanent and transcendent. —Consider first his *immanence*. Although remaining the Holy and Exalted One, God is, and from the beginning has been, immanent in our world by his spirit and power. His strong arms uphold the stars in their courses, and his near presence is, as we have seen, felt in the consciousness of every man. But it is not of this that at the moment I am speaking. It is of that other, more redemptive immanence which we call the *Incarnation*. The Incarnation is inseparable in Christian thought from the Crucifixion and Resurrection of our Lord, it being the precondition of these. But it is not in that relation and context that I now wish to contemplate it. I wish only to point out that God is *able* to hear and understand our prayers, not merely because he is *personal*, but because he became *incarnate*. He took up residence in our world, assumed our flesh, subjected himself to the conditions of our existence, participated in our weaknesses, and shared our sorrows—in short, he *identified* himself with us. He therefore knows, not merely by omniscient intelligence, but by concrete experience, by historical participation, by real involvement, and by actual endurance the quantity and quality of our hurts and pains, our perplexities and wonderings, our desires and aspirations. And so, when we call upon him, he not only *hears*: he *empathetically understands* what we are saying or

asking, detecting with sensitivity honed by real experience every nuance of our fevered cries.

3. A third reason God is *able* to hear our prayers is that he is *transcendent*—an inhabitant of *eternity*. Some people are skeptical about prayer, or at least perplexed by it, because they find it hard to believe that God can hear a multitude of prayers at once. How, they ask, is God able in one moment of time to attend to a million voices simultaneously raised to claim his attention? The solution to this difficulty lies in the fact that God transcends the temporal flux, and is not required to fit many things into one brief segment of time's duration. In his book, *Beyond Personality* (pp. 14–17), C. S. Lewis puts this whole matter in sharp focus when he says,

> God is not in Time. His life does not consist of moments following one another. If a million people are praying to him at ten-thirty tonight, he hasn't got to listen to them all in that one little snippet which we call ten-thirty. Ten-thirty—and every other moment from the beginning of the world—is always the *Present* for him. If you like to put it that way, he has all eternity in which to listen to the split second of prayer put up by a pilot as his plane crashes in flames. . . . God is not hurried along in the Time-stream of this universe any more than an author is hurried along in the imaginary time of his own novel. He has infinite attention to spare for each one of us. . . . His life is not dribbled out moment by moment like ours. . . . If you picture Time as a straight line along which we have to travel, then you must picture God as the whole page on which the line is drawn. We come to the parts of the line one by one: we have to leave A behind before we get to B, and can't reach C till we leave B behind. God, from above, or outside, or all around, contains the whole line, and sees it all. . . .

So much, then, for the *ability* of God to hear our prayers. But is he *willing* to do so? Is he *disposed* to be in communication with the members of the human race? Does he put *any store* in the attention that they pay him? Or is he perhaps *wishing* that they would refrain from bothering him?

B. The *willingness* of God to hear our prayers, as distinct from his *ability* to do so, is indicated on every page of the Bible. From the Bible we learn, indeed, not only that God is willing to listen, but that he is *eager* to do so. He *yearns* to be addressed and sought out. In fact, so desirous is he of our prayers that he *commands* us to offer them. To understand this state of affairs it will be helpful to consider two great acts of God (creation and redemption) and one essential feature of his being (his trinitarian nature).

1. First, then, *creation*. The world is not self-existent. The being that it has is *derived*. Though it now is, it once was not. It came into being when God called it forth out of nothing, encased it in time, supplied it with structure, set it on its course, supervised its development, and crowned it with man. By God's design man was set as the immanent head of all creation. In him the entire cosmos was centered and integrated, that by the ministry of man the whole human race, and its cosmic environment, might fulfill the

divine purpose in creating. And now, what was that *purpose? Why* did God create the world? He was under no necessity, under no external compulsion, to do so. His glory was complete before all worlds. Nothing was needed to enhance him. *Why*, then, did he do this thing? There is only one answer to that question: He did it because he is *love*. The *agape* that names his essence fixed and settled his determination *not to be alone*, but to *share* his blessedness and felicity with others. He created man in order that the intra-trinitarian community might be so enlarged as to allow *others* to be insinuated into the divine life. He did it in order that man might participate in the Kingdom and enjoy the divine fellowship. In short, *communion* was his goal—not for his own sake (for he was always in communion), but for the sake of man. This being the case, he could not but delight in man's acknowledgment of him, man's desire to speak with him, and man's resort to him for guidance and instruction in the ways of the Kingdom. Since God's purpose has never been abandoned, he still delights in this. Prayer pleases him because it betokens the reality of that *community* the establishment of which was the goal of the pristine creation.

2. Consider in the second place, *redemption*. .We need not, for our present purpose, linger long upon the saving acts that God performed in Jesus Christ. It is not that these acts are not of great, indeed, ultimate, importance. It is only that, in the context of the present discussion, the redemption of the fallen race may be viewed as the grace-induced act of God to restore the creation, to redirect it towards it earliest goal, and to bring back into fellowship with himself those who in mysterious perversity had fled him or rebelled against him. One can therefore understand that when, through the vast expenditure of God's costly grace, repentant sinners call upon him, he delights in their prayers, and is mightily *disposed* to give them all that they ask in his name and according to his purpose.

3. *Trinity*. We should note in the third place that, so desirous is the God of Love to benefit and enrich his human creatures that he himself by powerful impulses moves them towards himself, the only source and ground of their felicity. He does not leave men to their own resources, but by the employment of his full trinitarian energy, evokes their prayers, and ushers them with infinite solicitude into the community of God. C. S. Lewis puts this nicely in the following words:

> An ordinary simple Christian kneels down to say his prayers. He is trying to get into touch with God. But if he is a Christian he knows that what is prompting him to pray is also God; God, so to speak, inside him. But he also knows that all his real knowledge of God comes through Christ, the Man who was God—that Christ is standing beside him, helping him to pray, praying for him. . . . God is the thing beyond the whole universe *to* which he is praying—the goal he's trying to reach. . . . God is also the thing *inside* him which is pushing him on—the

motive power. . . . God is also the *road* or bridge along which he is being pushed to that goal. . . . So that the whole three-fold life of the *three-personal* Being is actually going on in that ordinary little room where an ordinary man is saying his prayers. The man is being caught up into the higher kind of life . . .; he is being pulled into God, by God, while still remaining himself (*Beyond Personality*, pp. 10-11).

Before ending this section on the nature of God, and on his ability and willingness to hear the prayers of men, it may be appropriate to highlight what has been implicit thus far, namely that, at the bottom, and in its purest state, prayer is not a way to get things out of God, but rather a way to receive what he freely offers—fellowship with himself. At the heart of prayer is *communion*, communion characterized at both poles by concern and fidelity. . . . God's concern is for the welfare and ultimate blessedness of his creatures. . . . The believer's concern is for the accomplishment of God's redemptive purposes both in his own life and in that of all God's creatures. Prayer, therefore, and the divine response to it, is the token, and indeed the substance, of a divine-human fellowship and *communion* in the accomplishment of a single purpose—the final and perfect establishment of the Kingdom of God.

III. GOD AND THE WORLD

We have come now to the third and last part of this essay, and here we must consider, not whether God exists, or whether he is able and willing to hear our prayers, but whether he can *effectually respond* to them—that is, whether his power and mastery is such as would enable him to alter things and influence events, and thus be of help. A full discussion of the subject would consider the nature of his response to such elements of prayer as praise, adoration, and communion. But, considering the limitations of space, and having special regard to the relation of prayer to providence, I shall focus on petitionary prayer—the type of prayer which to many people is particularly problematic. It should be remarked in passing that included in petition is intercession, and in its train, when things are properly ordered, is of course thanksgiving.

A. *Providence.* To get a hold on the problem before us I shall begin by giving the briefest possible account of the Christian doctrine of providence. Let it be said then that the Christian who believes in providence believes that the world and all of its inhabitants is *upheld* by the supremely good, infinitely wise, all-powerful, and personal Creator God, who not only *preserves* that world in its being and form, but also exercises such superintendency and *governance* over it that it is teleologically directed toward a *goal* which he has set and to the attainment of which all events, great and small, are *sovereignly* employed or utilized.

Out of this summary statement two things may be lifted out for further elaboration:

1. The first thing to be observed is that one of the two chief elements in providence is *preservation*, a continuous act of God required because the world is not self-sustaining, but utterly contingent. The idea here is that the world which was called forth out of nothing hovers over an abyss of nothing-ness and would plunge into it were it not for the preserving grace of God. As I have elsewhere said,

> The God Christians believe in is not only the Creator of the world; he is also its sustainer. What God once made he now supports and constantly renews. He gives existence to every being, energy to all that moves, and life to every living thing. He does not do this once and for all and then depart; he does this incessantly. All things are constantly upheld and energized by his present Power.

It is especially to be noted that divine *preservation*, which reflects God's faithfulness to his creation, guarantees the constancy of nature and the order of its arrangements. This gives a lease to science, for a structured nature is the very precondition of the scientist's vocation. It is then by God's grace that the scientist has before him "an impersonal, objectively existing nature with stable characteristics, open to observation, amenable to analysis, and operating in ways susceptible of mathematical formulation" (H.S.). More than that, this preserved order is calculated to give to every man "a feeling of cosmic security." As Emil Brunner says, "The laws of Nature point to Him in whose hands it is good to *rest*, under whose mighty control we can live *quietly*, and in *confidence*" (*Doctrine of Creation and Redemption*, pp. 161–162).

2. The second element in providence is *government*. This is sometimes understood deterministically or fatalistically, as though everything that happens in the world happens by God's agency and according to a fixed and unalterable plan which he laid down before the world was framed. This is, I think, not the right or Christian view. God is not the sole agent of historical events. He is, in particular, not the cause or author of sin; sin was, contrary to the divine will, introduced by the errant creature. Also, the plan of God, though fixed upon a determinate goal, is flexible in the arrangements of its parts. The sovereignty of God, accordingly, does not mean such mechanical domination over man's will as would rob it of its freedom and responsibility. The sovereignty of God consists in his unlimited ability to *maneuver* in the face of opposition and resistance, and to so *over-rule* all evil that, so far from frustrating his ultimate design, it is woven into the divine web, and made

serviceable to his Kingdom. In this sovereignty, then, we may confidently trust.

B. Against this background what shall we now say of petitionary prayer? I don't know what, given a little more time and much more wisdom, I might be able to say. But now I shall make only four short remarks and bring this discussion to an end.

1. There is, as far as I can see, no obstacle in providence to freely offered requests for the exercise of divine agency. Although God's will is firmly settled upon the goal that he has fixed, it would seem that as the Living One who moves with infinite resourcefulness around the obstacles human agents place upon his path, he would be able, by the same token, to accommodate and domicile the supplications of the saints. It appears, in short, that God's plan is not so tightly woven as to prevent the insertion in it of what may be called the adventitious cries of his petitioning creatures.

2. It should further be observed that God is free, and that he can, and does, combine variability of action with consistency of purpose. As Langdon Gilkey remarks: "His actions are not restricted to certain universal and therefore invariable relations to the world, as if everything he did was everywhere and always the same. Rather, in agreement with his purpose, which does not change, his actions on the world can vary as he chooses" (*Maker of Heaven and Earth*, p. 97). And what he chooses may well be in response to a human request addressed to him.

3. It will be remembered that preservation guarantees the stability and reliability of the natural order. It would therefore seem likely that the established divine arrangements would set certain limits to what the believer is allowed to ask for. I suspect that one cannot, without impugning God's order and minimizing his faithfulness to it, asks God to make the climb up a hill as facile as the descent, or to heal a fractured bone overnight, or to keep aloft a plane which has lost all its engines.

4. On the other hand, it must be observed that, though "God stands by his law, because he stands by his creations" (Brunner), he is not *bound* to it. The God of Order transcends the order he has established and he can act and work in ways that are miraculous. As I said earlier, "God is free to plant his steps precisely where he will, and sometimes he plants them on unaccustomed ways—and performs a miracle. He does this, we may be sure, to serve some holy purpose. Perhaps he does it on occasion just to testify that he is free, and so reveal his glory." And sometimes, no doubt, he does it to succor and to heal the supplicating saint.

11

The Death-of-God Theology

DURING THE LAST FEW YEARS a new movement has arisen in the theological world, and the creators of it have managed to give the movement a voice. Being young, energetic, bold, and articulate, they have not stayed in their studies or even in their classrooms, but they have addressed the nation in a spate of books, articles, and speeches. And they have been heard. They have been read by students, listened to by popular audiences, and interviewed by reporters. And they have been commented on. Not only the religious, but also the secular press has analyzed, wondered at, praised, and denounced them.

All this puts a man in a quandary. On the one hand, how can one be silent about a thing everyone is vocal about? On the other hand, what need is there to speak after so much has already been said? If, as the appearance of this essay attests, I have broken out of the quandary, it is not because I am entirely sure that the moment calls for speech rather than silence. I write, I suppose, partly because, like everybody else, I am curious about the movement; partly because friends have idly wondered what I thought about it; and partly because a witness of some sort seems simply to be called for. Whatever the explanation may be, I herewith hazard some observations on the subject.

This essay first appeared in *The Reformed Journal* in March 1966, September 1966, and November 1966.

1. PHENOMENOLOGY

The people whose views we are to discuss are sometimes called the "Death of God" theologians. They themselves have chosen to call themselves "theological radicals." Gabriel Vahanian, who is sometimes numbered among them, but who is really critical of them, has called them "atheosophists" or "Christosophists." Others have called them "Christian atheists," and some have called them names too unflattering to repeat. In any case, the names already mentioned will suffice to label them.

Those so labeled are few in number. Thomas J. J. Altizer of Emory University in Atlanta is one of them. So is William Hamilton of the Rochester-Colgate Divinity School, and so is Paul van Buren of Temple University. Besides these there are hardly any at all—at least not yet—although the thinkers concerned do claim the support of such contemporaries as Rudolf Bultmann and John A. T. Robinson, of such recent theologians as Dietrich Bonhoeffer and Paul Tillich, and of such earlier ones as Sören Kierkegaard and Ludwig Feuerbach.

Mention of these European theologians provides the occasion to observe that the radical theologians are all American, and that, indeed, they are conscious of doing theology in an American setting in a typically American way. Says Hamilton: "The time of European hegemony is at an end. . . . The thing of being a Christian in America today is so wildly *sui generis* that our most precious clues are no longer expected to come from a *Zeitschrift* or a *Dogmatik.*"

It is this Americanism that presumably accounts for the worldliness, the secularity, the radicalness, not to say the brazenness of the theology under consideration. Says Hamilton: "America is the place that has travelled furthest along the road from the cloister to the world that Luther and the reformation mapped out. We are the most profane, the most banal, the most utterly worldly of places." An American theology, it is suggested, should in its mood and structure comport with this fact.

Speaking of mood and structure, it may be remarked that the radical theology is less a system than it is a thesis. Also, it is largely negative: it draws its strength from a denial, and its general mood is iconoclastic. This does not mean that it has nothing positive to propose. It is not without its affirmations, nor is it without a sense of direction. But the direction is still uncertain and the proposed alternative to traditional theology has as yet no fixed form. This is perhaps the reason why most academic theologians, unlike many writers in the popular press, have either ignored the new theology or have suspended comment and critique until something more positive and substantial shall have been said.

At the moment, indeed, not even Altizer, Hamilton, and van Buren know with any degree of certainty precisely what their colleagues are saying. There is obviously a bond of sympathy between them, but they hardly know each other personally, have conferred hardly at all (though plans are afoot to start a "school" journal), and there are indications that at critical junctures they differ with each other. The movement, conducted by men in their late 30's or early 40's, is obviously just getting off the ground, and its ultimate course, shape, destiny, and cohesion cannot with any confidence be predicted.

This points up, of course, the hazard anyone runs who attempts to expound the movement. In my own case, I wish it to be clearly understood that my analysis is tentative and extremely corrigible. It may be shamefully premature. Yet in the light of recent publicity given to the movement, one can hardly keep completely silent. Moreover, the radical theologians do have a claim upon the concern and the corrective influence of others who, with them, are trying, however weakly or mistakenly, to do theology in a world increasingly forgetful of Christ's name.

Before indicating how I propose to structure the exposition, I wish to declare that my posture over against the new radical theology is negative. But I nevertheless believe that there is something in the world and in the gospel which it has pointed out and which traditional theology has left unnoticed or unaccented. For that, in spite of all that must be opposed, we can be thankful. For this, too, we can be thankful: that these men, however perverse and mistaken their procedure and program may be, are trying to relate Christian teaching to the modern secular man. This every theologian and preacher must do, and there is reason to believe that we who confess the living personal God as Creator of the world and Jesus Christ as its divine Lord and Savior, have not been too successful at it. Perhaps the false start of the radical theologians will serve to enlist us for a better, more biblical, and more effective attempt to speak to our alienated generation.

There are obviously many ways of structuring an exposition of the new radical theology, and I am not at all sure that the way I have chosen is the best. But when I first heard of the movement I asked myself (1) who or what is the *God* whose death is being proclaimed? and (2) what is meant by saying that he, whoever he is, has *died* or is *dead?* and (3) who or what has come to *take his place?* and (4) what *moves* these theologians to speak as they do? Now, I suspect that others are asking these questions as well. I propose, accordingly, to pose these four questions anew, and to provide intelligible answers to them.

In eliciting answers to the first two questions I shall not restrict myself to the radical theologians, but will appeal as well to other people, including ourselves, who, like them, do also in some sense or other proclaim the death of God. In this way a *context* may be established for the unique and undoubtedly mistaken denial of God's existence by the radical theologians.

2. GOD

In order to enter fruitfully into a discussion of the God whose death is being proclaimed it is necessary to observe at the outset that, in a manner of speaking, the *existence* of God is not in question but only his *essence*. No one denies, I am sure, that something in the world, or out of it, is a proper object of ultimate concern, an entity or value worthy of man's unconditional loyalty, a final source of being and meaning. What men deny is not that "God" *is*, but that he is such and so. They oppose not divinity, but what they regard as a faulty conception of this. The God-question is, accordingly, not a question about *whether* there is something upon which all depends, but *what* that something is really like, and how it should be described.

What this concretely means is that the radical theologians, in their proclamation of God's death, are negating, not "God," but a certain *understanding* of him. They are repudiating a theology. When they say that God is dead they are saying that somebody's conception of him should be buried.

Now there can be no doubt that there are a number of such theological corpses in the world, and that the proposal to bury them is an eminently Christian proposal. There are, so to speak, a number of gods that are dead, and deserving of quick interment. The only question is who or what are they? The traditional Christian and the contemporary radical theologian cannot possibly differ on the question as to *whether* the death of some god should be proclaimed, but only on the question as to which gods these are.

What, then, are contemporary theologians concretely saying when they say that "*God* is dead"?

(1) They could be saying—and they no doubt are saying—that *the god of the primitive peoples is dead*.

This god, confined to the world, is a diffused nature spirit, diversified into many spirits in accordance with the diversity of nature. This god, multiplied by the numerous things in nature and by the many occupations and concerns of men, inhabits earth and sky, forest and field, lake and stream, and indeed every nook and cranny of the world, which by his presence he divinizes and makes sacral.

It is against this god that the Old Testament prophets inveighed, for they had heard from the Lord of all that the earth and the world were quite unsacral, neither divine nor suffused with divinity, but created and quite worldly and secular. Through the influence of their teaching—i.e., their proclamation that this god is dead—there was banished from large areas of the world the superstition and magic which is the inevitable consequence of animism. And through the influence of that same proclamation the foundations of modern science were laid: with the prophetic banishment of resident spirits and divinities men were made free to manipulate and control the inanimate world with that objectivity and detachment which is the hallmark of science.

Now I judge that we are enjoined by the Christ we serve both to endorse the prophetic judgment upon primitive animism and to embrace with thankfulness the scientific structure consequent upon it; and also to resist, in concert with the radical theologians, every spiritualistic attempt to compromise, by a kind of pseudo-religiosity, the genuinely Christian secularity which is our inheritance from the prophets.

(2) When the radical theologians say that "God is dead," they could be speaking too—and I judge they are—of the god the Apostles and the early Christians spoke against—*the god of the Greek Polis and of the Roman Imperium*. It is significant, and worthy of note, that on account of their negative speaking and acting the early Christians were called "atheists"—a name which in this case was a badge of honor. What the New Testament and the emerging church saw clearly was that God could not be identified with any nation, any history, any culture, or any race; that he stood above them all; that his grace and judgment rested upon them equally; and that one cannot worship at any national or racial shrine, or serve any cultural gods.

That we may not do so in America today—or in South Africa—we are perhaps beginning to learn. The radical theologians have learned it, and they are proclaiming the death of the god men have arrogantly invoked to justify their false superiority and spurious pride.

(3) Another god whose death the radical theologians are proclaiming is *the god of philosophical ontology*. This is the god of Plato and Aristotle, and of all who in the intellectual history of the West have followed in their path. This god was fashioned in accordance with the Greek notion of perfection. Being perfect, there was no motion in him; he could therefore neither create nor have emotions. Being perfect, he could love or desire only the best; he could therefore love neither the ugly nor the immoral, but himself. Being perfect, and therefore spiritual and rational, he could only be confronted by but not subdue matter and the non-rational. Being perfect, he was unchangeable, unable to respond to prayers or to move in empathy and compassion with creatures in time and space.

This god, qualified by biblical revelation, was introduced into Christian theology during the patristic and medieval periods and became a constituent of classical theism. Against this god Pascal inveighed when he declared "not the god of the philosophers, but the God of Abraham, Isaac, and Jacob."

Against this god the radical theologians, too, declare. They pronounce him dead. They repudiate an ontological god concept. They do this too indiscriminately, but they have laid their finger on what is, at least in part, a foreign import into Christian theology. In whatever terms the divine transcendence may be stated, it may not be stated in terms of metaphysical abstraction.

(4) There is another god which has come upon the Christian stage. It is *the god of the gaps*. This is the god who has sometimes been used by Christians to fill in the gaps of scientific knowledge. He is a deistically conceived god, a *Deus ex machina*, who is employed as an occasional hypothesis when scientific explanation is at a stand. This god is periodically inserted into the ordered pattern of created events and processes by "religious" people in order to account for otherwise inexplicable phenomena. In the presence of this god the radical theologians proclaim a scientific atheism, meaning thereby, not, or not necessarily, that the being of God is irrelevant to scientific studies, but that scientific method is, and ought to remain, the method by which one part of nature is explained in terms of another: i.e., that the scientific method is the method of natural correlation. The radical theologians have a point. There is a sense in which, to use the words of Nathaniel Micklem, "science must be atheistic." As he goes on to say, "For a physicist, a chemist, or a biologist as such, it would be as improper to ascribe an event to divine intervention as it would be for the scientific historian to break into his account of a campaign with the observation that at this point or that God interposed his hand to rout the enemy." It may, of course, well be that God *did* rout the enemy, and in a sense he certainly did, for his governance is over all, but this is a religious truth that cannot be domesticated into a scientific explanation. Here a healthy Christian secularity is what is wanted.

If, as Bonhoeffer has pointed out, we use God to fill up the gaps in our scientific knowledge, then when in the progressive advance of science these gaps are closed, God will be edged out of the world, and people will declare him dead. This is what must happen even in the case of the farmer of whom Father Walter Bado of Loyola University recently spoke. This farmer, the priest said, "prayed to God as if he were an agricultural factor which now can be replaced by more efficient fertilizers." Just so! Science must inevitably kill God, if God is only he who fills up the gaps in our knowledge. Indeed that god is already dead; science has killed him, and the radical theologians are approvingly proclaiming the fact.

(5) Another god in whom the radical theologians do not believe is the *god of the church*, sometimes called *the god of the religious ghetto*. This is the god whom one meets before the altar, and nowhere else. He is the god fashioned in accordance with the nature of the respectable bourgeois sitters in the comfortable pew. He is the god to be adored, reverenced, sung to, but not served. He is not met in the slums, nor does he environ the white man and the black who meet on the street. He is the god proclaimed in irrelevant, abstract, and other-worldly sermons, the god who does not goad his worshippers on to worldly participation in suffering and sorrow, in helpfulness and compassion.

This god has come, in the view of the radical theologians, to be identified with "religion," and this is why they advocate with Bonhoeffer a "religionless Christianity." Unlike Bonhoeffer, however, they also repudiate the church. The death-of-God theologians are vulnerable here. Their critique of churchly respectability, of Sunday religiosity, of pious insulation is certainly justified. But this need not involve the abandonment of religion or of religious services (the preaching of the Word and the administration of the sacraments) nor the repudiation of the institution of the church. Yet something is being said that may not be ignored. What is being said is that the church is Christ (or his body) and that it should be found where he was found: in the world, redemptively active among men, and not, or not merely, on the Mount of Splendor.

(6) If now these were the only gods the radical theologians were declaring to be dead, the Christian community could hardly do anything but applaud. Indeed, if this were their only thesis, they would be standing squarely in the best Christian tradition. But they are saying more than this. They are saying that the God whom the historic Christian faith has apprehended in the revelation preserved in the Bible is dead. The God who is an infinite, but nevertheless personal and individual being; the God who out of his own free will and in superabundant love created the world out of nothing, and ceaselessly upholds it; the God who is at once transcendent and immanent, this God is said to be dead. Or at least half of him is said to be this.

The God of the Bible is, as I have just said, both transcendent and immanent. He is both the Creator who stands above and beyond the world, radically independent of it, and the Governor who by his Spirit directs and controls it. He is the God who is both *out there* and *in here*. He is the paradoxical God who is in heaven, even beyond Olympus, and who is on every highway and byway that men walk. He is God and not man, yet he became not merely man, but flesh, man in sin and degradation. He is the God so highly exalted, so radiantly holy, that the very angels veil their faces in his presence, and yet the God who did not disdain a stable, a cross, and a tomb. It is this God—the God of the Bible and the churchly tradition—particularly this God in his transcendence—who is said to be dead.

But now we must ask what is meant by saying that this God is *dead*. Can a Christian really say that? Can he say that the true, the living God is dead? He can, I think, and because he can, we must reserve judgment upon the radical theologians until we discover what they mean by *dead*.

3. DEAD

When we ask what might be meant by "death" in relation to the true and living God, we need not, at the outset, look beyond the Bible and beyond our own personal religious experience to get the answer.

(1) That God—the true God—is dead may mean that we have passed the judgment of death upon him, that we have negated him, that we laid upon him the shroud of our *sin*. Now sin, as it is represented in the Bible, moves a man in two directions: away from God and toward (against) God. The man in sin is either in flight from God or in rebellion against him. He turns his back upon God or he turns his face against God.

The biblical representation of hell corresponds to this twofold movement. A man in flight from God moves toward the outer darkness or down into the bottomless pit—where he is enveloped by unspeakable coldness and blackness. But the man in rebellion against the holy God, who is all aflame with His glory, moves toward the fiery furnace of God's wrath—the place of infinite heat and blinding light.

But what is here more especially to be observed is the bearing this twofold movement has on the "death" of God. The man in flight from God "forgets" God; for him God goes increasingly "out of mind." Because his back is turned to God, he does not "see" Him. God becomes "hidden," "absent," as it were "dead." On the other hand, the man in rebellion against God (and he is paradoxically the same man who is in flight from Him, which is why there are not two hells, but only one), this man does not "forget" God, he faces God. He goes against God. Indeed, he attacks Him, and though there is a sense in which God is invulnerable, there is another sense in which God succumbs in the attack and expires.

Something like this is what happened in Palestine around A.D. 30. Immanuel—God with us—was turned upon and slain. The papers have lately been concerned with this event. The Roman Church absolved the Jews of deicide, absolved them not because no deicide had occurred, but because the blame for the occurrence rests not on the Jews as Jews but upon all men. We—all of us—nailed the God-man to the cross, and we let him hang there until he was dead.

I am not here trying, you will understand, to revive the ancient heresy of Patripassianism. I am trying merely to suggest that the event of the cross might have served to make us open for the adoption of death-of-God talk.

Now I wish I could report that the theological radicals had this kind of "death" in mind. But I cannot. I have been able to detect in none of them a biblical conception of sin, much less a conception of sin in its ultimate dimension of destructive rebellion. By the same token, there is not in them that unutterable sorrow and weeping repentance which is the prelude or accompaniment of God's forgiveness for so loathsome a crime as the "destruction" of God that took place on Golgotha.

(2) What, then, do these theologians mean by saying the true and living God is dead? In some of their moods they seem to be saying what we all can understand. They seem to be making a simple personal confession. They seem to be saying what the man in flight from God (which at times and in

degrees is all of us) must say: "God is dead for me." They seem to be saying: "I don't believe in him any more; God has gone out of my life; I am unaware of him." The proclamation of God's death is in this reading nothing more or less than the confession of one's own faithlessness.

If this is what the death of God means—an account of *man's* non-openness to God—then there can be no objection to the proclamation. One may regret that this non-openness is true, or is a fact, but one cannot blame anyone for confessing the fact. It is good and right to be honest. If for anyone the heavens are as brass, if God appears to anyone to be not only distant but unreal, let him say so. He is then at least in a position to be helped.

(3) Talk about the death of the true and living God may, however, be not talk about man's faithlessness at all, but truly talk about God. It may mean, for example, and it does in part mean in the mouth of the radical theologians, that the God of the Bible has himself withdrawn from human society. God is therefore not "really" dead, but he acts as if he were. He deliberately absents himself. He never puts in an appearance. He arrests his power, stops up the fountain of his grace, pours no mercies and blessings upon men. His wonted place is empty. He is present neither as benefactor nor as an avenger. He is simply absent. Where once he stood there is now nothing but a void, a nihil, a nothing, an impenetrable abyss.

It is at this level that there comes into view the *Existentialism* that has affected and conditioned the death-of-God theologies. In a sense the radical theologians have passed beyond existentialism. There is in them little of the *angst*, the despair, the giddiness of classical existentialism, not even of the classical existentialism of the Christian sort, as in Kierkegaard and the early Barth. In another sense, however, the radical theologians are veritable existentialists. They "sense" God's absence, or what is experientially the same thing, they sense their "cosmic loneliness." They feel homeless, isolated, forsaken, alone. They feel what the orthodox theologian would call the "judgment" of God, the divine decision "not to be" a God to man, and this divine decision "not to be" they translate into the "death" of God. Hamilton can therefore say: "God is dead. We are not talking about the absence of the experience of God, but about the experience of the absence of God." He means to say: I actually experience the withdrawal of God. I experience his absence. I do actually peer into the consequent void. Where God once was, there is now nothing. God has gone away, gone away for good; he will never return; we are on our own. God is dead as far as human existence is concerned. God has reprobated us; we can expect from him no help, no comfort, no instruction. There can, therefore, be no faith, and certainly no hope. God is dead.

(4) One can, and one must, give another meaning to the word "death," however. When the radical theologians say that the God of the Bible is

"dead," they also mean to point to or describe a social fact, a cultural phenomenon. All three of them are fond of saying that a historical event has taken place. They mean that in the Western world God is simply not reckoned with. People find that they cannot fit him into their lives. Social existence has been secularized, thoroughly dedivinized, desacralized. The life of Western man, not only in science, but in business, in the university, everywhere, has been rationalized, *entzaubert*. God is someone who, as John Robinson has said, "no longer connects with anything in most people's life." If people believe in him at all, they believe in him as "that which is left over when all the vital connections have been made." He is really irrelevant to the concrete problems that we face. God does not mean anything to the modern man who solves all his problems in and through the techniques that science provides.

There is something here for us to ponder. We, too, are modern men. We, too, in one way or another, proclaim the "death" of God. What modern Christian, when his child is doing poorly at school, thinks of God as the solution to the problem? What Christian does not put his trust in the technical competence of the teacher or, when that fails, in the sociologist, the psychologist, or the psychiatrist? God, for many of us, is the icing on the cake, the "plus" that is not needed in the practical and ongoing daily solution of our problems. And what need is there really of the "plus," of the "religious luxury"? Why don't we simply declare, as the modern man does, that God is "dead" as far as the conduct and order of our life is concerned? For, as far as that is concerned, he *is* dead. This it is that the radical theologians declare; they proclaim a cultural fact. God "died" when in the Renaissance and in the post-Renaissance period man came of age, and when human competence and resourcefulness took the place of God.

(5) It is possible, however, that when God is said to be dead another thing is meant. What may be meant is that the *term* "God" as a linguistic symbol, as a grammatical entity, as a simple locution, no longer functions meaningfully in human discourse. What may be meant is that people can no longer use the term "God," for they don't know any more what it means.

In this interpretation of the death-of-God theology one would have to understand the radical theologians as declaring, not that God is dead, but that the word "God" is dead, that the term "God" conveys no sense, that the locution "God" is moribund, unusable, meaningless.

In this interpretation the reality that was once designated by the word "God" must now be designated by another word or words. If people cannot be brought into touch with ultimate reality through the mediation of the word "God," if that word has functionally died, then let other locutions be employed. Let secular words be used. Let the ancient verities be expressed in a "worldly" idiom. Let there be, what Hamilton has attempted, a restatement of Christian truth. Let there be a theology that entirely dispenses with the word "God," and that presents in contemporary language "the secular meaning of the Gospel."

This is certainly part of what the radical theologicans are saying. They are people who have drunk at the fountain of contemporary British linguistic analysis. Under the influence of this philosophy they have been convinced that to speak meaningfully the theologian must use not "ontological," but only "empirical" terms. Unless what one says can be expressed in language that refers to actual or possible states of affairs in concrete experience, one is talking nonsense. Since the term "God" refers to no such state of affairs, it must be abandoned. "God," as a term, is dead.

(6) I have suggested a number of things that the radical theologians could mean, and in part do mean, when they say that God is dead. If what I have set down were all they did in fact mean by declaring that God is dead, no orthodox Christian would have reason to be perturbed or alarmed. He might indeed make common cause with the radicals.

But what the radical theologians mean when they say that God is dead is more than what has hitherto been noticed. What they mean, in the final analysis, is that the personal, living, individual, transcendent God of the biblical revelation is a fiction. He simply does not exist. "God" is not the entity that is proclaimed in the Bible, or delineated in the Christian creeds, or proclaimed from orthodox pulpits. God is not "out there" or "up there"; he is not "beyond" the world in any sense; there is no transcendence.

The death-of-God theologians have sometimes been thought of as disciples of Tillich. This, in my judgment, is not the case. Tillich, too, denies supranaturalism. He denies that God is intrinsically personal and individual. But he nevertheless affirms a kind of transcendence. Tillich is, in the last analysis, an ontologist. He posits Being as ultimately real. This Being is "God beyond God," that is, God beyond the personal, individual god that functions in the religious life of man.

The radical theologians, on the other hand, are thoroughgoing empiricists. Whatever god they have is not outside of or beyond process. He exists only on the plane of history. Beyond the here and now there is nothing. God is dead.

4. ATHEISM

What the contemporary radical theologians mean by saying that "God is dead" is that the God professed in the classical Christian creeds is non-existent. From the point of view of these creeds, therefore, the radical theologians could be called atheists, just as from the point of view of the Graeco-Roman religion the early Christians could be so called. Now it happens that the radical theologians are in fact called atheists. What is particularly arresting is the fact that they are so called not only by some of their orthodox critics but also by themselves. They have boldly adopted the atheistic label. They wish to be known as atheists.

By classifying themselves as such the radical theologians have not eased the burden of their interpreters; they have simply compounded the difficulties of understanding. The introduction of the term "atheism" into religious and theological discourse almost always creates confusion. It does this because the term is hopelessly ambiguous. As appropriated by the radical theologians the term serves to indicate the fact that they do not accept the account given of God by orthodox Christian theologians. But does it mean more than this? Does it mean, for instance, that they repudiate deity altogether, that they simply cancel out the sacred? Does it mean that religion, in every sense of that equivocal word, is for them utterly reprehensible? Does it mean that they consider theology a spurious undertaking? Does it mean that for them Christianity is unacceptable in any form?

It seems that in their use of it in application to themselves the term "atheism" means none of these things. In whatever sense these radical thinkers are atheists, they are not atheists in what they choose to call the "traditional" or "classical" sense. They recognize that the old-fashioned kind of atheism cannot be combined with Christianity. The "atheism" they espouse, however, is regarded by them as being quite compatible with it. When therefore they say that "God is dead" they must be understood as saying, not that "There is no God," but only that "There is no God corresponding to the ancient formulas."

In a significant sense, therefore, the radical theologians appear upon the scene not as atheists but as revisionists; what they deny is not the presence of divinity but the authenticity of inherited understandings of the sacred. Accordingly, they do not regard themselves as having abandoned the field of theology nor as having forsaken Christianity. They wish to be received as nothing less than Christian theologians. "Radical theology," say Altizer and Hamilton in the preface to their new book *Radical Theology and the Death of God*, "is a contemporary development within Protestantism . . . which is carrying the careful openness of the older theologies toward atheism a step further. It is, in effect, an attempt to set an atheist point of view within the spectrum of Christian possibilities" (p. ix).

What is being proposed in the new theology, it may be said, is not so much an a-theism as a non-theism. The proposal is to dismantle the theistic or supranaturalistic framework of the sacred and enclose it in a this-worldly or secular form, "a form of theology which can exist in the midst of the collapse of Christendom and the advent of secular atheism" (p. xii). Altizer and Hamilton declare: ". . . radical theology, as here conceived, . . . reflects the situation of a Christian life in a seemingly neutral but almost totally secular culture and society. Hopefully it also reflects the choice of those Christians who have chosen to live in Christ in a world come of age" (pp. xii–xiii). In accordance with these representations, Emerson W. Shideler says: "Those today who, from within the environment of Christian theology, announce the death of God, put themselves forth as the saviors of the tradition, not its funeral orators. They declare the death of God, not in order to get rid of a religion which stands in the way of man's fulfillment, but in order to release that religious faith and its institutions to do its work" (*Theology Today*, July 1966). It seems that what the new theology is trying to do is not to discredit Christianity but, by reinterpreting or remodeling it, to make it meaningful for modern man.

The remodeling takes place by locating ultimate meaning, radical freedom, ethical ideality, the enduring Sacred, the saving "Word," not in a celestial realm "out there" but in the world "down here," within the stream of history. In the new understanding the figure in whom divinity becomes concentrated is not a "Father in heaven," an individual divine person existing in ontological separation and independence, a "God" highly exalted, omnipotent, and aweful; but a "Man," the man who is or represents the whole of Christian life and meaning, the man Christ Jesus. In the new understanding Jesus takes the place of God. The "God" who is more or other than Jesus, who is the Father of the son, who is not incarnate in our world, who is not part of the texture of our existence, who is not wholly "here," is not (or is no longer) a god at all; he is either a construct of man's imagination, or a god who, having once existed, has since died.

In these representations transcendence, as it has been conceived in Christian theism, is decisively negated. The negation itself, taken strictly as such, is certainly no new thing. It is indigenous to all peoples who, not having been instructed by the scriptural revelation, have not come to know the Creator-God. For all such peoples reality is homogeneous. For them there is not, as in biblical Christianity, a great gulf fixed between the Being of the Creator and the being of the created; all is of one piece. It is in this broad tradition of thought that the radical theologians stand; they are committed basically to a metaphysical monism—even those among them who eschew metaphysics. By the force of this monism they are driven to deny transcendence and to regard the sacred, in so far as they regard it at all, as nothing more than a feature or dimension of worldly existence. It is a happy circumstance for the radical theologians that Jesus, even in orthodox teaching, is a "worldly" being, a veritable man, really in history, and existentially involved with us in our sufferings and strivings. This enables them, with a show of reason, to manifest a "Christian" concern for the sacred and the divine without breaking out of the secular frame; with apparent biblical support they can refuse to look beyond Jesus of Nazareth in their search for ultimate meaning and they can thus resist all overtures to posit a radical transcendence.

Transcendence, then, as traditionally understood, is what the radical theologians deny. Transcendence is dead, and by that token God is dead. There is a curious expression in this connection that both Altizer and Hamilton employ. They say, not merely that God is dead, but that he "died." They wish to tell us, apparently, that something happened, not merely to men's thought about God, but to God himself. God's death, we are asked to believe, was an occurrence, an event, something that took place in history. Their thesis is "that there once was a God to whom adoration, praise, and trust was appropriate, possible, and even necessary, but that now there is no such God" (*Radical Theology and the Death of God*, p. x). This is puzzling and, taken literally, it is absurd. How *could* God die? A philosopher is willing to acknowledge that God can be conceived in many ways, but he can hardly acknowledge that a conception of something that does not endure is a veritable conception of God. Immortality is surely an inseparable note of deity. It is easier to think of a round square than to think of a God who actually goes out of existence. I cannot believe, therefore, that this is what the radical theologians really mean to say when they assert that God once was but now no longer is.

It is likely that an approach to their meaning can be made by asking: If God died, when did he die; when precisely did this event occur? In their recent joint publication Altizer and Hamilton themselves raise this question, but they do not clearly answer it. On the one hand they suggest that God died in the nineteenth century. They say,

> ... radical theology is being more and more drawn into the disciplines of intellectual history and literary criticism to answer the when question.... One of the major research tasks now facing the radical theologians is a thorough-going systematic interpretation of the meaning of the death of God in nineteenth-century European and American thought and literature, from, say, the French Revolution to Freud.... The nineteenth century is to radical theology what the sixteenth century was to Protestant neo-orthodoxy. For only in the nineteenth century do we find the death of God lying at the very center of vision and experience (pp. xi–xii).

These words appear to say that in order to date the death of God one must look to the nineteenth century. But these words also suggest that the "death of God" is not an actual dying of God, but only the loss in nineteenth-century Western man of belief in God as a personal transcendent being. God's death, in this reading, is no more than the death of a God-concept which once prevailed in the occident but which during the nineteenth century ceased to dominate men's minds. The change indicated by the word "death" was a change in men, not a change in God.

But there is another answer to the "when" question, an answer given particularly by Altizer. God died, he declares, God really died, in the first century of our era. He died not merely, nor even primarily, on the cross; he died in Bethlehem; he died in the incarnation. When God became man, when he became Immanuel, he emptied himself and ceased to be God. In the incarnation there was a total emptying, an absolute kenosis. Accordingly, ever since the incarnation God is contained wholly and irrevocably by the world. He is no longer "up there" or "out there," but only and exclusively "down here." He poured himself out in Christ, and thereby ceased to be the exalted one. In the incarnation God laid aside his transcendence; he ceased to be God and became man. God therefore is dead; he died in the first century. Altizer believes this to be a uniquely Christian assertion, and he thinks that it is precisely as a Christian that he is obliged to proclaim the death of God: "Only the Christian can celebrate an incarnation in which God has actually become flesh, and radical theology must finally understand the Incarnation itself as effecting the death of God" (p. xii).

God is dead, but Jesus is there in his stead. The radical theologians have no interest in God—except to proclaim his death; their interest is in Jesus, God's substitute. As Hamilton and Altizer say: "The radical theologian has a strange but compelling interest in the Figure of Jesus. This must not be confused with the nineteenth-century liberal quest for the historical Jesus. The new theologian has died to the liberal tradition and is in quest of that Jesus who appears in conjunction with the death of God" (p. xii).

5. APOLOGETICS

The radical theologians are saying not merely that modern man's notion or representation of God has undergone a change, but that God himself has changed. God in their view—especially in the view of Altizer—has undergone an alteration. He did not die a literal death, but he did undergo a veritable transformation. He became man. At a given moment he laid aside his primordial transcendence and became completely immanent. Only in this sense did he "die." He "died" as the Wholly Other, the Independent, the Distant One in the process of becoming the Historical, the Secular, the Involved One.

God, in "speaking" the Word, "emptied" himself of his exaltedness and autonomy, and as a result of this "kenosis" he ceased to be "God" in any traditional sense. Having become flesh, having entered history and become "worldly," God is now dead as "God." This does not mean that the sacred has ceased to exist; it means only that the sacred is now resident exclusively in the profane. The divine is no longer in heaven or in the beyond; it is since the great event of God's "death" only in the here and now; it is exhaustively enclosed in the incarnate Word. Indeed, there is no heaven any more, it having been vacated by God and reduced thereby to nothingness. The "beyond," the Transcendent, the "other-worldly" has ceased to exist. Now there is only the earthly, the mundane, the secular, with its focus in the human.

Supernaturalism must therefore be rejected. What is needed is an authentic naturalism. It is of course not a materialistic naturalism that is needed, for the natural has in the incarnation—i.e., in the "death of God"— become divinized, and a merely profane and nakedly atheistic naturalism can hardly do justice to this fact. What is needed is a humanistic naturalism, a man-centered secularism. This means that classical theism, which is but a form of supernaturalism, must be rejected. What must be substituted for it is a humanism not merely of the scientific but of the religious sort. To be exact, what must be substituted for it is a Christian humanism, one that takes Jesus with utmost seriousness. This must be done because Jesus as the Christ effects and signifies both the death of God and the apotheosis of man. The Christ-event supplies both the death-blow to supranaturalistic theism and the warrant for a truly "worldly," even though "spiritual," humanism.

This, at any rate, is how Thomas Altizer conceives of the matter, and we are bound to ask why he thinks and speaks as he does.

Altizer is best understood, I think, when, in spite of his uniqueness and radicalness, he is contemplated as a member of that large group of contemporary neo-liberals who, after lifting the Barthian ban on apologetics, have undertaken the task of relating the Christian faith to human culture and to modern man's self-understanding. This is always a delicate and hazardous undertaking, and it is seldom well done. This is one of the reasons, I suppose, why apologetics is so often both shunned and denounced. Yet, in spite of the denunciations, theology has not been able to suppress for long the nisus toward apologetics which is inherent within it; apologetic theology has periodically reasserted itself and today, with figures like Bultmann and Tillich in the van, it dominates the field.

The last time within recent history that this was the case was in the period which lies between the late nineteenth century and the end of the second decade of the twentieth. In Protestant circles this was the age of classical Liberalism. During this time Christian thinkers sought to appropriate the valid insights achieved by the scientifically formed mind of modernity, and they also sought to interpret and present the Christian faith in such a way as to make it understandable and palatable to the sophisticated intelligence and taste of modern man. Soon after 1920 it began to be recognized, however, that Liberalism, in its otherwise wholesome attempt to "meet" the modern mind, had made undue concessions to it and had in effect evacuated the faith of its distinctively Christian meaning.

No one of like consequence saw this as soon or as well as Karl Barth. He inveighed against the culture-Christianity which the Liberals had espoused, and he substituted for the theology of experience, elaborated by Schleiermacher and Ritschl in accommodation to the then reigning empiricism, a biblically oriented theology of the Word. Barth dominated the theological scene from 1920 to 1945—the entire period between the two world wars. During that time most theologians, under the impact of his teaching, eschewed apologetics, and those that did not do so were either ignored or forced to occupy a place off stage. The Gospel, Barth insisted, was not to be accommodated or adjusted to the mind of the natural man. Indeed, he said, there was nothing in the self-understanding of the man outside of Christ with which the Gospel had the slightest affinity. The Gospel never comes, he said, with "fitting" answers to men's good questions or as a fulfillment of men's sound but partial yearnings; it comes only as grace and judgment upon the whole of human culture. It was not apologetics but proclamation that he advocated. The Gospel, he believed, must not be tailored to the "situation" but thrown into it, as a stone.

After the second world war, however, a revolt set in. Much of the inspiration for it was released by Dietrich Bonhoeffer, particularly through his *Letters and Papers from Prison*. Bonhoeffer, an erstwhile admirer of Barth, began in his prison years to fear that the Barthian method of reaching the increasingly unchurched and irreligious European was ineffectual; it was, he feared, too "religious," too dogmatic, too disoriented to the cultural situation. To make the Gospel really impinge upon modern man the preacher and theologian must, he judged, take man as he really is today—secular, mature, estranged, and godless. What the times call for is the presentation of Christianity, indeed, but only of a religionless Christianity; of the Gospel, to be sure, but only of a Gospel that accepts and does not discredit the secular and profane. One must, in preaching Christ, respect modern man's maturity, recognize and validate his insights and achievements, and in general reckon with him as he is.

When Bonhoeffer was laying out this program Bultmann and Tillich were already implementing it—how well, and at what cost to the purity of the Gospel, is not now the question. The point is that under the aegis of thinkers like Bultmann, Tillich, Bonhoeffer, and others a theology with marked cultural orientations began to emerge. It was a new apologetic theology, a theology which saw Christianity as the answer to questions implicit in human existence, a theology which saw the Gospel as an essence which was not dependent on the time-bound forms and myths with which it was initially associated, a theology which saw the faith as a prophetic anticipation of that eclipse of God which modern man is currently experiencing.

Now Altizer is part of this general movement. He wishes to do apologetic theology; he wishes to interpret Christianity for contemporary man; he wishes to do justice to the Gospel while appropriating and reflecting the values and realities that reside within the "situation." That he does not succeed I shall hereafter attempt to show. What is now of interest is not how

well he does his job but what job it is he is attempting to do. He is attempting, as I have already suggested, to indicate how one can be both a Christian
believer and a modern man; how one can endorse the Gospel without surren-
dering one's claim to contemporaneity; how one can be existentially involved
in the problems and currents of the age without losing one's hold on Christ.

This is in itself not an evil thing; it is in fact a very good thing that sorely
needs doing. But to do it appropriately two conditions must be fulfilled: the
Gospel must be read aright, and the situation must be accurately discerned.
These two requirements are clearly interdependent. We read the Bible with
eyes formed and focused by our temporal stance in the world and by the
apperceptive mass we have accumulated in the course of our experience; and
we read the cultural situation in the light of the Gospel that has been declared
to us. But these two operations can nevertheless be disciminated and be
separately considered.

How, then, does Altizer read the situation? What is for him the mark of
modernity, the sign of contemporaneity? In different contexts he gives different answers to these questions, but the one that is relevant to the present
discussion is this: to be modern is to *be* able and to *feel* able to "make it"
without God. Modern man—i.e., every mid-twentieth-century person who
has sensitively responded to his history and not sought asylum in some
bygone age—is a man who with his hands full of techniques and controls
knows no way of "fitting" God into the pattern of his existence, and has, in
the exercise of a new-found freedom, taken upon himself full responsibility
for the conduct of the world's affairs.

Modern man feels quite able to get along without God in the manage-
ment of his external life. He doesn't need God to stop floods, for he knows
how to construct dams and dykes. He doesn't need God to prevent disease,
for he knows about the structure and functioning of the human body, and he
knows how these can be regulated and repaired. He does not need God to
enrich the soil or to raise good crops, for he knows about fertilizers and
irrigation systems. And so it is with all the aspects of his environment. In the
affairs of heart, soul, and spirit the situation is similar. The sense of guilt can
be removed by psychoanalysis; fear and anxiety can be eased or dissolved by
knowledge; forgiveness can be experienced through social approval and self-
acceptance.

If the modern man does not raise the question of existence per se, which
he obviously does not, for else he would come face to face with God; if he
does not inquire why anything should be at all, perhaps because he regards
the question as part of a meaningless metaphysical venture; if he simply
accepts the world and the human race as a datum, or sheer "given," as he
appears to do; then the totality of the world's facts must be taken as sufficient
for the explanation of any selected fact, and, by the same token, the totality
of the world's resources must be taken as sufficient for the solution of any one

of the world's many problems. There is then no need to appeal to anything or anyone outside the world; and modern man, come of age in the time of scientific triumphalism, does not in fact make such an appeal. He has unlearned the racial habit of using God as a problem-solver; he knows that he, or his environment, and not God, is responsible for his mistakes and faults; and he believes that whatever increment of good the world contains is referable centrally to quite human actions and decisions. The world, with man at its center, is conceived of as independent, self-explanatory, and free of all outside determinants.

This means that the present age is pervasively "atheistic." The contemporary situation is one in which man lives by and large "without God" and without a "sense" of God. This man, this typically modern man, was conceived in the Renaissance, he was born in the Enlightenment, he came to self-consciousness in the nineteenth century, and he reached maturity in the twentieth century. He is a thoroughly secular man.

Now, Altizer observes, this secular man is, from the point of view of any individual, not merely some other individual whom one meets along the way; he is oneself as well. The secular man is not merely the non-Christian; he is also the Christian. He is every man who truly "exists" in the twentieth century, in the time of the "death of God." The secular man is therefore both the preacher of the Gospel and the hearer of it. No twentieth-century man, be he Christian or non-Christian, preacher or hearer, can, without fleeing reality and dooming himself to irrelevancy, circumvent the secularity, the "religionlessness," the profanity of the age. It is in him and around him. It is his fate to be secular. As a consequence of this the hearer of the Gospel must either be addressed in and through the secularity which is the distinguishing mark of him, or not really be addressed at all. Similarly, the preacher of the Gospel must either articulate a secular version of the faith or fall into that class of men who, speaking in a foreign and unintelligible tongue, find themselves at last offering stones instead of bread.

This in substance is Altizer's account of modern man. This is his reading of the situation. I think the picture is distorted. Although I acknowledge that many people in the West have been led by the reigning horizontalism to lose vital touch with the height and depth dimensions of existence, I hold with Calvin that the "sense" of God is not extinguished in them and that, like men everywhere, they are centrally religious, even though their religion may take the form of what the Bible calls idolatry. I further hold that, though scientism and historicism have formed a type of man who in his observable aspects has been quite adequately described by Altizer, Christianity continues to form men of quite another sort, men who in their "peculiarity" are not one whit less modern or contemporaneous than their secular or "atheistic" counterparts.

However that may be, there can be no denying that there exists in the twentieth century the being called "secular man," and that *in some sense* the contemporary Christian is also this. This fact gives point to two questions of apologetic import: How can a man be both a Christian and in some sense secular? And, how can a Christian who because he is a Christian and in some deeper sense non-secular, present a Gospel of supernatural grace and judgment to those who, unlike himself, claim to be without any intimations of deity and are on this account satisfied atheists?

These two distinct but related questions must be candidly and thoughtfully faced by every Christian thinker. I believe that they are being thus faced by many orthodox theologians, but what is of interest here is that they are also being faced by the radical theologians. It may be said, indeed, that their theological positions have been elaborated in direct response to questions of this sort. I say questions of this sort because, of course, the radical theologians formulate the questions differently than I have done. Paul van Buren, for example, puts the first question in some such form as this: In what way is a Christian compelled to reinterpret the Gospel if, as is proper and needful, he wants to be and remain a twentieth-century secular man in full communion with the anti-supernaturalistic spirit of the age? This is obviously not an orthodox way of stating the problem. Indeed, the very form of the question precludes an orthodox answer. Clearly underlying it is the assumption that not the Gospel as traditionally understood but only existence as currently interpreted has integrity and canonical significance. The assumption is that when the Gospel contronts the age, the Gospel must yield and take on the contours of the age. The Gospel, it is assumed, must allow itself to be repatterned in conformity with (what are regarded as) the brute factualities of scientific experience; it must consent to be brought into adjustment with the cultural forms and institutions in which contemporary man expresses his self-understanding. Van Buren does, in fact, impose upon the Gospel the pattern of Western industrialized modernity and he thereby removes all tension between Christianity and secularity. In this way he can live happily in two worlds; he can present himself to the world both as a Christian and as an atheist. But only, of course, because he has previously reduced the one to the other.

Van Buren, interestingly, does not go on to ask the second question I have posed—not even in his own peculiar form. He has no interest in the apologetic or evangelistic dimension of "Christian" existence. He is content to allow the reality of "human freedom," which in his judgment is the essence of the Gospel message, to make its way through the world by the force of simple contagion. This is not the case with Altizer. He asks both questions. He formulates the first question in essentially the same way that Van Buren does, and he answers it in like fashion. The second question he formulates in some such way as this: What understanding of the Gospel will enable the Christian to present it to secular man without calling his well-founded "atheism" into question? How may the Gospel be interpreted so as to affirm rather than deny the reality of man's history, particularly the history of Western man during the period stretching from the Renaissance to the present? What understanding of the Gospel is calculated to justify modernity, validate man's coming of age, and thus enlist the secularist's adhesion to the faith?

This, it will be observed, is a radical version of the apologetic question which was posed by classical Liberalism. By the same token Altizer's theology, which is an answer to this question, is a radical version of Liberalism's acculturated Christianity. Radical theology is an extreme new Liberalism; new because it is disconnected from the old by the Barthian interlude; extreme because it is a passionate reaction to certain questionable elements in the Barthian stance.

The fact is that some Barthians, if not Barth himself, sought to interpret the Christianity-culture relation in a way reminiscent of Tertullian. Gospel and world were set over against each other in an absolute way. An antithesis was established between them as radical as the antithesis between grace and sin. As a consequence of this the possibilities for good resident in nature and history, and the actualities of goodness and truth which emerged from these under the general superintendence of God's Spirit, were ignored or negated. The judgment upon the world which the Gospel undoubtedly announces was separated from the world-affirmation which the Gospel also entails.

In reaction to this view of things the radical theologians are attempting to bring Gospel and world into a more positive relationship. They unfortunately end up doing a great deal more than this: they bring the two into accord. In fact, they make the two identical. All tension is thereby removed. How Altizer proceeds the reader already knows. He takes a Christian theme—the incarnation of our Lord—and represents this on the one hand as an absolute and unconditional world-affirmation, and on the other as a final and irreversible disappearance of transcendence. In this way he evacuates the universe of "God" and addresses a radical "yes" to autonomous man. He makes Christianity modern and relevant, not by making its message, in all its integrity and uniqueness, impinge with healing power upon man's broken existence; he does it by representing the Christian "Word" as the hitherto unrecognized, but surely beneficent, force which through many centuries has been shaping Western man into a mature and self-conscious atheist. When therefore the Gospel is now preached to secular man it is preached not in order to change him but in order to explain him. The preaching does not enjoin him to become right; it declares him right. Sin and judgment are thereby eliminated from secular existence and so, in consequence, is every vestige of divine grace. Man is indeed "justified," but not in virtue of something that happened in his behalf through a merciful divine agency; he is justified just as he is because God for reasons unknown once committed suicide and allowed man to become Lord by default.

But this "Lordship" man had already assumed in the Fall, or so the Scriptures say. Was this assumption of power, this declaration of independence, merely premature? Is the biblical notion of justification now to mean nothing but divine acquiescence in the premature seizure of lordship and power by precocious man? Has Christianity nothing to offer secular man save endorsement and corroboration?

For Altizer, it appears, the world has replaced the Gospel, and culture has replaced Christianity. This, I suggest, is apologetics turned on its head. Altizer wants to keep the Christian name, but the desire to do so is surely gratuitous. Why keep the name if the thing which the name denotes is better and more immediately known by other names, like "human autonomy," "atheism," "secularism," "scientism," and the like. Why come with the Gospel when what the Gospel says has all along been known, at least outside the church? Why come with a mere endorsement? Why should this be necessary or even helpful; is it not agreed that man is independent and autonomous, not in need of support or praise, even from Christianity?

12

Christianity and Other Religions

IN THIS ESSAY I shall maintain that Christianity is the one absolute and final religion, the only way that leads from man to God, since it is concerned with the single way in which God confronts man redemptively, the Way called Christ, who himself once said: "I am the way. . . . No man cometh to the Father but by me."

Before I proceed, however, I must indicate what I mean by the term "Christianity" and by the term "Absolute." By *Christianity* I mean that sacred deposit of grace and truth which came in Jesus Christ, was anticipated in God's saving dealings with his chosen people Israel, was proclaimed by the Apostles, and is preserved in the church, which communicates it through the preaching of the Word and the administration of the sacraments, in the power of the Holy Spirit.

By the *absoluteness* of Christianity is meant that quality of Christianity which lifts it above the relativities of time and circumstance and gives it final and unconditional validity. The English word "absolute" is derived from the participial form of the Latin verb *ab-solvere*, which means to be "cut loose" from, or to be "set free" from. An absolute religion is therefore a religion which is free from temporal limitations. In theological and philosophical usage the word is frequently used to describe God, or the highest power or principle which is taken as God, and when so used it is employed to indicate that this person or principle is not dependent upon or conditioned by the complexities of finite existence: he or it is "free" of flux and process, raised above the changes of time and history, "cut loose" from the determinants which condition all other entities.

THE PROBLEM

Now, there are some thinkers who refuse to predicate absoluteness of *God*, for to predicate absoluteness of God is, they believe, to conceive of him deistically, as out of all relation to history, as uninvolved in our problems and pains, as out of touch with our experiences. The absolute God is, in their view, the Wholly-Other God. But this god, they say, is a non-existent, certainly a non-existential god, the figment of the philosopher's imagination; and they refuse to acknowledge him, preferring instead an immanent god who is joined with us in our struggles on the concrete plane of history.

If there are some who refuse to predicate absoluteness of *God*, there are more who refuse to predicate it of *religion*, and by that token, of the Christian religion. Religion, they observe, is precisely what is *not* cut loose from process and the relativities of our existence. Religion, they point out, is a human affair, and like everything human, it is finite, imperfect, partial, changeable. How then, they ask, since Christianity is a religion, can anyone speak of it as absolute? It is temporal; it arose in time and is even now in process. Being relative it is *essentially* no different than any other religion. It may differ from other religions *accidentally*, in measure or degree, but at bottom it is as conditioned by time and circumstance as others are; it has no monopoly of truth or grace; it is not the only, the absolute, the final, the definitive religion. It may be the religion best suited to some men, and even the highest and best religion yet conceived, but it is not absolute.

What are we to say to this? Is there not force in these anti-absolutistic remarks? Is it, for example, not true that Christianity arose at a definite time and place; that its sacred books reflect the mind and spirit of the Jewish people, modified by the philosophical ideas elaborated by the Greeks and transmitted by the Romans; and that its institutions and practices express the genius of the Northern European peoples? Is Christianity not essentially Western in nature, and if not Western, then Near-Eastern or Semitic? And is it not on that account limited, partial, particular—ill-suited to other places and peoples, and even to other times?

Adolph Hitler thought so. Under the tutelage of Friedrich Nietzsche and Alfred Rosenberg he came to ascribe Europe's ills to the super-imposition upon the Nordic race of a Semitic religion entirely out of accord with the deepest impulses of the Aryan spirit, and he resolutely opposed Christianity as well as Jewry in the interest, he thought, of restoring Europe's spiritual health and saving it from religious schizophrenia. And was not Hitler right?

Isn't it the duty of an awakened nationalism and a self-conscious racism to throw off, not indeed religion, but a non-indigenous religion which arrogantly exercises, as it has historically fostered, a culture-destroying spiritual imperialism? Should not different people, in different countries, in different historical contexts, find their own way to God and develop a religion suited to their own peculiar needs and circumstances? And will not political co-existence and international peace come into being and flourish only when on the spirituo-religious level extravagant and self-preferential claims are dropped and each is allowed in utter freedom to pursue his own spiritual destiny? Or, if in one world, one single religion is to weld all peoples together by the power of one spiritual force, must not this religion be an amalgam of the best in all religions, a synthesis of the religious insights of the entire race, and not the expression of a narrow and intolerant particularism?

The *Laymen's Appraisal* of fifty years ago, which was set down in a book called *Rethinking Missions*, thought so. In this book Jesus is regarded as no more than the world's most eminent religious genius. Jesus was a fellow-seeker with us after God, and we bear his name because in our quest of God we follow his lead. Christianity is not a religion *about* Christ but the religion *of* Christ. To ascribe an absolute finality to Christianity is to give expression to a spiritual arrogance entirely foreign to the spirit of the Master. Christianity is an ethical system which ought to be generously proffered to inquiring people, but it is not a way of salvation that must be urged upon people as an alternative to eternal death. The central aim and purpose of Christian missions is to serve men, not to change or rescue them. Too long, it is complained, have we regarded conversions as the zenith of missionary achievement, and a soul as a kind of spiritual scalp in our wigwam. We must remember that we are commissioned not to rob other people of their faith, but to "assist them to a truer interpretation of their own meaning." Christian missions are not proselyting agencies but only means of coming to terms with the ethnic religions. What the missionary asks of non-Christian peoples is not repentance and conversion, but greater depth or consistency in the practice of their native faith, for it is not only at Jerusalem nor only on Mt. Gerizim that God may be served, but on every way men walk in sincerity and uprightness, whether in the company of Gautama, Confucius, or Jesus. What can we say to this?

SCRIPTURE

The first thing we can say is that this is not the view entertained of Christianity in the Bible, which for us is the divinely given rule of faith and practice, and which, on any theory of inspiration, must be taken as an authoritative source of Christian teaching. The Bible clearly teaches not merely the superiority but also the exclusive validity of the Christian way.

In *John* 14:6 Christ says of himself, "I am the way, the truth, and the life; no one cometh unto the Father except through me." In the light of this pronouncement the command of Christ in *Matthew* 28:18-20 stands forth in all its authority and urgency. Christ here proclaims himself Lord of the world, saying, "All power is given unto me in heaven and earth." He announces himself as the one Lord whose imperious claim on men's lives, though gracious, is comprehensive and unending, "even unto the end of the world."

This understanding of Christ animates the preaching of the Apostles, as can be seen, for example, from Peter's sermons in *Acts*. In *Acts* 2:36, 38 we read, "Therefore let all the house of Israel know assuredly, that God hath made that same Jesus, whom ye have crucified, both Lord and Christ. . . . [Wherefore] repent, and be baptized every one of you in the name of Jesus Christ for the remission of sins." And why repent and flee to Christ? The answer is given in *Acts* 4:12: ". . . in none other is there salvation, for neither is there any other name under heaven, that is given among men, wherein we must be saved."

Because this is so, Paul, who determined not to know anything among men save Jesus Christ and him crucified, could say in *Galatians* 1:8, "Though we, or an angel from heaven, preach any other Gospel unto you than that which we have preached unto you, let him be accursed." Paul, it is evident, regarded the gospel as final.

THEOLOGY

The reason the Christian gospel is absolute and final is that its content, Jesus Christ, is absolute. As John tells us in *John* 1:1, "In the beginning was the Word, and the Word was with God, and the Word was God." Wherefore Jesus said in *John* 10:30, "I and my Father are one." Jesus Christ is no mere prophet; he is certainly no mere hero or genius; he is not a spark struck off the human block; he is no mere man reaching up to God. He is God identifying himself with man; he represents an incursion into this world from another world; he is God incarnate. In him God has come to men completely, fully, finally. There cannot be a revelation beyond this revelation. In Jesus Christ we have the absolute God standing in the most intimate relation to mankind without himself being thereby relativized. Here is Eternity standing in time yet not being temporalized. Here is Finality in touch with process and giving it the only meaning it has.

What is true of Christ's person is true also of his *work*. He came for one purpose only: to reconcile man to God. And since the reconciliation could be effected in one way only, it may be said that he came to die. To this end was he born. And when he died and arose again there was accomplished what need not and could not ever be done again. At the cross and on Easter the power of sin was forever broken, the sting was taken out of death, and the grave was robbed of its victory. About the finality or once-for-allness of Christ's work the Scriptures do not leave us in doubt. Paul says in *Romans* 6:10: "For in that he died, he died unto sin *once.*" Peter says in *1 Peter* 3:18: "For Christ also hath *once* suffered for sins, the just for the unjust, that he might bring us to God." And the author of the Epistle to the *Hebrews* says in 9:26, 28, "But now *once* in the end of the world hath he appeared to put away sin by the sacrifice of himself. . . . So Christ was *once* offered to bear the sins of many."

RELIGION

Because Christianity is concerned with the person and work of Christ, it is final and absolute. Christianity is not a way of man to God (then it would be temporary and relative), but an account of God's dealing with men and of man's graciously initiated response to the divine activity. As such it is unique, distinguishing itself from all other religions, every one of which is the product of man's search after God while in flight from him or in rebellion against him. Christianity, therefore, must be radically distinguished from every ethnic faith. To all such faiths it stands in a relation of antithesis. With none of them can it come to terms or be combined.

ANTITHESIS

Christianity in its uniqueness and absoluteness is set over against the ethnic faiths, but it is important to understand just wherein this antithesis resides. I suggest that what are set-over-against each other in the antithesis are not, primarily, two histories, nor two lives, nor even two theologies, but rather two principles, the principles of sin and grace.

1. The antithesis in all its radicality is not between two concrete *historical entities,* between historic Christianity and, for example, historic Buddhism. The history of these two magnitudes is governed to a large degree by common factors. Each is in great part the product of cultural, economic, political, and generally human causes and influences. In respect of these influences each may be compared to the other and subjected to a single analysis. Because they lie on the plane of history these two religions change their aspects with the times, and are at different times more or less true to themselves; the

course described by each is not steady and linear, but full of ups and downs, of defections and reformations. On this plane Christianity as well as Buddhism stands under judgment, for it is here not only affected by the relativities of finite existence but also by human depravity.

2. The antithesis is also not, in the most radical sense, between two *lives*. A recognition of this fact will keep us from making a comparison of the behavior of a Buddhist and a Christian, and save us from the embarrassment which often attends such a comparison. It is a well-known fact that non-Christians are often more dedicated to their faith, more meticulous in the observance of their duties, more willing to sacrifice their private interests than is the Christian. There is always the noble pagan to shame the Christian. In this situation it must be remembered that it is no part of Christianity to say that our lives are better than those of the heathen. It is, as Christians, not our virtue we confess but our sins and weaknesses. We confess that we are unclean and undone, and this is not merely a pious mouthing but a declaration of literal truth. We acknowledge that we are not so much good as *declared* good in the juridical act of justification. And even when, through God's sanctifying Spirit, our lives are radiant with love, our failings are there to temper our pride, and to keep us from boasting or making odious comparisons. It is forever un-Christian to say, "Lord, I thank thee that I am not like that publican." A recognition of this general truth will keep us, too, from intellectual confusion. It will help us unmask as pseudo-philosophy much discussion as to whether there is any knowledge or any virtue among the unbelievers. Of course there is such knowledge and virtue, and on the empirical level it often exceeds our own.

3. The antithesis is also in its deepest sense not between two *theologies*. Theologies, too, are human products, inevitably influenced by natural and human factors, which render them imperfect, changeable, criticizable. Theologies, including Christian theologies, lie in the judgment as well as human lives and historical institutions. Although against Barth we must maintain that there do actually exist what he calls the "Blessed Possessors," yet it will never do to identify our theological constructions with the truth as it is in Jesus Christ, for then we cut off every possibility of reformation, and make ourselves guilty of a spurious absolutism. It should be observed also that on the level of theological reflection the antithesis is modified by the fact that Christian theology and *theologia-falsa* employ common intellectual instruments (methods and categories), and address themselves to much the same problems. A good illustration of this is found in the theological work in Europe in the twelfth and thirteenth centuries, when, with a common appeal to Aristotle, Christian and Mohammedan alike were fashioning different theologies around a common set of problems, such as the authority of sacred Scripture, the relation between predestination and free will, the bearing of

philosophy upon theology and vice versa, and the relative value of Scripture and tradition.

4. The antithesis that exists between Christianity and non-Christian religions is effected by the supernatural and absolute power of grace which is mediated to the world through Jesus Christ and his Spirit, and through no one else. This grace, which separates men and cuts the human race in two, was promised (and indeed imparted) in the early dawn of human history, soon after man yielded to the temptation of the devil and fell away from God. By that fall man came into the power of sin, from which there is no final release except through a counter-power, the power of grace, which God released, in pre-Christian times, in view of Christ's sacrificial death, and, in Christian times, upon the basis of that sacrifice. Through grace there is called out of the mass of men those who by faith in Christ's name are saved from condemnation and ushered into life. And between those who are thus called out and those who remain under judgment there is a great gulf fixed, a gulf that none can cross unaided. And those on either side are very different, the one being in Christ, the other being outside of Christ; the one living from the principle of grace, the other from the principle of sin. Now, in so far as the term "Christianity" means the vehicle and expression of grace (and this is what it centrally *does* mean) it stands opposed to other religions as light to darkness; for other religions, though they could not exist without the indelible sense of God impressed upon the soul, are nevertheless expressions of man's determination to serve not the one true God but only some creature that God has made; and from such creatures, who themselves are alienated from God, no way can be found that leads to God and blessedness. There is only one way to God, the way laid by God himself—his only begotten Son, the Savior of the world—the way upon which Christians walk, the way which, if one walk upon it, makes one a Christian, an adherent of the Christian religion, a member of the Christian church. The Christian way is therefore unique, absolute, imcomparable, for it is Christ himself, very God of very God. This, then, is what we mean when we say that Christianity is absolute, and opposed antithetically to all other religions.

CHRISTIAN AND NON-CHRISTIAN RELIGION

What does this mean for our understanding of religion in general, and for non-Christian religions in particular?

It means, negatively, that, standing within the perspective of Christianity, we cannot take the phenomena of the non-Christian religions as the key to the meaning of religion or to the meaning of the religious life, but rather that this key must be found exclusively in the revelation set down in the Christian Scriptures, the Bible, by whose light alone man and his works can be truly understood. It means, too, that we cannot regard non-Christian religions evolutionistically as approaches or stepping stones to Christianity. They are rather deviations from Christianity, lapses from the true religion, movements away from truth and beatitude. They are at bottom *false*, being animated centrally by the sinful rejection of God's right to define himself and to prescribe how he should be worshipped. It also means, therefore, that we do not represent Christianity as merely relatively different from non-Christian religions (separated from them by degrees), but rather as radically other than these religions, remembering always that this is a judgment of faith, and not empirically verifiable, and remembering, too, that since it is a judgment of faith it will give offense to those who stand outside the faith. It means finally that we are obliged to press the non-Christian worshipper, not merely for improvement, but for repentance and for a decision to break with his false gods.

If the true nature of all religions is disclosed within the perspective of the Christian religion, this enables us not only to pass a *negative* judgment upon non-Christian religions, but also to appraise certain positive features in these religions—i.e., it enables us to explain the characteristic *complexity* of these religions, to explain that curious play of lights and shadows which is such an undeniable feature of their existence. For though all religions, other than the religion of Christ, are false at the center, displeasing to God, and unable to save, there is yet in them an unwitting acknowledgment of God, there is power in some of them to raise the level of men's moral behavior, and all of them keep alive in men's consciousness the reality of the Unseen. They are so far forth a protest against atheism, immorality, and radical secularism. Now, far from denying that these features exist in ethnic religions, Christianity calls our attention to them and provides us with the principles in terms of which to account for their existence. There are at least four such principles disclosed in Scripture. They are:

1. The *sensus divinitatis* or the *cognitio dei innata*—an inner, unquenchable awareness of God, owing to man's being made in God's image, and retaining it in the broader sense in spite of all the ravages of sin.

2. *General revelation*—a display in nature and history of God's might and divinity, a display which does not entirely escape the notice of sinful men, for the reason that God's display or revelation of himself is always effectual after its kind. The power of sin which reigns in the heart of the unregenerate is not strong enough to shut God out. His witness still comes through the barrier of their resistance, and, though non-Christians try to suppress, and though they fundamentally misinterpret what God is saying, they do apprehend something of him, and what they apprehend is recognized by the Christian to be of value.

3. *Common grace*—a disposition and power of God which, without working regeneration and salvation, arrests the power of sin to blind and destroy, and gives good gifts to the rebellious.

4. *Special revelation*—which appears in non-Christian religions in a twofold way: First, as a *borrowing* from the Jewish and Christian faiths. A good example of this is Mohammedanism, many of whose brighter spots are owing to a kind of orientation to Old and New Testaments. Other examples are found in certain reform movements in Hinduism. —Special revelation appears in non-Christian religions, *secondly,* as a *memory* or tradition, a memory dim and distorted of the original revelation to Adam in paradise, and to himself and his descendants before the formation of God's special people Israel.

When once we have gotten these principles and facts in view, when once we give due weight to the innate sense of God, general revelation, common grace, and the indelible memory of God's dealings with men before the separation of his chosen people, then we will understand that it is contrary to both fact and Scripture to regard the ethnic faiths as (simplistically) *nothing but* the outworkings of sin, *nothing but* the work of Satan. There is grace in them too—not saving grace, and there is no salvation in them—but grace nevertheless, the presence of which is, of course, not an occasion to congratulate the sinner, but to magnify the Lord.

It is this complexity which makes true on the one hand the declaration of Paul in *Romans* 8:7 that "the carnal mind is enmity against God," and on the other hand that the sinner in some sense is a seeker after God, being restless until he rests in him, as we learn from *Acts* 17:27, "that they should seek God, if haply they might feel after him and find him."

We see, accordingly, that Christianity is both the *denial* of the ethnic faiths and the fulfillment of them. It is a rejection of them, and an answer to their questions. It is this complex relationship which gives significance to the missionary enterprise.

Missionary work is *necessary* because the natural man is lost without Christ, no man being able to be saved by even the most diligent observance of the prescriptions of the ethnic faiths.

And missionary work is *possible* because God has been beforehand with the people to whom the missionary addresses the Gospel, and because he has provided in their religious existence a living point of contact for the Good News that is addressed to all.

INDIVIDUAL DESTINY

A question unaddressed in what has been said so far concerns the fate of those who die, without knowing Jesus Christ and without making any profession of his name. I therefore here append what I regard as a biblically informed address to the issue of "ignorance" and "non-profession." The question is: Are all those who have not known the name of Jesus, and all those who have not acknowledged the Galilean as the world's Redeemer, consigned to hell?

The answer to this question is, quite obviously, No! As everyone will acknowledge, the Old Testament saints, though they believed the promise, had no conception or image of the historical Savior, and therefore made no concrete or existential profession of his name, and yet they were saved on his account. It is likewise universally acknowledged that the children of believing parents who die in infancy are without their knowledge, and without confession, and even without baptism, received into heaven. It is also held by such Calvinists as B. B. Warfield, Charles Hodge, Robert Breckenridge, Robert Candlish, and others (whose opinion I share) that all who die in infancy, whether born of believing parents or not, are the children of God and enter at once into his glory.

The fate of others who, not knowing the Christ in his historical concreteness, remained external adherents of pagan or heathen cults (as, e.g., Socrates); and the fate of those who, having heard of the Christ, made no public profession of his name and continued to bear some non-Christian label (as, e.g., Gandhi)—the fate of these must be left in the hands of God; we are not here entitled to enter into judgment. We are only to remember that God is sovereignly free in his election and that the Spirit of God bloweth where he listeth.

The one thing we are authorized to declare with certainty is this: *If* anyone is saved it is because of what God did in Jesus Christ, who by his birth, death, resurrection, ascension, and kingly session became the only Savior that lost sinners will ever have; who, in short, is and will ever remain the one and only mediator between God and man.

13

Calvin and Aquinas

JOHN CALVIN has been—and remains—my own chief mentor, and I have no disposition whatsoever to minimize the profundity of his thought, the soundness of his conclusions, or the scope of his influence. Yet anyone who surveys the topography of Christian thought cannot help noticing that in the mountain range of sanctified reflection two peaks stand out above the rest. These mountain peaks are St. Augustine and St. Thomas. These two estimable thinkers have, I think, effected a vaster and more influential synthesis of Christ and culture, theology and philosophy, than have any others in the history of the church; and every thoughtful and well-directed Christian student, interested in these central issues, has had to go to school with them. It would be futile, and perhaps perverse, to inquire which of these two—the Plato and the Aristotle of the Christian tradition—should be given primacy. Protestantism has, to be sure, been shaped predominantly by St. Augustine, but no responsible Protestant has thought it fitting to ignore St. Thomas, and none has found it possible to evade the thrust of his searching analyses. By Protestants, as by Roman Catholics, both men have been taken as accredited teachers; and both have in fact been the molders not only of Christian thought but of large portions of the intellectual history of the West.

It is not necessary to dwell at length on the many virtues of St. Thomas. No one who has even the slightest acquaintance with him can fail to be impressed by his deep piety; his vast erudition; his capacity to make relevant

---

This essay first appeared in *The Reformed Journal*, May-June 1974.

distinctions; his willingness to face any and every objection, actual or imaginable; his genius for systematization; his courage in appropriating the New Learning which filtered into late twelfth-century Europe; his skill in rescuing Aristotle from the misinterpretation imposed upon him by his Jewish and Arab commentators; his contribution to the establishment of university scholarship alongside of monastic piety; his endorsement of nature and reason in opposition to every type of world-denying mysticism; and—not to be forgotten—his affirmation of the core truths of Christianity: the priority of God in his power and goodness and the centrality of Christ in his incarnation, death, and resurrection.

All this and more could and should be mentioned in any catalogue of the virtues which adorn St. Thomas. But it would serve no good purpose to proceed farther along this laudatory path. What is likely to be more helpful is some indication of why Protestants, particularly those of the Reformed persuasion, do *not* heed the admonition of Leo XIII to pattern themselves strictly on Thomistic lines. To that end I shall comment not on one or another of the more particular tenets of Aquinas, but on his general approach to what I think is the central issue in the Christian's intellectual engagement with the wider world of thought and understanding. That issue is: *What is the relation of the Revelation in Christ, the eternal and incarnate Logos, to that Reason, or immanent Logos, which prevails in universal culture?* Can a Christian who in grace-induced faith embraces the Gospel still participate with the generality of men in the rational pursuit of truth, goodness, and beauty; and if so, in what way, in what measure, and on what grounds? This single issue, which has engaged thoughtful Christians since at least the second century, lies at the very center of the Thomistic synthesis, and it pervades and determines the very shape of his constructions. It is the issue of the relation between religion and science, Christ and culture, revelation and reason, theology and philosophy, grace and nature, and the like.

*   *   *   *   *

To get hold of this issue, one must first cast a glance backward on the time when the Gospel, and the theologico-philosophical conceptions implicit in it, first confronted the sophisticated Gentile world. What then comes into view is a most dramatic clash of two quite diverse understandings of reality, of two importantly different wisdoms—the Judeo-Christian and the Greco-Roman. These wisdoms differ in origin, form, and content.

As for origin, the Judeo-Christian wisdom was rooted in and sprang forth from faith in a spoken word and from a grace-induced perception of the meaning of certain historical events and enactments. The Greco-Roman wisdom sprang forth from unaided and unsanctified reason operating on the static and dynamic structures of created reality. The one was due to a special divine revelation; the other to a human quest or inquiry. The one was an authoritative disclosure; the other a disputable discovery.

As for form, the Judeo-Christian wisdom appeared in narratives, psalms, prophecies, and the reports of witnesses. The Greco-Roman wisdom appeared in essays, disquisitions, and treatises. The one was told forth, proclaimed; the other, reasoned and argued.

As for content, the Judeo-Christian *Ultimate* was a living and speaking person. The Greco-Roman Ultimate was an impersonal and silent principle or form. For the one wisdom the absolute was a loving subject; for the other it was an attractive but immobile object. For the one wisdom the world was a creation out of nothing in or with time; for the other it was an eternal emanation from an infinitely expansible substance. For the one wisdom history was linear, tending toward a final judgment; for the other it was endlessly circular without *a telos*. For the Greek, man was partly divine and partly non-being; for the Christian he was quite undivine but yet a real being, and in his native constitution wholly good. For the Greek salvation was an achievement; for the Christian it was a gift. For the former it came through the force of human aspiration on the way of eros; for the latter it came through a divine descent in agape. For the Greek the good life consisted in humanistic self-realization; for the Christian it consisted not in purposed ego-fulfillment but in self-denying service in the interest of the neighbor and to God's greater glory.

In the first three centuries of our era these two wisdoms confronted each other and were soon locked in combat. It was not immediately apparent how the issues between them would be eventually resolved. When Christian missionaries first took the Gospel into the Hellenistic world, not many members of the philosophical schools embraced it. It was foolishness to them. It was, they charged, against all reason. But some there were who, although bred in the schools, became disciples of the Christ. It was these who first raised the question which has agitated Christians ever since: What is the *real* relation between the wisdom of God and the wisdom of men? Must one to follow Christ cease to be a Greek? To live the life of faith is it necessary to deny the claims of reason? Does Christianity stand in radical and thoroughgoing antithesis to pagan philosophy? Or is it perhaps, despite appearances, at bottom identical with it? Or is Christianity, while importantly different from paganism, congruous with its nobler insights and able to incorporate into itself significant elements of Greek wisdom?

It is a fact of history that these three questions were given affirmative answers in precisely these three ways by representative Christian thinkers in the patristic period. In answer to the question whether Christianity and paganism are in any sense compatible, Tatian and Tertullian answered *No*. Christ and Aristotle are radically out of accord, they said. There are no positive connections between the Christian faith and the Greek ideas, no concourse between Jerusalem and Athens. The two wisdoms are simply antithetical. At the other extreme were the Christian Gnostics and, to a considerable extent, the well-known apologist Justin Martyr. These tended to think that underlying the two wisdoms is a basic unity. Although there are surface differences between them, they are essentially the same. Both are products of the same Logos. The Christian differs from the enlightened pagan only in that one knows and the other does not (yet) know that the Logos became flesh.

These two positions, however—antithesis on the one hand, and identity on the other—never achieved ascendancy in the church. To the question, "Are the two discriminated wisdoms—the Judeo-Christian and the Greco-Roman—in accord?" the answer the church gave was neither a simple Yes nor a simple No, but a complex and dialectical Yes and No. The Christ that the church most decisively confessed was neither the Christ *against* culture, nor the Christ *of* culture, but either the Christ *above* culture or the Christ who *transforms* culture. What came to be almost universally advocated in Christendom was some sort of *synthesis*.

$$* \quad * \quad * \quad * \quad *$$

Now, it is on the level of this synthesis that St. Thomas and John Calvin meet. Both stand, with St. Augustine, in the mainstream of Christian thought and life. Neither of them is a follower of Tertullian or of Justin. Each rejects the radicalism of the right as well as the radicalism of the left. Both wish to distinguish supernatural revelation from philosophical and scientific inquiry, faith from reason; but both refuse to break the connection between them. They do not wish to surrender the uniqueness and exclusiveness of grace, but neither do they wish to surrender the universality and commonness of nature and of culture. Both want to preserve both creation and redemption, nature and grace, culture and Christ. Against this commonness of outlook and purpose, however, an important difference emerges between John Calvin and St. Thomas.

To get the difference between Calvin and Aquinas into focus, it is necessary to recall that, in order to understand and appraise anything at all from a Christian point of view, we must have recourse not merely to two controlling concepts but to three: nature, sin, and grace, three concepts which correspond to the three great events affecting all mankind—creation, fall, and redemption.

It is an often uttered complaint that, in contrast to Catholicism, Protestantism has lost its hold on nature, and therefore on human culture (which is nature rationalized and ordered), because in quasi-Tertullian fashion it equates nature, reason, and culture with sin. There is ground for this complaint, for in Lutheranism at least there is a tendency to employ only two controlling concepts: sin and grace. But a similar complaint has been uttered against Catholicism, particularly St. Thomas; and Calvinists as well as Lutherans have uttered it. They have noticed, or think they have, that Thomas tends, no less than Luther, to employ only two controlling concepts: not this time sin and grace, but nature and grace. In consequence, the deeper meaning of the fall seems to escape Aquinas, and the devastating effects of sin tend to be ignored or glossed over. Calvinists wish to join Thomas in asserting the rights of the natural, but they wish also to join Luther in asserting the reality and all-pervasiveness of sin—all the while holding in common with all Christians the renewing power of grace. Calvinists find the key to philosophico-theological issues such as those we are now discussing in the ineluctable unity of nature, sin, and grace.

It is because Tertullian equated Greek thought with sin, and did not recognize the precipitate of created nature in it, that Calvin rejected Tertullianism. It is because Justin equated Greek thought with Logos-filled nature, and did not see the perverting power of sin on and in it, that Calvin rejected the identity theory. And, although Calvin recognizes that St. Thomas comes closer to the center of Christian truth than Justin, inasmuch as he reserves a unique place for the supernatural and for grace, he finds that Aquinas, apparently unmindful of the sin that everywhere pervades the thought of unredeemed mankind, is too quick to adopt wholesale and unmodified the disciplined ratiocinations of what St. Paul calls the natural man, and to allow these to serve as a purely rational foundation on which to erect a Christian superstructure. For Calvin, as for St. Thomas, nature is basic, because creation is. But nature and natural reason, Calvin recognizes, have been despoiled by sin, and they can be retrieved and utilized only after they have been renewed by grace, and only after they have been viewed and exercised in the closest possible association with faith.

Calvin, consequently, and most of his followers with him, have taken exception to a number of things in St. Thomas—among them his too uncritical endorsement of Aristotle as the paradigm of the philosopher; his too rigid distinction between philosophy and theology; his denial of the possibility of a Christian philosophy; his rationalistic arguments for the existence of God; his uncompromising empiricism; his ethics of natural law; and the like.

What this all comes to is well stated by H. Richard Niebuhr: Aquinas confesses a Christ *above* culture, while Calvin confesses a Christ *transforming* culture.

14

A Note to Young Seminarians

THE SACRED MINISTRY can never be lightly undertaken, for it makes very heavy demands upon a man. A minister must be many things at once. He must be a theologian, and as such disciplined by logic, history, and philosophy. He must be a pastor and by that token a psychologist and friend. He must preach and as a preacher be a rhetorician and a prophet. And above all he must be a man of God.

If, then, in addressing you as ministers, actual or prospective, I limit my discussion to theology and the theologian, it is not because I am either unaware of the other aspects of your calling or in any way inclined to minimize their importance. Aside from accidental determinants, the limitation is rather imposed by my desire to remind you that you are, or ought to be, *also* theologians. I want to remind you of that because, although theology, considered as an intellectually articulated account of revealed truth, still enjoys the primacy among us, we are constantly being tempted either to divorce theoretical theology from practical pursuits like preaching and counseling, or to pursue the study of theology with the activistic, functional mind of the day. And both of these temptations we should, I think, resist.

We should resist the temptation to divorce theology from the practice of our calling, because the divorce is bound to impoverish both our theology and our practice. Each can, and should, support and vivify the other. The theologian who does not remain in intimate touch with the teeming life to

This essay first appeared in *The Calvin Forum,* January 1950.

which as preacher and pastor he is called to address himself, is making overtures to a barren scholasticism. And the preacher who neglects the discipline of theology gives hostages to an empty psychologism.

But, while keeping theology and practice in relation, we ought not to compromise the integrity of the former. Theology is a means, indeed, of enriching our practical service, but it ought not be pursued as a mere means. It has its own worth and its own ends. It ought not therefore to be reduced to common utility. One does not study it well when one studies it with half an eye on next Sunday's sermon or on the imminent board examination. One studies it best when one regards it as a system of truths that is valid independently of its functional efficacy; when one approaches it as a system of meanings that is worthy in its own right of being *understood*. Your pursuit of theological learning should, therefore, not be confined to a mastery of what is narrowly and practically useful in your job. Theology is not a technical instrument; it is a liberalizing discipline. Its study is not mere vocational training. On that account "useful" theological information should not be accepted in lieu of cultivated theological judgment. You should so direct your efforts that you are not merely *informed*—i.e., provided with information, data, "facts"—but also *formed*—i.e., intellectually and spiritually enlarged, enriched, and deepened by your studies. As educational media here encyclopedias, compendia, digests, surveys, and schemata cannot substitute for the classical theological literature that our culture provides in such lush profusion. You may not be content merely to acquire the results of theological reflection, but should learn also to participate in the process of theologizing by studying the writings of Athanasius, Augustine, Aquinas, Calvin, Luther, and the like. In this way there is every likelihood that you will be formed and disciplined by your tradition, and perchance be used of God to extend and enrich it.

The theology we learn, embrace, and construct must of course be a *living* theology, and I should like to suggest a few of the characteristics of such a theology.

THE LIVING WORD

A living theology should be in contact with the Living Word—i.e., the Scriptures.

There is, of course, a sense in which a word, any word, and by that token the whole complex of words which make up the text of Scripture is dead. Words are lifeless symbols which seize, incarcerate, and freeze the meanings they connote and press life and movement out of them. When, nevertheless, the Word is said to live, we mean that it is an authentic and authoritative witness to an historical and ever-present reality—the gracious and loving presence of God in Christ. As such it is not dated. It is always contemporaneous, ever new. It spans the ages, and speaks to every situation. It addresses itself to changing moods, rises to meet each circumstance, suits itself to every need. It is as it were a thing alive. And such indeed it is, for brooding over it, and speaking through it, and making application of it is the Holy Spirit himself.

It is alive, too, in that it is a narrative, a history. The Book is not a collection of propositions, dicta, abstract truths. Truth is there, and principle, but never nakedly, never separated from the context of life. The truth lies embedded in great creative and redemptive acts and in the lives and experiences of saints, within the context of existence.

A theology, as such, is not alive in quite that way. Theology, like all theory, is abstract. Being the product of thought, it is constructed through detachment from the flowing stream of life. It is therefore a step or two removed from the concrete reality that it points to and intends. As long as it borrows its force and authority from this reality—the living and life-giving Word of God—its inevitable detachment will work no harm but rather enhance its symbolical and interpretative function. But there is always the danger that, having raised itself above its data for a better look, it will return to them no more, yield no longer to the pressure of the facts, and harden into a system inhospitable to further truth. In order to prevent this, theology must remain sensitive to the revelation, responsive to its importunities. It must allow the fresh winds of the ever-present living Word, the pulsating life of the biblical witness, to flow clean through itself. This means that the theologian must be empirical. He must descend continually to the Word and allow his formulas to be tested by it. Recognizing the priority of the living Word, he must acknowledge the essentially fluid character of his constructions and be ready at all times to bring them into greater conformity with the truth. Only so will his theology remain alive.

A LIVING FAITH

A living theology must emerge out of a living faith. Theology is jargon until there is commitment and involvement. Ritschlian subjectivism is rightly repudiated by Reformed theologians, for Ritschl substitutes the religious consciousness for the objective revelation of God in the incarnate and inscripturated Logos. But this much perhaps we may learn from Ritschl and from subjectivists: that unless a man's theology has something of himself in it, it is nothing.

I suspect that the reason we are frequently unmoved by discussions on the Trinity, the atonement, regeneration, and similar Christian doctrines is that we have never deeply *felt* their truth, or have never consciously related our experience of them to our theologizing. Theology, to be alive, must, while setting forth the meaning of the objective Word, be at the same time a delineation of one's own deepest spiritual experiences. The truth will then be personalized and vital and proof against the dry-rot of barren and abstract scholasticism. And when truth and lived truth are joined, one will also discover, I think, that the life formed within one by the prayerful reading of the Scriptures becomes itself a clue to the meaning and significance of the Word.

THE LIFE OF THE CHURCH

A living theology should be in contact with the life of the church, the experience of the religious community.

It is sometimes said that theology is proper to academic halls, and to the minister's study, and that it is less proper to the pulpit, and entirely out of place at sick beds. This is not true. What is out of place at sick beds is academic palaver; but then this, without more, is out of place in the classroom, too. Theology must stand in vital relation to the congregation, the people, the church; forming it, and being formed by it.

Theology must be formed by the church. It must emerge out of the matrix of human need and be augmented and enriched by the common experiences of the redeemed society. It must bear upon itself the stamp of the life of the religious community. The best theology is therefore written in the manse, by a man in daily contact with the flowing life of the people; or, if not in the manse, then by a man who understands that Christians constitute a Kingdom, which in its turn provides the context for all Christian truth.

Not only must theology reflect the character of the church life; it must also speak to it and form it. I submit that a theologian is bound to exhibit the significance for Christian living of the distinctions he makes between *homoousia* and *homoiousia*, and the like, or to drop them altogether, and I think he should not drop them. There is a relevance in Christian theology to the temptations, trials, hopes, struggles, anticipations, and frustrations of people, and that relevance must appear. The formulas and distinctions of theology must be so interpreted and mediated, kept so alive and dynamic, as to make a difference to the practical and moral conduct of people. Its truths must be truths that liberate, enrich, direct. Theological truths are truths to live by, and the theologian has the awful responsibility of ensuring that their existential import becomes apparent.

CONTACT WITH CONTEMPORARY THOUGHT

A living theology should be in contact with contemporary thought.

It should take note of the issues, problems, and perplexities agitating the contemporary mind, and respond to contemporary challenges.

It should take note of the present state of theological learning, on the theory that the Spirit of God is still in the church and not limited to our segment of it; and that theological maturation, like every other kind, is an historical process in which many and diverse forces are operative. This means that the theologian should carefully consider what those say who differ from him in doctrine, lest some segment or aspect of the full truth be lost to him. It means *a fortiori* that he should address himself to theological issues arising within his own communion, especially when the issue raised has profound implications for the significance of the present cultural crisis.

A living theology, finally, should find in contemporary heresies a reason for critical self-examination; for heresies, it may be believed, do not come forth exclusively out of a sinful heart, but are frequently occasioned by the deficiencies and imbalances of the essentially true theology they oppose.

A living theology should be contemporaneous, historical, personal, and, above all, oriented to the Living Word. To construct it is no small task, but its construction is, I suggest, our common duty.

Part IV

REVELATION

15

Jesus and the Old Testament

WHAT WAS JESUS' VIEW of the Hebrew Scriptures? What did he teach, by word and attitude, respecting the place and authority of the Old Testament writings? Did he regard the Jewish canon as comprising the inspired Word of God, supernaturally communicated and preserved, and exercising unconditional authority over the lives of men? Or did he perhaps repudiate it—in whole or part? Did he distinguish between the Written Word and the Scribal Tradition? If so, what was his attitude toward each? Did he conform his own life to the precepts of Scripture, recognizing it as binding, or did he on occasion appeal to a higher authority? Did he recognize, besides the Hebrew Bible, an additional source of knowledge of God's will and purpose? How, according to him, was one to understand the Scriptures? Was he conscious of transcending or superseding the Old Testament revelation?

That these are not idle questions every serious reader of the New Testament will acknowledge. They emerge from the main stream of the Christian records. The synoptists unquestionably accept the inspiration and authority of the Old Testament; they freely quote it, are at considerable pains to vindicate its prophecies respecting the Messiah, and report words of Jesus which imply its unconditional validity. Yet they represent him as in constant conflict with the Pharisees about matters of the Law, and include sayings of his which suggest only a qualified acceptance of the inspired writings. What view of Scripture, we should like to know, could enable the Lord to speak at

---

This essay first appeared in *The Reformed Journal*, January 1955.

one time as though the Law and the Prophets had ceased with John, and at another to declare them to be eternal—unchangeable in respect even of one jot or tittle? In terms of what principle are we to reconcile his condemnation of the elders for making the Word of God of none effect, and his words enjoining obedience to those who sit in Moses' seat? The student of Paul confronts the same problem. What enabled that apostle, who recognized the Law to be holy and "the commandments holy and good," to declare in the name of Christ that we are no longer under the Law, but under grace? The Christian church recognizes Jesus as its Lord; in fidelity to what in him did it include the Old Testament in its canon, while failing to observe its ceremonial injunctions? By what understanding of the mind of their Master did Christ's followers break with Judaism and shortly thereafter repudiate Marcion?

* * * * *

Jesus, the Liberals tell us, was a child of his age. There is truth in the statement. If it means, however, that Jesus was merely a product of Judaism, and, in the fulness of his character and work, dependent upon the succession of history in time, it is false. There is, as the church has always confessed, something superhistorical about Christ. Though in history, he is not of history. He is unique, *sui generis*, of the order of Melchizedek. He is the Son of God incarnate. There is an eternal moment in him that refuses to be pressed into temporal categories. In Jesus God's love cuts through all historical and psychological mediacies. This it is necessary to affirm in opposition to the modern historicism and psychologism that is offended by the skandalon of an eternal revelation in Christ and by the paradox of a universal man.

Yet Jesus can in a sense be regarded as a child of his times. He was born out of the house of David, into a particular community, at a definite point of history. He was a Hebrew, born under the law, and trained according to its precepts. His language, his conduct, his themes, and his thought forms were in the tradition of his people, and we are learning that his teachings differed but slightly from those of the Judaism of his day. Klausner is even prepared to say that "throughout the gospels there is not one item of ethical teaching which cannot be paralleled either in the Old Testament, the Apocrypha, or in the Talmudic and Midrashic literature of the period near to the time of Jesus," and adds: "Without exception Jesus is wholly explainable by the Scriptural and Pharisaic Judaism of his time" (*Jesus of Nazareth*, p. 384).

With this last a Christian will not agree. Jesus himself was conscious of his own originality, and as Scott says, "There can be no doubt that he came forward as a teacher under an irresistible impulse to proclaim something new" (*The New Testament Idea of Revelation*, p. 85). What he brought could not, he believed, be poured into old skins. Yet Klausner and others have served to remind us that Jesus did not live and preach in a vacuum. He taught in a definite milieu, and his teachings found their roots in the past. Though himself a revelation, he witnessed to a revelation already existent. He came proclaiming the truth of God as set down in the Scriptures of the Old Testament. It was not in opposition to, but in confirmation of the Law that he delivered his message. He came not to destroy, but to fulfill.

*   *   *   *   *

Fidelity to Scripture is basic in Jesus. It was this fidelity as much as anything else that involved him in quarrels with the Scribes and Pharisees. It was not because they upheld the Law, but because they perverted it and made it of none effect, that he lashed them (Mk. 7:8; Mt. 15:3). When called upon to defend his teachings, it is to Scripture that he appeals (Mk. 2:26; 11:17; 15:34). When a seeker after eternal life asks him the way thither, he refers him to the Word of God (Mk. 10:19; Lk. 10:26). When a certain newness in his utterances renders him momentarily suspect, he declares: "Think not that I came to destroy the Law and the Prophets; I came not to destroy, but to fulfill" (Mt. 5:17).

It was on them that he nurtured his own soul. He was brought up in and breathed the atmosphere of the spiritually minded circle represented by Zacharias, Elizabeth, Simeon, and Anna, and with them he "walked in all the commandments and ordinances of the Lord, blameless" (Lk. 1:6). To what extent the Scriptures had become a part of him is evident from his habit of resorting to Scriptural language in the deepest crises of his life. It is by the word of Moses that he repulses Satan in the wilderness, and David furnishes him with speech as he agonizes on Calvary. It cannot be doubted that Jesus' acceptance of the Torah is final and complete. It is the foundation on which he builds.

*   *   *   *   *

It is important to remember this basic loyalty of Jesus to the Scriptures. There are those who presume to find warrant in his life and teaching for the setting up of an authority higher and more vital than any combination of written words. It is not, we are told, by consulting any external oracle, be it pope or book, that we know the will of God; it is by attending to the promptings of God's Spirit in our hearts. To the authority of any book or creed we must oppose the authority of our spiritual intuition and religious experience. The highest revelation of God is in the depths of the individual soul sensitive to the universally operating Spirit of God. "The children of the Father, in virtue of their filial relation to Him, know Him directly, and spontaneously maintain communion with Him apart from temple and synagogue" (Mackinnon, *The Historic Jesus*, p. 325). This, it is alleged, is what Jesus taught us, and he himself appealed to the inner guide in opposing his "But I say unto you" to the "Ye have heard" of the religious tradition.

In answer it must be said that Jesus' "religious experience" (the phrase is not apt) was throughout conditioned by his study of the Scriptures. He entertained not only a theoretical regard for these; they were woven into the very fibre of his life. Furthermore, the deliverances of his "consciousness" were always in corroboration and establishment of the revelation contained in the Old Testament writings. It was on the basis of and in fidelity to the Scriptures that he proclaimed his message. This fact did not escape his followers. It was not a gratuitous whim that moved the Christian Fathers to combine the Old and New Testaments into one authoritative book to be used by them for the nourishment of their spiritual life. It was loyalty to Christ that impelled them. They, at any rate, never understood him to have supplanted the Scriptures by an inner witness.

This insistence by Jesus on an objective revelation as the seat of authority in a religion does not, of course, involve a rejection of the inner witness; the two are complementary and interactive. It merely makes plain that the inner witness is a *witness*. It does not stand alone; it testifies of something. The inward condition of the heart is always an *attitude;* faith is a *responsive* activity; the spirit is a *testifying* spirit; "experience" is an experience of *something*. And it was always to the objective reference of the spiritual life—to God and his Word—that Jesus recalled his hearers.

*   *   *   *   *

It is obvious, however, that in some sense Jesus stood above and beyond the Written Word. However true it may be that he searched the Scriptures and commanded his followers to do likewise, it is equally true that he marks an advance upon the past, bringing a revelation which, if it does not contradict the Old, at least heightens and improves it. The fact is patent enough. How is it to be interpreted?

Some, as was suggested above, would explain it in terms of a "religious experience" not qualitatively different from that of other men. This explanation is unacceptable, however, inasmuch as our "experiences" are not so much critics of as they are criticized by the revelation of God. Moreover, the Scriptures themselves supply a different interpretation. They affirm that the phenomenon in question is to be looked at from the point of view of the supernatural process of revelation.

Jesus, according to Christianity, is both the revealer and the revealed. As a revealer he stands in the succession of the prophets. Like them he believed himself to be sent from God (Lk. 4:43; Mt. 21:37; Jn. 3:17, 34) and to have a message not his own. "I speak," he says, "not from myself; but the Father that sent me, he hath given me a commandment, what I should say and what I should speak; . . . the things therefore which I speak, even as the Father hath said unto me, so I speak" (Jn. 12:49, 50). It is this special communication from God, the same God who spoke to Moses and the

Prophets, that Jesus feels constrained to proclaim. It is as a servant, as a bearer of a message, as under a kind of spiritual duress, that he appears on the scene.

Considered under this aspect, Jesus' authority was not his own; the prophet's authority is never the authority of man. The rights, privileges, and powers of a prophet are never to be regarded as definitive of the rights, privileges, and powers of a man per se. The revelations borne by them may never be psychologized down into deliverances of their own consciousness. It is the possession of something wholly underived from "experience" that is the genius of prophetism. The prophets are characterized not so much by the fact that they spoke, as by the fact that they were spoken to. They did not discover God's will while on a religious quest; they were arrested and conscripted into God's service, frequently against their will. Their authority lay not in their own excellence, piety, or earnestness, but solely in the fact that they were chosen by God, and by a supernatural act made receptive for his word. They knew themselves to be bearers of a revelation, and revelation is more than religious experience. It is the divine criticism and transformation of religious experience.

Two things then emerge from a consideration of Jesus as a prophet. First, his advance upon the Old Testament revelation is not made on the basis of a religious experience of a kind common to the race of men. And second, the advance was not at the expense of the Old Testament, but on the basis of it. It did not supplant; it supplemented. It did not destroy; it fulfilled.

*   *   *   *   *

However we view the matter, therefore, we cannot, with appeal to Christ, set up our "experience" as a standard in terms of which to criticize the revelation of God contained in the Scriptures of the Old and New Testament. If it be indeed a revelation (and Jesus regarded it so), there is no possibility of standing above it. It stands above us as a judge and we have no alternative but to obey. It was precisely this that Jesus taught us. Not mystic intuition, not this or that experience of an individual or group, but the Law and the Prophets—here one finds the will of God.

In what sense Jesus "went beyond" the Law and the Prophets must now be considered. There are sayings of his which seem to supersede the Law. By fulfilling it he seems at times to disallow it. In view of this how can one still maintain his full fidelity to the Scriptures?

*   *   *   *   *

To answer properly we must first distinguish between the written Torah and the Scribal Tradition. Much of what Jesus opposed was in the latter and not in the former. It is true, of course, that the Judaism of Jesus' day ascribed to the oral law a character as binding as that possessed by the written. It, too, was believed to have been revealed to Moses. "The whole revelation of God was not comprised in the Sacred books. By the side of Scripture there had always gone an unwritten tradition, in part interpreting and applying the written Torah, in part supplementing it" (Moore, *Judaism*, I, 251). To this supplementary part the Scribes accorded absolute validity. Pirke Aboth even goes so far as to say: "it is more serious to offend against decrees of the Scribes than against the decrees of the Law" (Brenscomb, *Jesus and the Law of Moses*, p. 44). On the other hand, Judaism did differentiate between Torah and Tradition, Canon and Commentary. "When the last prophets, Haggai, Zechariah, and Malachi died, the Holy Spirit ceased out of Israel" (*ibid.*, p. 41). And Josephus says: "From Artaxerxes to our own time the complete history has been written but has not been deemed worthy of equal credit with the earlier records because of the failure of the exact succession of the prophets" (*Contra Apionem*, I, 41). Canon and Tradition were, therefore, distinguishable, and it is evident that Jesus did distinguish between them. There is no evidence, however, that he regarded the Tradition as in itself reprehensible. With much of it he was in apparent agreement. He "would not suffer that any man should carry a vessel through the temple" (Mk. 11:16). He observed the rules for celebrating the passover (Mk. 14:22, 26). He seems to have worn the fringed garment prescribed for every good Jew (Mk. 6:56). But, and this is the significant thing, he did not regard the Tradition as apriorily binding. It was not inviolable, as the Scriptures were. For that reason he could oppose it on occasion in the name of Scripture. The Scribes were the objects of his scorn because they exactly reversed the true relation, leaving the commandments of God and holding fast to the tradition of men (Mk. 7:8). Many of these traditions Jesus believed to have no scriptural warrant and to be subversive of man's best interests. For that reason he was careless about the frequent cleansings and fastings, opposed the ceremonial washing of cups before eating, and inveighed against a fettering legalism that tithed mint and cummin and neglected the weightier matters of the Law. Human tradition no less than human intuition had to bow before the revelation of God in the canonical Scriptures.

*   *   *   *   *

But, it will be said, did not Jesus retouch the Old Testament itself so as really to change its complexion? Did he not inwardize and spiritualize its ethics? Did he not introduce a comparative principle by the application of which one scriptural precept was rejected in the interest of another?

That Jesus interpreted the Torah differently than his contemporaries cannot be denied. Therein, among other things, lay his originality. He was the great interpreter, and his followers can never properly read the Old Testament save through his eyes. From him we know what the law against murder really means (Mt. 5:21), and how strictly the prohibition of adultery must be taken (Mt. 5:27). He lay bare the very heart of the whole law, summing it up in love (Mk. 12:28-34; Lk. 10:25-28). He provided us with a new perspective, teaching us that the Law is meaningful only in the measure that it transforms itself into an inner witness. Where the Scribes had enjoined obedience to an abstract Law, he enjoined obedience to God *through* the law. He made plain that trust in God is the active principle of all goodness, and insisted that the moral quality of an act is largely determined by the intention that lies behind it. In all this he far transcends the Judaism of his day and casts a new full light upon the Scriptures.

It is evident, however, that in the class of passages here referred to, Jesus strengthens the Law rather than weakens it. He reveals to us its true scope and meaning. The fact is, he *interprets* it: he indicates what God meant the Law to say. By so doing he establishes it. He was here, as elsewhere, the True Light, illuminating the Scriptures, dispelling its darkness, making plain its obscurities, and casting into bold relief its mountain peaks while preserving its hills and valleys. His discourses are one long answer to the question: What say the Scriptures? What really do they mean?

*   *   *   *   *

There are a number of passages, however, which seem to imperil the thesis we have thus far been maintaining. These passages suggest that Jesus definitely abrogates certain parts and provisions of the Scriptures. He replaces the scriptural law of revenge with the law of forgiveness and non-resistance; he controverts Moses on the question of divorce, and forbids swearing, which the Law allows. He fails to observe the Mosaic regulations pertaining to the Sabbath, and permits the eating of forbidden foods. Apart, too, from any specific utterance there seems to be in his tone, bearing, and conduct a general magisterial indifference to the peculiarly ethnic and ceremonial aspects of Israel's religion. Walker notices that Jesus "wholly subordinates the ceremonial expression of reverence for God to the humanitarian expression of it" (*Jesus and the Jewish Teaching*, p. 306). And Mackinnon is of the opinion that "his attitude toward the ceremonial law practically implies its abrogation" (*The Historic Jews*, p. 325).

How are we to square this important element in the teaching of Jesus with his fidelity to the Scriptures? The answer, it seems to me, lies in the question; the problem suggests the solution. It will be noted that it is the "peculiarly ethnic and ceremonial aspects of Israel's religion" that Jesus abrogates. The significance of that fact cannot be overestimated, for it is precisely in respect of their nationalism and ceremonialism that the Old Testament

Scriptures *are by their own witness* temporal and provisional. When Jesus attacks them at these points, therefore, he is doing what they themselves anticipate and in a sense demand.

In this light we can understand the utterances referred to above. When Jesus declares that the Law and the Prophets have ceased with John, he is merely announcing the presence of the new era toward which the Law and the Prophets pointed. All prophecy had been concerned with one great far-off divine event. Now it had happened; the Messiah had come. Hence prophecy must cease. As for the Law, the very peremptoriness of its moral imperatives promised a Perfect and Sinless One in whom it would be justified. In its ceremonial aspects the essence of the Law lay in its prospective reference. All its sacrificial lambs pointed to the Lamb that taketh away the sins of the world. Now the perfect lamb had come. Hence the Law, too, must cease. This does not mean that the Law and the Prophets are broken and discarded; it means simply that they are completely vindicated.

In Israel church and state were one; religion and politics were practically identical. This was inevitable in a theocracy. This peculiar organization was, however, in its very nature provisional. Jewish nationalism existed for a larger end. Abraham was chosen that in him "all the nations of the earth should be blessed" (Gen. 18:18; 22:18). God's special revelation, in the Old Testament, was temporarily confined to this narrow national channel in order that in the fulness of time it might the better irrigate the whole world (Ps. 107:3). What Jesus says in effect when he speaks about divorce and Sabbath observance is that they are to be raised out of their socio-political matrix and personalized. He does not condemn the old order; he merely affirms that it is passing away. And in so doing, it must be remembered, he is saying what the Scriptures themselves say. Jesus is here again the great interpreter. He is being true to the Word.

But was there nothing new in his own revelation? Was he merely an expounder of the Old Testament Scriptures? There was something new. The new and vital message that Jesus brought was this: not that nationalism and ceremonialism was dispensational, but that their dispensation had *now* come to an end. His unique message was that the universal, spiritual, and unceremonial kingdom adumbrated in the sacrificial system, implied in God's choice of a special people, and promised by the prophets, had *now* come. This is the really distinctive element in his teaching. His contribution lay not so much in his ethics; Klausner, Abrahams, Strack-Billerbeck, and others have helped us to see that more plainly. His contribution lay not in the rejection of a book-religion; he was throughout loyal to the scriptural word. His contribution lay in the announcement of the Kingdom; his teaching was a setting forth of its rules; his life was a display of its spirit; his death was the seal of its establishment; his resurrection was the sign of its triumph.

16

The Doctrine of Revelation in St. Paul

T HE CHIEF SOURCES for Paul's thought are, of course, his epistles. Without entering into the critical questions respecting the authorship of the disputed letters, I have limited myself for the most part to those which are generally acknowledged to be genuine—namely, Romans, Galatians, First and Second Corinthians, Philippians, and Philemon. The book of Acts is valuable as a secondary source. The essay falls into three main parts: the nature, the contents, and the reception of revelation. The division seemed natural inasmuch as every revelation must contain three moments: speaker, word spoken, and hearer.

THE NATURE OF REVELATION

General.—Paul firmly believed in the universality of revelation. The fact has been adduced as evidencing his Hellenism. Judaism, it is argued, was particularistic. It restricted God's communications to a single people especially chosen to receive them, and regarded the rest of mankind as lying in ignorance and sin. The Greeks, on the other hand, were expansive. They had discovered that God spoke a universal language and that he had left himself nowhere without witness. With a broad and exemplary tolerance they ad-

This essay first appeared in the *Calvin Theological Journal,* November 1966.

mitted all men into favor with God, and it was from them that Paul derived
his belief in general revelation.

The fact is, however, that Paul's position is wholly Jewish. The idea of
revelation found no place in Greek thought and was foreign to its very
genius. Not transcendence, personality, dualism, faith, and obedience, but
immanence, monism, reason, and inquiry were the key words in Hellenic
thinking. God was not someone to be received, but someone to be inquired
after. The world was a datum, not a voice. It did not reveal something
beyond itself; there was nothing beyond to reveal. There was no supernatural; there was only the supersensuous. The gods were not Other; they
were simply higher. They lived on Olympus, not in the heavens. The universe was single, and the gods themselves were caught up in the unitary
process. There were no transcendent references, no vertical planes. The
world reflected back upon itself, and all thought moved in a circle. Nature
was not articulate; it was merely provocative. It was complete, self-contained,
and self-explanatory. The universe was a question to be answered, not a
revelation to be heard.

It was otherwise with the Jew. The whole world was a witness to a
transcendent reality. Nature was Gothic in structure with every line vertical.
It was a finger pointing upward, a sign and symbol of something beyond. It
testified not of itself, but of an Other. The world was a creation; it was made
and fashioned by another hand whose power it displayed. It was vocal with
praise of the Creator. Nature was warm with the breath of the Spirit, and her
every mood was a divine communication. The whole universe was a revelation, a letter written in God's own hand and intelligible to all who could read.
"The heavens declare the glory of God, and the firmament showeth his
handiwork. Day unto day uttereth speech, and night unto night showeth
knowledge. There is no speech nor language in which their voice is not
heard. Their line is gone out through all the earth and their words to the end
of the world" (Ps. 19:1-4). God, the Jews believed, had made a universal
revelation of himself.

Paul was of the same mind. The world, considered both as a divine
creation and as the instrument of God's providential ministrations, reveals,
Paul teaches, something of God's mind and disposition. "The invisible things
of him since the creation are clearly seen, being perceived through the things
that are made, even his everlasting power and divinity" (Rom. 1:20). To the
pagans at Lystra he declares, "God left not himself without witness, in that
he did good and gave you from heaven rains and fruitful seasons, filling your
hearts with food and gladness" (Acts 14:17). But that not alone. God also
discloses himself in the consciences of men, being "not far from each one of
us" (Acts 17:27). His law is written in the heart (Rom. 2:14), and all men
know that he hates unrighteousness, for God "manifested it unto them"
(Rom. 1:19). Man is the image and glory of God (I Cor. 11:7), and there is

that in him which is turned toward his maker and which acknowledges his will as righteous (Rom. 7:15).

Whatever knowledge of God there is in the world is due, therefore, to God's own free activity, not to the activity of man. God is not a fact to be discovered, a kind of spirit to be ferreted out from its hiding place in the crevices of the universe or in the mystic shadows of the human heart. That would reduce him to a datum amenable to investigation. It would make him a mere object, while he is in fact the absolute subject. Whatever truth there be, whatever virtue, whatever religion—it all goes back to a primitive revelation, a personal communication. Do all men possess the idea of God? Are all agreed that the good is to be preferred to the bad? Then it is due to the fact that God has declared himself. These ideas are not human constructs. They are owing to a self-disclosure of God; they are stray wisps from the great light that originally diffused the course and structure of the world.

This light, however, is now very dim, and wholly inadequate to the needs of men. Sin entered the world through Adam, the first man (I Cor. 15:45), who by his fall and disobedience broke covenant with God and thereby brought himself and all his posterity into a state of misery (Rom. 5:12). Had this not occurred, almost completely quenching the light, man would doubtless have attained to an ever-increasing knowledge of God. This is no longer possible. The light, though not completely withdrawn, is obscure. More than that, the power to follow it is lost. Man may recognize the right, but he is quite unable to perform it (Rom. 7:15). It is impossible to follow the gleam. Both the divine revelation and man's capacity to receive it are seriously mal-affected. Nature itself is subject to vanity (Rom. 8:20), and "we know that the whole creation groaneth and travaileth in pain together until now" (vs. 22). The principle of deterioration and estrangement is especially operative in the hearts and minds of men. Because, knowing God, they did not glorify him as God, they "became vain in their reasonings, and their senseless heart was darkened" (Rom. 1:21). Failing to retain God in their knowledge, God gave them up to a reprobate mind (vs. 28), and they began to worship idols, exchanging the "glory of the incorruptible God for the likeness of an image of corruptible man, and of birds, and four-footed beasts, and creeping things" (vs. 23). In so doing men honored the creature more than the Creator, and withheld obedience from him to whom alone it is due. They gave allegiance to the weak and beggarly rudiments, and "not knowing God, were in bondage to them that by nature are no gods" (Gal. 4:8). It was only after Christ was preached to them that the Galatians came to know God, or rather to be known of him (vs. 9); and when the Ephesians were without Christ, they were "without God in the world" (Eph. 2:12).

All so-called natural religion is therefore not only inadequate, it is subject to condemnation. The natural light men have is just sufficient to condemn them, to leave them without excuse (Rom. 1:20). Paul admits that the

Athenians were religious, but it is precisely of their religion that he asks them to repent. Their inaccurate knowledge and ignorant worship God formerly overlooked, but now he "commandeth that they should all everywhere repent, inasmuch as he hath appointed a day in which he will judge the world in righteousness by the man [Jesus] whom he hath ordained" (Acts 17:30). Paul nowhere tempers this harsh estimate of natural religion. All attempts to please God on the basis of natural aptitudes and dispositions are vain. "The carnal mind is enmity against God" (Rom. 8:7). It cannot know him because he is spiritually discerned (I Cor. 2:14). It will therefore not do to plead the universal presence of God. God is indeed everywhere present, but he is present as a judge. Conscience still speaks, but its mandates cannot be carried out. There is some sense of a goal, but where it lies men cannot tell. There is desire, but no fulfillment; there are questions, but no answers; gropings, but no satisfactions.

This is Paul's doctrine of general revelation. It contains two judgments, both of which must be maintained. On the one hand, natural revelation is obscure and incomplete, and the religion based upon it is false and idolatrous. This religion cannot yield certainty, provides no proper sanctions for morality, and is unable to attain to salvation. Its instruments—reason, mystic contemplation, and moral endeavor—fail to touch God. At best they only discover the need of him. On the other hand, natural revelation (which, strictly speaking, is not natural, having come from God) preserves man from gross error, enables him to do a kind of good, and awakens in him a longing and expectation for something higher. It is for this reason that the natural man and his religion is redeemable. God's image is not completely destroyed. Man is made for God, and there is a dim apprehension in him of his higher destiny. Man's religion is false, but his capacity for religion and the impulse to religious expression is divinely caused. His questions are poorly expressed, and his answers are wrong, but they imply the consciousness of a lack. On that consciousness and impulse any special revelation, if there is to be one, will have to build. If there is to be another and clearer word of God it will have to come as an answer to a question. Paul knew that. Christ came, he believed, to fulfill a *need*. It is on this point that the early Barthians seem to have misread Paul. The apostle never completely severed the natural and the supernatural. The God whom the Athenians but dimly discerned and ignorantly worshipped, Paul openly declared (Acts 17). The process of revelation is characterized by a living interdependence between question and answer, answer and question.

Progressive—Natural revelation, therefore, demanded another and special revelation. Men needed more light to understand clearly what nature teaches, and they needed to gain additional information concerning God's own nature and his will for man. But they needed more than that. The situation demanded a revelation that was effectual as well as informative, a force as well as a fact. It was not only knowledge men needed; they needed a new heart. Power had to accompany light. Revelation had to be redemptive. Such a revelation Paul came proclaiming as a reality. He preached that God had revealed himself in Christ, and was in him reconciling the world unto himself (II Cor. 5:19).

The Christian revelation, however, was not a sudden emergence, a startling and unlooked-for bolt out of the blue. It had been long in preparation and was a precipitate of a definite process. God did not choose to reveal himself in one blinding flash. He preferred to supplement and correct the natural by a revelation historical in character and moving slowly and progressively on the plane of time. Not ideas, but facts were to be his instruments. For that reason he chose a special people in order that in the life and fortunes, the transactions and practical experience of that people he might realize his redemptive purpose. Abraham was called to be its father, and his children were conscious of the unique place they occupied in God's vast plan. Through them God entered in a special way upon the plane of history. He guided and directed them, legislated their law, controlled their national fortunes, inspired their singers, and spoke through their prophets. He revealed his will and plan not all at once, through the enunciation of eternal ideas, nice maxims, bare principles, or abstract philosophical truths, but gradually and progressively, through events, happenings, and activities. History and time were integral to his plan, and Christianity is part and parcel of its development. The Old and New Testaments are inseparable. They constitute an indissoluble unity.

All this Paul maintained. He taught that God had revealed himself not only in and through Christ, but also in and through the history of Israel. To the Israelites, in distinction from all other peoples, God had spoken in a special way. Theirs was "the adoption, and the glory, and the covenants, and the giving of the law, and the service of God, and the promises" (Rom. 9:4, 5). Theirs also were the fathers, and of them was Christ born according to the flesh. Of this progressive revelation he conceived Christ to be a real, though dominating, part. Christ was for him not an isolated fact. He stood in a particular succession and was part of a special redemptive history. It is sometimes said that Paul did not so regard him. It is at this juncture, we are told, that he differs from the author of the epistle to the Hebrews, who represents Christ as the last of many voices (Heb. 1:1). Not evolution, but revolution expresses Paul's meaning. This, however, seems hardly true.

Here, as elsewhere, Paul moves almost completely in the Jewish world. He, no less than his kinsmen after the flesh, regarded revelation as an historical process. The light did not suddenly break. Dawn preceded noon. There, for example, stood the law. Through it was the knowledge of sin (Rom. 3:20), and by it the righteousness of God was witnessed (vs. 21). It was holy and spiritual, and the commandments holy and righteous and good (Rom. 7:12,

14); and Paul is at pains to establish it (Rom. 3:31). Most significantly, its function was to lead men to Christ (Gal. 3:24), who is the end of the law for righteousness (Rom. 10:4). This, then, was the definite context in which Christ stood. He did not emerge as a strange and foreign element. He was demanded by all that had gone before. It was to him that everything had pointed. His revelation was of one piece with those that had preceded. The scattered rays of the Old Testament were focussed in him. He completes God's redemptive purpose. In him the anticipation and ideal of Israel is fulfilled (cf. Luke 24:27, which reflects Paul's teaching). It was this antici-pated and promised Christ that Paul preached. He declared himself to be an apostle "separated unto the gospel of God which He promised before through his prophets in the Holy Scriptures concerning his son" (Rom. 1:2). In Christ "a righteousness of God hath been manifested" which was "witnessed by the law and the prophets" (Rom. 3:21, 22). To the Thessalonians he mentions Jesus in the same breath with the Hebrew prophets as victims of Jewish violence (I Thess. 2:15). If one admits the letter to the Ephesians as Pauline, it follows that Paul regarded the Christian church as being built on a founda-tion which includes, besides Christ, the apostles and the prophets (Eph. 2:20). The conclusion seems inescapable. Paul regarded revelation as a special, historical, progressive, unitary process culminating in Jesus Christ, who was at once its goal and highest term.

Supernatural.—Perhaps what is meant when Paul's conception of Christ is said to be revolutionary rather than evolutionary is that Paul did not attain to a knowledge of him through the ordinary channels of information. In that case the statement is perfectly true. It was not through acquaintance, study, or discovery that Paul came to know Christ. It was solely through super-natural enlightenment, through the gracious approach of God in his Son.

Paul is certain at any rate that his knowledge of God is not human in origin. His apostleship, he declares, is "not from men, neither through man" (Gal. 1:1). Nor is his gospel. "I make known to you, brethren, as touching the gospel which was preached by me, that it is not after man. For neither did I receive it from man nor was I taught it" (Gal. 1:11, 12). He emphasizes the fact that he did not confer "with flesh and blood" (vs. 16) and thanks God "without ceasing" that the Thessalonians, when they received from him "the word of the message," did not accept it as "the word of men" (I Thess. 2:13). He is anxious lest even in peripheral matters he be regarded as speaking "after the manner of men" (I Cor. 9:8), and when certain Corinthians boast "We are of Paul," he upbraids them for their carnality of mind (I Cor. 3:4). He makes plain, therefore, that the gospel is not his gospel. He neither invented nor discovered it. Once or twice, it is true, he speaks of "my gospel" (Rom. 2:16), but the phrase must be interpreted in the light of the whole and understood as referring to the fact that he was its preacher.

Paul is reinforcing here what he elsewhere intimates about the incapacity of man to attain to a knowledge of God. It was the error of Greek gnosis to suppose it could learn God's will and purpose through the exercise of reason; and the Jews, the pragmatists of his day, erred in supposing that God could be controlled through moral activity. Paul rejects both. Whether ethical or intellectual, both are human approaches and thus vain. He, at least, did not receive the truth in that way. Nor, indeed, does anyone else, for the things of God cannot be known by the natural man (I Cor. 2:14).

Whence, then, did Paul receive his Gospel? He tells us explicitly: "It came to me through revelation of Jesus Christ" (Gal. 1:12); "God revealed it through the Spirit" (I Cor. 2:10); or simply, "by revelation was made known unto me the mystery" (Eph. 3:3). He speaks of "visions and revelations of the Lord"; of being "caught up even to the third heaven" and "up into paradise" where he heard "unspeakable words which it is not lawful for a man to utter" (II Cor. 12:1-4). No one can read Paul without noticing in him a strong conviction of being in a peculiar sense a recipient and trustee of immediate revelation from God. He claims to be a chosen organ of communication from Christ and does not hesitate to seal his claim with an oath. "Behold, before God, I lie not" (Gal. 1:20).

What is here especially to be noted is the supernatural character of these communications. Revelation is first and last a divine activity—free, sovereign, and gracious. There is nothing man can do to elicit it, and when it comes there is nothing he can do but believe and obey. It comes with an authority all its own and constrains even against one's will. The movement is entirely one-way. Man does not reach up to lift the veil; it is God who discloses himself. Revelation is divine self-communication, a movement of reality towards man, an active incursion from a supernatural Other. That was Paul's teaching, and that was his "experience" on the way to Damascus.

What was the nature of that experience? Is it to be psychologically explained? That it touched the psychological plane cannot be denied. After all, it was an *experience*, and experiences are the subject matter of psychology. But one doesn't get far with psychological explanations. As a matter of fact, psychology doesn't explain at all. It is merely a descriptive science. It can only give a surface account. It is merely photographic. Psychology can at best note the mental, spiritual, and physical *attendants* of an experience; it cannot touch the experience itself. This, indeed, is the limitation of every science. As Karl Heim has pointed out, this limitation is intimately bound up with the nature of time. The chief characteristic of the experience of time is the irrevocability of the time-direction. Each moment is only once present, then it is over, never to return again and never to be recalled. The essence of time lies in the passage during the present moment from a state which is arbitrary to one which is determined. Every occurrence which crosses the present moment passes over from a fluid aggregate state in which there are possibilities still unlimited to a solid aggregate state in which one possibility has once and for all become a reality. Any "experience" lies in the present; its psychological explanation lies in the past. Experience is fluid, living, intangible, mysterious, fluctuating, awesome; science can deal with it only after it has precipitated itself into a solid. Then it can be measured, weighed, and analyzed, but only from the point of view of a spectator not himself involved in the situation. No real explanation can therefore be given. Psychology is able in no case to decide whether a given experience is natural or supernatural. It can at best cast only a sidelight.

Looked at with such light the experience bears all the earmarks of being what Paul always regarded it as being—a real appearance of Jesus Christ; "whether in the body or out of the body" is immaterial. Doubt has sometimes been cast on the narrative in Acts from the fact that Paul makes so little of it in his epistles. The fact is, however, that he does make much of it, as all his references to the revelation he received amply witness. What he does not do is give space to psychological and biographical notitia, and that because the experience was meta-psychological. His conversion was not so much moral (although that, of course, was included) as it was intellectual. He came into possession of a *fact*, or better, the *meaning* of a fact. He learned that Jesus was Lord, that Christ had died for the sins of the world. Intelligence was brought to him of an action on the part of God. He was told of something that had happened in the supernatural world. That could not be "experienced"; it had to be told him.

Paul, therefore, would never admit that he, by reflection or any other kind of personal activity, had arrived at the truth that stood in the center of all his preaching. He knew that it was beyond reason to attain. It was in fact contrary to "reason." To the Jews it was a stumbling block, and to the Greeks, foolishness (I Cor. 1:23). There was nothing in it to recommend itself to the natural mind. It was in fact a criticism of it. Paul never laid the emphasis upon "knowing" it; it had to be believed. It is not so much that we know God as that God knows us (Gal. 4:9). As was this revelation to Paul, so was the revelation in Christ. Something objective and cosmic had happened. A great light had broken, and a great redemption had been accomplished.

The conviction of having been immediately spoken to by God accounts for the note of authority in Paul's voice whenever the Gospel in concerned. He comes not with knowledge that man's wisdom teaches (I Cor. 2:4). He preached Christ, the power of God and the wisdom of God, a wisdom that made foolish the wisdom of this wold (I Cor. 1:24; 1:20). For this reason Paul could give no quarter and brook no compromise. This was due not to mere ardor of conviction, or to a propensity to indulge a natural positiveness and spirit of domination. It was due to the fact that God had spoken. "Though we or an angel from heaven should preach unto you any gospel other than that which we preached unto you, let him be anathema. As we have said before, so say I now again, if any man preacheth unto you any gospel other than that which ye received, let him be anathema" (Gal. 1:8, 9).

What Paul teaches, therefore, is that we cannot solve the question of God in our own strength. We cannot lay hold of his reality either by individual study or by logical reasonings or by exertion of the will. He must reveal himself if we are to find him at all. And his love and grace is therein manifested that he has revealed himself, not in this or that thought, aptitude, inclination, or impulse of man, but in an historic figure of the past, who lived and died and rose again, effecting thereby our redemption and making us what we were not before, sons and daughters of God. In this word once spoken, and in this redemption once and for all accomplished lies, Paul teaches, the only hope of the world.

THE CONTENT OF REVELATION

Tradition.—It is a fact worthy of note that though Paul always claimed to have received an independent revelation, he never claimed it to be new or different. To those who presumed to doubt his apostleship he declared that he was not a whit behind the chiefest apostles (II Cor. 11:5). Christ had appeared to him no less than to them, even though it was last of all, as to a child untimely born (I Cor. 15:8). He prefaces nearly every letter with an assertion of his apostleship and reminds the Corinthians that he wrought among them the signs of an apostle (II Cor. 12:12). His authority is therefore equal to that of the others. But Paul never regarded his authority as being superior to theirs, so that his gospel had a claim to be received in preference to that of the other apostles, or to the detriment of theirs. The fact is, they were in essential agreement. If Paul was greater than they, his greatness lay in the clearness with which he recognized the implications of the generally accepted Christian position and the consistency with which he preached and lived it. The Galatian Judaizers were not apostles, but Jewish Christians who had failed to think out in any thoroughgoing fashion the position to which their Christian confession committed them. When Paul rebuked Peter at Antioch it was not for error in doctrine, but for a lapse in conduct. He charges Peter with hypocrisy. Peter knew better; he knew that Christianity did not involve an observance of the ceremonial regulations. It was because he did not have the courage to conform his conduct to his confession that Paul upbraids him.

That there was a Judaistic and a Hellenistic strain in primitive Christianity no one can deny, but they were not in the strict sense opposites. At bottom they were one. Both confessed Christ as Lord and salvation to be through his death and resurrection. They differed in the completeness of their understanding of that fact, in the recognition of its full implications.

Paul always stands on the common Christian tradition. What he pleads for is thought and conduct appropriate thereto. It was not appeal to different revelations that characterized the Christian Council at Jerusalem. That would have effectually deadlocked it. It was discussion of the commonly accepted truth and consideration of what it meant in relation to Judaism. The decision there reached was possible only on the basis of a deeper agreement.

Paul must therefore not be regarded as having obscured the primitive gospel by obtruding a Hellenized and perverted Christianity. Not the teachings or example of Jesus, but his death and resurrection were of first importance to the early church, and in emphasizing these Paul is but expressing the faith of his brethren in the Spirit. When he wrote, he wrote not to change or modify, but to establish and confirm their faith. Moreover, though Paul exceeded all the others in the firmness with which he grasped the distinction between Judaism and Christianity, Christ and the Law, he neither originated nor discovered it. It was implicit in the teaching of Jesus and was early apprehended by the Christian mind. The Christianity that Saul the Pharisee opposed was one in which this distinction was openly acknowledged and acted upon.

Jesus.—Assuming then that Paul's gospel was not substantially different from that already in vogue, what was its central message? What was the revelation he received? A complete answer is, for obvious reasons, impossible. It would involve a discussion of Paul's whole theology, and for that there is in the present instance neither call nor warrant. Yet the question cannot be wholly ignored inasmuch as it is substance as well as form that gives character and meaning to revelation.

In answer to the question proposed it may be said that the whole content can be summed up in two words: Jesus Christ. That Paul meant to indicate by that name an historic figure of the immediate past cannot be doubted. Whether he uses the name Jesus (Rom. 3:26; 8:11; I Cor. 12:3; II Cor. 4:5f; 11:4; Phil. 2:10; I Thess. 1:10; 4:14) or Christ (Rom. 5:6; I Cor. 1:23; II Cor. 5:16; Gal. 2:21; Phil. 1:18) or Jesus Christ (Rom. 1:1; I Cor. 1:1; II Cor. 4:6; Gal. 2:16; Phil. 1:8), the reference is always to the same individual. Moreover, no conclusion can be drawn from the fact that Paul uses the name "Jesus" here, and the name "Christ" there. He employs them quite indiscriminately. His terminology provides some basis for the distinction frequently drawn between the historic Jesus and the theological Christ (he never speaks, for example, of being "in Jesus"), but it must be noted that, contrary to our common usage, he speaks of *Jesus* as the one who justifies sinners (Rom. 3:26); it is at the name of Jesus that every knee shall bow (Phil. 2:10); and it is Jesus who delivered us from the wrath to come (I Thess. 1:10). On the other hand, it is *Christ* who died (Rom. 5:6) and was raised from the dead (I Cor. 15:12), and it was Christ whom Paul knew after the flesh (II Cor. 5:16). It is one individual whom Paul has in mind. The identification is verbally made in Paul's recurrent use of the name Jesus Christ or Christ Jesus. It is he who is the subject matter of revelation and the central figure in Paul's gospel.

What did Paul think of the Rabbi of Nazareth, the so-called historic Jesus? The paucity of references to the words and deeds of Jesus in the epistles has frequently been remarked. It is significant, too, that Paul always insists it was through direct and immediate revelation of Jesus Christ that he received his gospel. He did not "confer with flesh and blood" and did not "go up to Jerusalem to them that were apostles before" him (Gal. 1:16), to those who had known Jesus when he was on earth. One is tempted to conclude that he was uninterested in the character and career of Jesus. He himself seems to lend support to this view when he says that he will know Christ no longer after the flesh (II Cor. 5:16). These considerations do doubtless betray a fundamental attitude of Paul. It is safe to say, however, that they do *not* mean that Paul was ignorant of the life and teaching of Jesus, or that he regards such knowledge as inconsequential. He knew of whom he was speaking.

The passage in II Corinthians 5:16 presents at first a little difficulty. What is the reference of "flesh"? If it refers not to the flesh of Christ, but to Paul's own flesh, then we have no explicit disavowal of interest in the earthly Jesus, and we may assume that he had acquainted himself with the life and teachings of the Savior. If, on the other hand, it refers to Christ, then there is an open declaration of the fact that Paul had previously known Jesus, either directly or indirectly. In either case therefore we may assume a fairly complete knowledge of Jesus—his life, work, and teachings. This assumption is strengthened by a number of considerations. Paul was intensely interested in the death of Christ, and it is incredible that he did not inform himself of the events leading up to it. Moreover, merely as a Jew he must have known much about the man who had stirred the whole country. Jesus had not done his work in a corner. Furthermore, whatever may be said about Paul as a persecutor of the church, it must be admitted that he was an intelligent and deliberate persecutor. That means that he had informed himself respecting the claims and teachings of its Lord and founder. It must also be remembered that, though he preferred to go to Arabia before going to Jerusalem, he did afterwards come to that city and there conferred with the apostles for many days. That they avoided speaking about Jesus is unthinkable. To all this must be added the fact that the references to Jesus in the epistles are not so meagre as is sometimes supposed. Paul calls himself an imitator of him (I Cor. 11:1). He entreats the Corinthians by the "meekness and gentleness of Christ" (II Cor. 10:1); commends the humility of Christ as an example to be followed (Phil. 2:5); and refers to his self-denying spirit (Rom. 15:3). In speaking of divorce Paul refers to Jesus' teaching in the matter (I Cor. 7:10) and on a related subject confesses: "Concerning virgins I have no commandment of the Lord" (vs. 25). It is significant, too, that it is only Paul who preserves the beautiful words of Jesus: "It is more blessed to give than to receive" (Acts 20:35). It must be acknowledged therefore that Paul was neither ignorant nor unappreciative of the earthly life of Jesus.

Christ.—It is true, however, that Paul does not emphasize the earthly career of Jesus. This is the more significant in the measure one acknowledges that it was not owing to lack of acquaintance with that life. He knew how loving and lovable he was, how meek, and generous, and kind, and withal how steadfast and devoted to the truth. Yet it was not here that he found Jesus especially significant. There was something that Paul regarded as of much more importance. Not Jesus' life and teaching, but his death and resurrection were the true locale of revelation. It was this that constituted him Lord and Savior and the final revelation of God. It is the other, the divine, the transcendent aspect of Christ that Paul stresses—the crucified, risen, and ascended Christ. And between that and the purely human aspect there was, Paul sensed, a radical discontinuity. His death was a break with his purely phenomenal existence, and his resurrection was something wholly different than the mere survival of abiding elements in the human Jesus. It was life in a new mode of existence. Christ is indeed one, but he lives and moves on two planes. There is the historic Jesus and the superhistoric Jesus. There is Christ after the flesh, and Christ after the spirit. There is the human Jesus and the risen Lord. The question is which of the two is the real seat of revelation? Paul does not leave us in doubt as to his own understanding of the matter. "Even though we have known Christ after the flesh, yet now we know him so no more" (II Cor. 5:16). Christ after the flesh, on this side of the grave, is weak, human, temporal, contingent. On the yonder side he appears what he really is, the Christ, the eternal Word, the Savior, the critic and judge of the world.

This is the revelation Paul received; this is what he preached; and on this he staked his life. Not this or that word of Jesus, not the contagion of his personality, not the enchantment of an exemplary life, but an event—on this his hope was built. "If Christ hath not been raised, your faith is vain; ye are yet in your sins" (I Cor. 15:17). What Paul was taught to do, therefore, was to rise above the historical and contingent, to rise above bare facts to their significance. He did not preach the death and resurrection of Christ as mere fact. That Christ had died everybody knew; that he had risen was the established faith of the church. It was in the meaning and significance of those facts that the revelation was to be found. It was there that God spoke. It was not that Christ died that was significant; what was significant was that in a world where all men die, this death was of cosmic importance. That Christ died is a fact, historically attested and verifiable; that he died for our sins is revelation, not given with the event and capable only of being believed. That Christ arose is a fact of history; that he arose for our justification is a revelation from God. Neither of these truths is discoverable by human reason or congenial to it. They are beyond the human, the historical, the verifiable, the rational. They are divine truths, the "Word" that lies in and yet above the events, apprehendable only by a new, divinely implanted faculty called faith. "The Jews ask for signs, and Greeks seek after wisdom: but we preach Christ crucified, unto Jews a stumblingblock, and unto Gentiles foolishness; but unto them that are called, both Jews and Greeks, Christ the power of God, and the wisdom of God" (I Cor. 1:22-24).

This is the *mystery* that has been revealed. Under the apparent facts a deeper meaning lies hidden, a secret purpose impenetrable to man, and needing to be supernaturally disclosed. Professor Scott observes that Paul is fond of the word and uses it in many connections, as for example in Rom. 11:25; Eph. 5:32; I Cor. 2:7; 15:51; II Cor. 2:6; II Thess. 2:7; etc. It was current in the religious thought of Paul's day, and there are those who believe that Paul not only adopted the word but also the ideas involved in it and so changed Christianity into a mystery religion. Yet Professor Scott is probably nearer the truth when he says that Paul

> ... uses it in a sense which is quite opposed to that which it bore in Pagan worship. The mysteries of the various cults were to be kept absolutely secret; that was the outstanding fact about them, and the word itself had been coined to enforce it. Paul thinks of the mystery of the gospel as the great truth which he is bound to declare. He says that he has been called as an apostle in order that he may make the mystery known to all men; and to any votary of the cults such language would have sounded like blasphemy. With Paul, moreover, the whole stress is laid on the intrinsic depth of the mystery. It had hitherto been concealed because, in its nature, it was impenetrable to knowledge. No man, by his own wisdom, could ever have discovered the eternal plan of God, and even now, when it had been revealed by Christ, it had meaning only to those who possessed the Spirit. In the pagan rites, so far as we can guess at their character from the obscure hints preserved to us, there was no pretence of a truth beyond human understanding. They were significant for no other reason than that they were never to be divulged.[1]

It is only, therefore, from the point of view of the risen Christ that the historic Jesus can be known. To know him only after the flesh is not to know him at all. That is to know him superficially, externally, and inadequately. That is to leave the mystery in him undisclosed, the revelation unread. There is that in Jesus Christ which flesh and blood cannot discern, which does not move on the human and historic plane at all. Behind the man, the teacher, the companion, is the Son of God, the redeemer of the world, the Lord of all. That is the mystery that has been revealed.

And so for Paul, Jesus was the Son of God in a wholly unique sense. He was the Son whom God "promised afore through his prophets in the holy scriptures," who "was born of the seed of David according to the flesh," and who was "declared to be the Son of God with power ... by the resurrection

---

1. E. F. Scott, *The New Testament Idea of Revelation* (New York: C. Scribner's Sons, 1935), p. 150.

from the dead" (Rom. 1:2-4). He was "the power of God and the wisdom of God" (I Cor. 1:24). Paul knew only "one Lord, Jesus Christ, through whom are all things, and we through him" (I Cor. 8:6). Comparing Christ with Adam, the apostle declares: "The first man is of the earth, earthy; the second man is of heaven." It is his grace that Paul covets for the churches (II Cor. 13:14), and he it is who "is able even to subject all things unto himself" (Phil. 3:21). Jeremiah had asked: "Who hath known the mind of the Lord?" (16:26); Paul answers: "We have the mind of Christ" (I Cor. 2:16).

It was this figure, who for somewhat over thirty years lived on earth, was crucified and arose again, whom Paul acknowledged as his Lord. He was not only to be believed, but to be obeyed. Paul at the feet of Jesus is one of the most striking spectacles in all history. Paul was no menial. When he has been accused, it has been for his pride and dominating spirit. Yet this man, conscious of his genius, admitting that he outstripped all his contemporaries in ability and zeal, prostrates himself before the will and authority of another. Christ was his sovereign and Lord, implicitly to be obeyed. "Paul, a bondservant of Jesus Christ" (Rom. 1:1)—that was his self-designation. It was not a hero and martyr that was crucified; it was the "Lord of Glory" (I Cor. 2:8). "We preach . . . Christ Jesus as Lord" (II Cor. 4:5). Faith, for Paul, is nothing but the recognition of this Lordship; it is the reverse of the fact that Jesus is Lord over us.

Finality. —We are not surprised, therefore, to find Paul regarding the revelation in Christ as of ultimate and universal significance, and the Gospel, in the strictest sense, final. There is no going beyond Christ. In Christ is an eternal word. In him something happened that can never be superseded. In him history and humanity have been brought into judgment. The issues of life and death will thenceforth be decided only with reference to that which happened in Judaea in the first century A.D. That is the center around which everything revolves. "Though we, or an angel from heaven, preach any other Gospel unto you than that which we have preached unto you, let him be accursed" (Gal. 1:8). There is an uncompromising once-for-allness about the Christian Gospel precisely because it is the proclamation of *a work done.* Here, in the death and resurrection of Christ, something was accomplished which has cosmic bearings. Calvary is the eternal trysting place of man and God. For that reason the Christian message can never change. "Christ and him crucified" is the unvarying Gospel. This was the substance of Paul's revelation.

APPREHENSION OF REVELATION

The Holy Spirit and Faith—Revelation, if it were to be expressed by a geometrical figure, would take the form of an ellipse, and not that of a circle.

It revolves about two foci—God and man. That does not mean that it is a kind of cooperative affair in which the revelational activity of the divine Spirit is met by a synchronous activity of the human spirit. It does not mean that the divine revelation and the human quest are one and the same thing looked at from two different points of view. They are emphatically not the same. God's self-disclosure can never be regarded as a human search or striving. What the figure intends to convey is simply that revelation, if it be truly such, is revelation *to man*. Not only God's will, but also man's consciousness is involved. If the notion of revelation is expressed in the sentence "God speaks," it is no less expressed in the sentence "man hears." Voice and ear must be in tune. There must be not only a special and supernatural unveiling of truth by God, but also adequate provision for the reception and understanding of that truth.

What faculty or organ, we must now ask, did Paul discover in man for the apprehension of divine truth? He was certain that man could not of himself reach God, but now that God had come to man, could man receive him? Were the means of identification ready to hand? Were men's eyes adapted to the Light, and were their ears attuned to the Word? A study of Paul reveals that he found no such capacity in men. Had they possessed it, they could not have crucified the Lord of Glory (I Cor. 2:8). The reasons for this incapacity Paul understood, but we can hardly do more than indicate them here. In the first place, man, to use plastic language, was blind and deaf through sin. In the second place, the revelation, precisely because it was God's revelation, moved on a non-human, supernatural plane. It was contained not so much in historical events as in the significance of those events. Christ's death, for example, as a mere fact, tells us nothing save that which we already know—namely, that all men die, even good men. But that Christ died for our sins: to what faculty in man could that truth commend itself? That Christ was a good man and an excellent teacher was a truth consonant with men's mind, and could be readily accepted. But how could men be led to acknowledge that this was indeed the Christ: God himself in the flesh? That truth did not and could not float on the surface. It was there truly enough, but it was hidden to every natural faculty of man.

If man were ever to receive it, therefore, there would have to be a radical transformation of human consciousness. This was Paul's teaching. Belief in revelation was, he insisted, impossible to the natural man. Since he is carnal and the truth spiritual, the two are not *en rapport*. Belief was possible only through the Holy Spirit, through the activity of a second principle of revelation no less divine than the first. For the supernatural truth without there had to be a supernatural witness within. Without illumination revelation remains unintelligible and ineffectual. Unless the Spirit accompany the Word there can be no belief. To enable a man to grasp the truths conveyed to his mind by revelation a power of recipiency must be divinely imparted. The mere word, even when it comes as a living voice, is powerless without the Spirit in the heart of the hearer to move him to apprehension. That such a spirit has been given bespeaks the completeness of revelation. God "sealed us and gave us the earnest of the Spirit in our hearts" (II Cor. 1:22). That Spirit leads us into knowledge of the truth. "We have received, not the spirit of the world, but the spirit which is of God, that we might know the things that are freely given us of God" (I Cor. 2:12). Only by that Spirit can we honor the high claims of Jesus. "No man can say, Jesus is Lord, but in the Holy Spirit." It is God, therefore, who is both the Alpha and the Omega in revelation.

Faith is the instrument of the Spirit. It is the new divine organ with which the Christian has been endowed. In its uniquely biblical sense it is the property only of the "new creature." It is the result of a miracle—the deed and gift of God. It is founded neither on reason nor on experience, but only in the sovereign and gracious will of God. Though Paul frequently speaks of it as the instrument or avenue of salvation, he never speaks of it as a condition. It is not a "virtue" or a "work" in reward for which salvation is bestowed. Its possession excludes all boasting. Its presence is the result, not the cause, of God's activity in the soul. It may be regarded as both active and passive. As active it is that exercise of the spirit which apprehends salvation and appropriates its message. As passive it is an attitude of receptivity; a reaction to something that must be recognized, accepted, passively received; a kind of vacuum or *Hohlraum* that can be filled only by the eternal God himself. Though it is not a human possibility and does not grow out of human experience, it is nevertheless closely bound up with the human spirit. It is not something extraneous and superimposed, a kind of superadditum. It is a movement or condition of the whole personality—a complete life attitude. It is man in the attitude of subjection to God.

The Object of Faith. —By faith Paul does not mean a mere general trust in God, or an easy confidence in the moral structure of the universe. It is not a mood or attitude at all, except derivatively. It is belief in and obedience to a particular individual, and an acknowledgment of the truth of certain facts. Faith according to Paul has always a certain specific reference. It is belief in Jesus Christ and in the redemptive character of his death and resurrection. It is important to observe that Christ is in his own person the object of faith. It is faith in him that justifies men (Rom. 3:26). "He that believeth on him shall not be put to shame" (Rom. 9:33; cf. Gal. 2:16; 3:26; Phil. 1:29). But this faith is inseparable from belief in the redemptive acts. "If thou shalt confess with thy mouth Jesus as Lord, and shalt believe in thy heart that God raised him from the dead, thou shalt be saved" (Rom. 10:9). And if it be that Christ has not been raised from the dead, then Christian faith is vain (I Cor. 15:14). We can have no hope of eternal life except we "believe that Jesus died and rose again" (I Thess. 4:14). Faith is not a certain religiosity or a vague kind of piety; it is the acceptance of a history, belief in a fact accomplished.

Of this fact and its significance witness has been given, and faith is mediated through this testimony. Salvation comes through belief in Christ and the recognition of him as Lord, but "how shall they hear without a preacher?" (Rom. 10:14). Revelations and the witness to it must always go together, and behind that witness faith cannot go. That is to say, faith in Christ demands faith in the witness. Paul was such a witness. He was called to be an apostle (Rom. 1:1), and to him was committed the word of reconciliation, to wit "that God was in Christ reconciling the world unto himself" (II Cor. 5:18). He comes therefore with the truth and the authority of God, being an "ambassador . . . on behalf of Christ, as though God were entreating by us; we beseech you on behalf of Christ, be ye reconciled to God" (vs. 20). It is through such preaching that the salvation of God is effectuated. "For seeing that in the wisdom of God the world through its wisdom knew not God, it was God's good pleasure through the foolishness of preaching to save them that believe" (I Cor. 1:21). Faith, it appears, is inseparable from the word. "Belief cometh of hearing, and hearing by the word of Christ" (Rom. 10:17). Faith, therefore, whatever else it may be, certainly includes intellectual assent to definite propositions. It is belief in certain facts and in a certain interpretation of those facts. It is recognition of Christ's Lordship and of the redemption wrought in and through him. True, faith is more than that. It changes not only one's system of thought but also one's self. But what is to be noted here is that it involves the acceptance of a definite witness to a definite redemptive act.

This witness is contained in the Bible. For that reason the Bible must always occupy an important position in the Christian church. It was with a true spiritual perception that the Reformers made it their major business to recover the Bible from the desuetude into which it had fallen. And in so doing they followed the mind of Paul. He did not regard what he wrote as of merely temporal significance. He was conscious of bearing witness to a final revelation. It was not his words that he put down. Even if the classical text in Timothy be regarded as coming from another hand than Paul's it is plain that he regarded himself as nothing more or less than the mouthpiece of God. "We received not the spirit of the world, but the spirit which is from God; that we might know the things that were freely given to us of God. Which things also we speak, not in words which man's wisdom teacheth, but which the Spirit teacheth" (I Cor. 2:12, 13). And again: "For we are not as the many, corrupting the word of God; but as of sincerity, but as of God, in the sight of God, speak we in Christ" (II Cor. 2:17). We could perhaps take no better leave of Paul than by stopping a moment to hear him say: "Now touching the things which I write unto you, behold, before God, I lie not" (Gal. 1:20).

17

The Logos Doctrine in John

WHAT IS the meaning and history of the term "Logos"? John, it will be noted, feels under no obligation to define it. From this we may infer that neither the word nor the idea it conveyed was strange to his readers. As a matter of fact, the word had been in use for something like seven centuries. We first meet with it in Heraclitus, who used the term to designate the Reason, Law, or Order he believed to underlie and control the ceaseless permutations of the world. For Heraclitus the universe never quite *was*, but was always *becoming*. Everything was in perpetual flux, everything, that is, except that abiding and immutable principle without which it would be impossible to speak of change at all. For this fixed principle Heraclitus has many names. He calls it Law, Justice, Harmony, Order, and sometimes God. His favorite term, however, is Logos or Reason. The term in this usage denotes, therefore, the immutable, super-temporal principle of the universe, the all-pervading reason or intelligence that gives meaning to things. Personality it did not possess. Hidden from sense, it could be dimly discerned by reason, but only after reason had been especially trained and enlightened. Though super-temporal, it was not supernatural. It was the eternal, but immanent and pervasive energy of the universe, one with it in texture and function.

Anaxagoras, in the fifth century before Christ, preferred the related term "Nous" to Heraclitus' term "Logos." The reference is, however, to the same principle. Anaxagoras's advance upon his predecessor lies in the clear-cut distinction he draws between the Nous and the matter it pervades and influences. Mind, though operating on matter, exists independently of it. It is interpretable in terms of itself. This conception represents a significant improvement over the hylozoistic monism of Heraclitus. Though matter is as eternal as mind, the two are eternally distinct. It is Nous that made cosmos out of chaos, and that provides movement and life. As in all Greek thought, the Anaxagorian dualism is inner-worldly. The Nous is not transcendent; it is merely individual, distinct from, and other than, matter. Nor is it personal. It is a kind of force or energy that in some undefined way lends meaning to things.

Greek thought culminates in Plato and Aristotle, and the relation of God to the world constitutes the central problem in their philosophies. Neither, however, set forth a well-articulated doctrine of the Logos. They occasionally use the word, but never with such precision as one should like. In the *Timaeus* Plato names the Logos as the intelligent principle of creation, but creation does not mean for him what it means in Hebrew and Christian thought. Matter is conceived by him as in some sense eternal and as essentially intractable. The Logos merely pervades and orders it. Like the ideas, with which at times he seems to identify it, the Logos is eternal and super-sensuous. It is unknowable by sense. Being the final interpretative principle, the whole in the light of which the parts become intelligible, it is known only through intuition, through divine illumination. In his cave myth, Plato represents the "natural" man as chained and shackled in a dark, underground, cavernous chamber where he sees nothing but shadows. It is only when he is released by a power greater than man's that he sees things as they truly are. If Plato never actually reaches it, he does approximate the truth that the Logos is hidden not merely from the vulgar but also from the simply human. —Aristotle uses the word to designate human reason, which by its very constitution is articulated with the world-reason. He speaks of *orthos logos,* or right reason, by which he means the faculty of determining right action. For him, as for Plato, the Logos is impersonal and immanent. It is, however, eternal, super-sensuous, regulative, and authoritative.

We are indebted to the Stoics for the first systematic exposition of the doctrine of the Logos. It is significant that Stoicism was a religion, rather than a mere philosophy or ethic, and that its founder and many of its most ardent disciples trace their origin to Semitic Asia. It suggests that the Logos idea is essentially a religious idea; more particularly, a way of expressing and defining the nature and mode of God's revelation. The Stoics used the words "Nous" and "Logos" interchangeably to designate the vital, intelligent, divine principle that governed and quickened the universe, making it a kind of living being (zōion). It was related to the world as soul to body, a sort of primal ordering force. Under one aspect it was single and divine, and under another, the sum of the seed powers which are the germs of future individual existences. The doctrine was pantheistically construed, and the Logos impersonally conceived. It was regarded as the manifestation of God in the world.

*   *   *   *   *

The Logos idea was no less present to the religion of Israel than it was to Greek religious philosophy, but the emphasis was differently placed. In Greek thought the Logos denoted Reason, or thought inwardly expressed by the mind. The Hebrews regarded it as Word, or thought outwardly expressed through language. In Greece God was regarded as manifesting himself through the natural processes of mind, within the circle of the finite. In Israel God's transcendence was stressed, and he was regarded as manifesting himself through specific acts, appearances, and words. God was recognized as a person, standing in an I-Thou relationship with man, and he was held to communicate himself not through influences or impulses but through speech. It is, accordingly, the Word that is prominent in Hebrew religion. It was by this Word that the heavens and earth were called into being. "By the word of Jehovah were the heavens made, and all the host of them by the breath of his mouth" (Ps. 33:6). It is referred to as an instrument of judgment (Hos. 6:5) and as an agent of healing (Ps. 107:20). In Psalm 147:15 it is endowed with a kind of personality. It is this word that comes to Abraham with divine promises (Gen. 15:1), and we are told that "Jehovah revealed himself to Samuel in Shiloh by the word of Jehovah" (I Sam. 3:21). Isaiah speaks of the word being sent into Jacob and lighting upon Israel (9:8). It seems to have been a messenger that, though distinct from God, was yet in some sense divine.

The Greek Logos idea finds an especially close analogy in the Hebrew Wisdom idea. Job accords to Wisdom a quasi-personality and regards it as underlying the laws of the universe (28:23-27). It may be that we have in the eighth chapter of Proverbs nothing more than a poetical personalization of Wisdom, but Sirach "represents Wisdom as existing from all eternity with God"; and in Baruch, "sophia is distinctly personal—the very image of the goodness of God."[1] The Targums, too, introduce the Word, the Angel, and Wisdom as the three chief mediating factors between God and the world.

*   *   *   *   *

The Hebrew and the Greek meet in Philo, who blends the Logos and the Word. In this Jew of Alexandria "the all-prevading Energy of Heraclitus, the archetypal Ideas of Plato, the purposive Reason of Aristotle, and the immanent Order of the Stoics are taken up and fused with the Jewish concep-

---

1. A. Alexander in *ISBE*, 3, 1912.

tion of Jehovah, who, while transcending all finite existences, is revealed through his intermediatory Word."[2] It is not certain that Philo conceived of the Logos as personal, although his language supports the contention that he did. He calls him the "heavenly man," the "Son of God," and even the "second God." In another connection he is spoken of as the "Intercessor" or "High Priest." This would seem to be sufficient to establish his identity as a person. Yet Philo is thoroughly imbued with the Greek spirit and shares the Hellenic predilection for abstract and impersonal ideas. He seems to hover between personality and impersonality in his conception of the Logos, regarding him now as a kind of superior angel, and then as the impersonal thought of God expressed in the rational order of the universe. As for his being and existence, the Logos is neither eternal like God, nor temporal like man. "It is neither without beginning as in God, nor begotten as you are [mankind], but intermediate between these two extremes."[3] Intermediate in nature, the Logos is also intermediate in function. It is that which unites God and man. "The Father who engendered all has given to the Logos the signal privilege of being an intermediary between the creature and the creator."[4] The Logos was the instrument God employed in creation and it is that which constantly interprets God to man.

* * * * *

We meet with the Logos again in the prologue of the fourth gospel, although it is here considerably modified both in conception and application. The notion has sometimes been regarded as peculiar to John among the New Testament writers. It is true that the word is found only in the Johannine literature. But the idea is prominent in both Paul and the author of the Epistle to the Hebrews, and it may be said to underlie every New Testament writing. All ascribe to Christ divine names, honors, and excellencies. He is everywhere regarded as in a peculiar sense the mediator between God and man. One need not appeal to Ephesians and Colossians for Paul's high estimate of him. He is declared in Corinthians to be the "power of God and the wisdom of God" (I Cor. 1:24), and he alone of all men is "of heaven" (I Cor. 15:47). He is of the very image of God (II Cor. 4:4), and through him "are all things and we through him" (I Cor. 8:6). The author of Hebrews, it is generally recognized, teaches a Christology fully as high as John's, and though there are other writings to whose immediate purpose this stress on the divine nature and cosmic significance of Christ is foreign, yet the high estimate placed on Christ's person and function is everywhere in evidence.

The fact that John alone among the New Testament writers employs the

2. Alexander, p. 1912.
3. J. Philo, as quoted in the *Catholic Encyclopedia*, 9, 330.
4. J. Philo, p. 330.

term "Logos" does not seem to me to be especially significant. It argues neither the date of the gospel, nor its character, nor the philosophic predilections of the evangelist. The term appears to have filtered down into the ranks of the people and to have been common property in the first century of our era. It had lost its special, well-defined signification, and was capable of bearing a wide variety of meanings. John uses it in a very general sense, merely as a convenient vehicle to convey his own message. To serve as such a vehicle it needed, of course, to bear a certain character, but John's message is gathered not from a consideration of the term, but from a consideration of the meaning he puts into it.

It will therefore not do to proclaim John a philonic philosopher because of his use of the term "Logos." As Harnack points out: "The reference to Philo and Hellenism is by no means sufficient here, as it does not satisfactorily explain even one of the external aspects of the problem. The elements operative in Johannine theology were not Greek theologoumena. Even the Logos has little more in common with that of Philo than the name."[5] This is fully borne out by a comparison of Philonic and Johannine ideas. In John the Logos is religiously, not philosophically construed. "The significance of the term for John lies altogether in the religious department."[6] Philo's Logos is metaphysical, abstract, instrumental, and only quasi-personal. John's is concrete, historical, equal with God, and the agent, not the instrument, of creation. He is, moreover, identified completely and exclusively with a particular man who was the very incarnation of the Logos. On the other hand, not only was the idea of incarnation alien to Philo's thought; he could not possibly have made that particular identification which is at the heart of John's gospel and of the Christian message as a whole.

Why, then, did John use the term? Neander suggests that "the name may have been put forward at Ephesus in order to lead those Jews, who were busying themselves with speculations on the Logos as the center of all theophanies, to recognize in Christ the supreme revelation of God and the fulfillment of their messianic hopes."[7] This seems to be a satisfactory explanation. It accords with the now generally recognized purpose of John to lead minds away from gnostic speculations back to the historic Christ who was to John the very reality of the Logos idea, the Logos made flesh. That the true locale of the fourth gospel is Jewish-Christian rather than Greek has often been remarked by students of this writing. Weiss, accordingly, finds the closest analogy to John's Logos doctrine in the Old Testament teachings concerning the *Word*, and Hofmann suggests that John's thought grew up out of the primitive Christian community, which designated as "the word of

---

5. A. Harnack. *History of Dogma*, I, 97.
6. O. Kirn in the *Schaff-Herzog Encyclopedia*, 9, 330.
7. A. Neander, as quoted in *ISBE*, 3, 1912.

God" the evangelical message. John's essential agreement with Paul and the author of the Epistle to the Hebrews tends to confirm this view.

* * * * *

What does John teach concerning the Logos? His views are set forth in the prologue to the fourth gospel. There are two other passages in the Johannine literature where the word is used (I John 1:1; Rev. 19:13), but these add nothing to the material contained in the gospel. There are doubtless many ways in which to construe the material of the prologue. It will be convenient to consider first the nature of the Logos and then his functions.

That the Logos is eternal appears from the first clause of the first verse. "In the beginning," says John, "was the Word." Some have urged that it is impossible to deduce the eternity of the Logos from the phrase *en archē*. So, for example, Reuss, who objects: "If we infer from these words the eternity of the Word, we must infer also from the beginning of Genesis the eternity of the world."[8] This is doubtless true, so far forth. The obvious allusion here to Genesis determines the word *Archē* as the temporal beginning of things. But that this is not John's meaning seems to me to be evident from the tenor of the whole passage. He does not hesitate to identify the Logos directly with God. One can only conclude that for John the Logos is as eternal as God. This, indeed, is borne out by the language he uses in the clause under consideration. As Godet observes:

> If the notion of eternity is not found in the word itself, it is nevertheless implied in the logical relation of this dependent phrase to the verb *ēn* (was). The imperfect must designate, according to the ordinary meaning of this tense, the simultaneousness of the act indicated by the verb with some other act. This simultaneousness is here that of the existence of the Word with the fact designated by the word beginning. When everything that has begun began, the Word *was*. Alone, then, it did not begin; the Word was already.[9]

John affirms here the eternal coexistence of the Logos with God. The claim is ascribed to Jesus himself in 17:5 where he is reported to have prayed: "Father, glorify thou me with thine own self with the glory which I had with thee before the world was."

It is in recognizing this preexistent Logos as a person that John advances beyond the speculations of the schools. The identification of the Logos with the historic Christ would be sufficient to establish his personality, but it is also implied in the language of the first verse. "The Logos," says John, "was with God [*pros ton theon*]." The preposition *pros* is significant. It expresses the fact of perpetual intercommunion, affirming union while excluding the idea of fusion. The Logos, John teaches, was and is in eternal fellowship with God. This means that he, no less than God, is a person. "The use of the

8. Quoted by F. Godet in his *Commentary*, p. 245.
9. *Commentary on the Gospel of John*, I, 245.

preposition *pros* has evidently no meaning except as it is applied to a personal being. . . . It is not of abstract beings, of metaphysical principles, that John is here pointing out the relation, but of persons. . . . The idea of the second proposition is that of the *personality* of the Logos and of his intimate communion with God."[10] The essential deity of the Logos is affirmed in the third of the opening propositions. "The Word was God." In this statement John resolves the duality of the preceding proposition. Substantial Godhead is ascribed to the Word. God and the Logos are held to constitute an essential and indissoluble unity. The Word, therefore, is no mere attribute or action of God; he is God himself. It is perhaps necessary to observe that John is here not primarily interested in making a predication about God. What he says is not that God is Word (the Greek permitting that reading—"Theos ēn ho Logos"), but that the Logos is God. This is overlooked by Prof. Bertling, who understands John to be interested in affirming that God is a revealing God. That John does teach this truth is doubtless true, but he is here and now interested in describing not God, but the Logos. Having affirmed that the Word is eternal and eternally in personal fellowship with God, he now affirms his substantial unity with God.

* * * * *

The function of the Logos is to reveal God. That, plainly, is John's teaching. Here, as elsewhere, the appropriateness of the terms for his purposes becomes evident. The word "Logos" had always borne that connotation—in Greek as well as Hebrew usage. How is God revealed? How is he mediated to the world? By what signs is he identified? These are the questions the various Logos doctrines were designed to answer. John, too, has his answer. He describes revelation in terms of the Logos, God's own Word, graciously operative in the history of the world.

The Logos appears first as the organ of the entire creative activity of God. "All things were made through him; and without him was not anything made that hath been made." This was the first act of divine revelation. Almost every word in the first clause of John's statement is significant. The first word, *panta* without the article, indicates the most unlimited universality. Everything, including the primeval matter of Plato, was called into being by God through the Logos. Whatever exists exists by virtue of his sovereign will. The second word, *dia*, "does not lower the Logos to the rank of a mere instrument." It is often applied to God himself (Rom. 11:36; Gal. 1:1; Heb. 2:10). It does signify, however, that "no being has come into existence without having passed through the intelligence and will of the

---

10. Godet, *Commentary*, p. 245.

Logos."[11] The fourth word, *egeneto*, indicates that all things *became*, in distinction from the Logos, which always *was.* In all this John is careful to avoid any identification of the Logos with the world. They are absolutely distinct, being related only as Creator to creation. In and through this relation God is revealed, his power being manifested through his works.

But not only so. God is also revealed in the spirits of men. "In him was life; and the life was the light of men." The Logos is not only the agent of creation, the origin of all existences; he imparts life to and accounts for the progress in creation. He illumines the hearts and minds of men and is the potent cause of such knowledge of God as men may be found to possess. But it must not be supposed that in John's opinion such knowledge was anything more than fragmentary. The life and light imparted by the Logos was moral, not physical, in character. It could be quenched and rejected. Man, simply because he is man, could turn his back upon God and thus blind himself to the light. That he has actually done this is the world's great tragedy. God witnessed of himself but his witness went unheeded. There are few words more pathetic than these: "The light shineth in darkness, and the darkness apprehended it not."

It is at this juncture—verse seven—that John introduces the message for which all the preceding was merely preliminary. Abruptly, quite without warning, he turns from the universal revelation of God in the consciousness of men to a single historical fact and occurrence. "There came a man, sent from God, whose name was John. The same came for a witness, that he might bear witness of the light." Of what light? Of the light in nature, or of the light in the hearts of men? No. He bore witness to a fact and to a person, to that at which he could point a finger, to an individual existence on the plane of time. For the wonder of God's grace and the heart of the Christian Gospel is precisely this that "the Logos became flesh and dwelt among us." The same Logos who was in the beginning, who was with God, and who was God; he through whom all things were made and who was always the light of men, he himself became man. John's meaning is unmistakable. He does not say that a certain man was peculiarly sensitive to the influences of the Logos and so displayed in himself a wealth of spiritual grace beyond that of all other men. He speaks of a great renunciation, an emptying, a humiliation. This is the utterly profound foolishness of the Gospel: that the Logos himself became flesh; that the eternal became temporal; the universal, particular; the infinite, contingent. This, for John, is the significance of Jesus. He was not a man in touch with God; he was God in touch with man—God concretized, limited, confined. It was because he was so confined—hidden, as it were—that, being in the world, the world knew him not. But those who did receive

11. Godet, *Commentary*, p. 249.

him, who recognized in this historical figure the super-historical and eternal
Word, "to them gave he the right to become children of God." This reception
and recognition was for John the all-important thing. That is why he wrote
his gospel. "These are written that ye may believe that Jesus is the Christ, the
Son of God, and that believing ye may have life in his name."

18

Philosophy and the Bible

THE TITLE of this essay contains two terms: "Bible" and "philosophy." Although the entire essay will be, in one sense, an attempt to clarify these terms, it may not be amiss to characterize them in a provisional way at the very outset.

By "Bible" I shall mean: (1) The Christian Scriptures—i.e., the specific canonical writings which the Christian church accepts as the authoritative rule of faith and life. (2) An authentic report of and witness to a veritable divine revelation. The revelation which it communicates is not itself a human achievement, but a divine gift. It is not one of man's many approaches to reality, but a movement of reality towards man. It is not the product of a religious quest, but a divine and gracious disclosure. It is an incursion from another order of existence. It is a word from beyond. (3) A set of existential as well as value judgments. It is a word directed not only towards the will and the emotions, but also towards the understanding. It is, among other things, a communication of facts, truths, ideas—a body of propositions setting forth the actual and the real. (4) The medium of a message to be received and of an assertion to be affirmed. The Bible conveys God's Word, and this Word, when it is recognized as such, is that with respect to which the only legitimate attitude of man is one of unconditional submission. That Word cannot

This essay originally appeared as Chapter IV in *The Word of God and the Reformed Faith*, ed. C. Bouma (Grand Rapids: Baker, 1943).

be critically appraised in terms of our immanent tests and standards; it is that which criticizes and revises all our standards as such.

By "philosophy" I shall mean: (1) A theoretical knowledge and systematic interpretation of the cosmos as a whole. Its task is deliberately and persistently to note the interrelation and interaction of things. In its ideal form it is a set of mutually implicated propositions—a coherent, logically articulated system of truths. (2) A human achievement—a theoretical construction which is the result of analytic and synthetic thinking, a product of the human spirit. As such it is a temporal, finite magnitude, never absolute, and always subject to revision. (3) A construction to be argued and critically appraised; something to be judged on its merits, according as it does or does not render man's life and experience intelligible.

Our problem is to determine how these two very different magnitudes— the Bible and philosophy, or revelation and philosophy—are or may be related. Several possibilities present themselves.

I.

A. Philosophy and the Scriptures may sustain *no relation at all*. The former may be completely independent of the latter.

In the ancient period of European culture philosophy did exhibit this absence of all relation to the Bible. Greek philosophy, it is now generally agreed, was developed in entire ignorance of the Old Testament Scriptures. It fell neither directly nor indirectly under their influence, and assumed neither a positive nor a negative attitude towards them. It appeared as a product of the human spirit working in complete independence of God's special revelation.

It is obvious that the sort of relation to God's Word exhibited by Greek thought is no longer possible within occidental culture. Such a relation can exist only there where the Scriptures have not been preached—i.e., there where their claim on the loyalties of men has not been voiced. Where they have been heard, there some sort of relation to the mind of man has been set up, there some attitude towards them must be assumed. It follows that a modern thinker in the West cannot, on this question, assume the Greek position. Christianity has intervened and some account must be taken of the fact.

Since the advent of Christianity three theories of the relation between philosophy and Scripture have found acceptance.

B. *In modern times* the view has prevailed that philosophy and Scripture sustain what may be called *a negative relation* to one another.

This view traces its lineage to Greece. The modern thinker will point out that, though Greek philosophy did not define itself against the Judaic-Christian Scriptures, it did do so against the Homeric and Hesiodic scriptures; and, he will add, its attitude towards the latter was consciously *critical*. Greek thinkers questioned the traditional account of things. They did not unhesitatingly adopt the ancient cosmologies, nor uncritically endorse the various wisdoms of the poets. On the contrary, they held them all suspect. They made them stand trial at the bar of reason. They set philosophy in judgment over an always questionable tradition.

The modern thinker proposes to do the same, or what appears to him to be the same. He proposes to be critical of the Scriptures. As a philosopher, this, he holds, is not only his prerogative; it is his duty. His charter forbids his admitting any authority other than the human spirit.

In taking this position the modern thinker makes a significant assumption. He assumes that the Christian Scriptures are documents embodying nothing more than a human tradition. He assumes that they are no more than a complex of human insights.—This is formally the same assumption that the Greek philosophers made with respect to the poems of Homer. The correctness of the latter assumption the Christian does not dispute. He is prepared to grant that Homer, whatever the excellence of his sentiments, gave expression to insights merely human. For that reason, too, the Christian has no quarrel with the critical spirit of Greek philosophy, purely as such. Greek philosophy appraising Greek religion is nothing more or less than the human spirit in process of self-appraisal. There is every justification for that. Nothing human is beyond the range of human criticism, and as long as philosophy observes these bounds no other limits can be set upon it.

It is, however, quite another thing for philosophy to hold critical sway over the Christian Scriptures upon the assumption that they are merely human documents articulating nothing more than human discoveries. From the Christian point of view that assumption is simply false. The Christian, by virtue of his Christianity, recognizes the Bible as mediating the veritable Word of God. He holds it to be that which bears reliable witness to a supernatural incursion into our world. This is his assumption, and this assumption, among others, *defines* him as a Christian. He cannot, as a Christian, think constructively on any other assumption than this. He must therefore reject the counter-assumption implicit in the typical philosophies of modernity.

C. *In medieval times*, more particularly within Thomistic circles, another view of the relation between philosophy and Scripture prevailed. The Thomistic position has two facets that must be clearly distinguished.

On the one hand, the Thomist *subordinates philosophy to Scripture*. As a Christian he acknowledges the supreme authority of the Scriptures. They are held to contain a wisdom higher than that of man. They are, as far as their central message is concerned (the divine proclamation), beyond the reach of philosophic criticism. More than that, they constitute the final criterion of philosophic truth. Any conflict between the Scriptures and his philosophy the Thomist regards as a sure sign of philosophic error.

On the other hand, the Thomist *insulates philosophy against the Scriptures*. He holds the two to be only externally related. Philosophy purely as such is a self-contained, wholly rational, enterprise. It has its own method, and goes its independent way. As Gilson describes it: "Based on human reason, owing all its truth to the self-evidence of its principles and the accuracy of its deductions, it reaches an accord with faith spontaneously and without having to deviate in any way from its own proper path." Absent from philosophy, on this view, are all the "mysteries" of the Christian faith—that is, all the truths which make Christianity distinctive. The Scriptures are a merely regulative, not a constitutive, principle of philosophy. Though they embody the highest wisdom in the world, only so much of that wisdom is taken up into philosophy as is susceptible of direct rational demonstration. Philosophy, accordingly, can never be "Christian." Philosophy is simply philosophy; integrally it is wholly independent of grace and faith.

The trouble with this view is that it is compartmental and divisive. It juxtaposes what ought to be integrated. It separates the religious and the scientific in man. It permits one to accept transcendent mysteries which lie beyond the power of reason to attain, but it forbids him to incorporate these into that total vision of the universe which it is the aim of philosophy to achieve.

It is for this reason that another theory of the relation between philosophy and Scripture needs to be suggested.

D. It is suggested that *philosophy and revelation should be integrated*. The Word of God should be taken up into, made constitutive of, philosophy. The resultant philosophy would (in principle) be "biblical" or "Christian."

Such a philosophy is seen to be possible as soon as one notes that all philosophy is *based upon a non-theoretical, a priori, religious commitment*. The fact is that all philosophy rests on a fundamental existential loyalty. It is founded on a radical pre-scientific choice. It has a "religious" root. No philosophy maintains a purely theoretical standpoint. All thinking is based on assumptions that transcend theoretical thought.

In support of this thesis two things may be pointed out.

II.

The first thing to be said is that *man is a "religious" being*. The word "religion," in this usage, has a restricted meaning. Religion is sometimes uncritically identified with theology. I do not make that identification here. In calling man religious I am not denominating him theological. Religion is more often identified with cultus—with prayers, sacrifices, ceremonies, and worship. It is not in this sense either that I use the word. I am not affirming that all men engage in religious exercises, or even possess what we sometimes call the "religious temperament." There may be men who have no "flair" for religion in that sense.

By religion I mean a fundamental divine-human *relation*. Man is religious because he stands in an unavoidable relation to God. God is an inescapable, ever-present fact. Man may love him or hate him, acknowledge him or ignore him, be aware of him or be unconscious of him—in any case he assumes an attitude towards him. And it is this attitude that—subjectively—constitutes man "religious."

It might be objected that if man is to be defined in terms of the relations he sustains, it is arbitrary to define him as religious inasmuch as he is the center of a complex network of relations. If it be true that he is related to God, it is also true that he is related to nature and to the realm of spirit, and by that token it is as legitimate to denominate him physical or rational as it is to call him religious.—On this I should like to remark the following.

It is true that man is the concentration point of various relations. It is also true that these relations condition him and so contribute the elements to a final definition. It is significant, however, that all these relations, with the single exception of the "religious," are intra-cosmic, and as such subordinate to and determined by the extra-cosmical relationship that man sustains to God. Let me illustrate. Man is related to nature—to the organic and inorganic worlds—and may on that account be characterized as physical and biological. It would be a mistake, however, to *define* him as such, since he is more than extension and more than life. Man is related to the world of values and may on that account be characterized as rational, social, and moral. But again, it would be a mistake to *define* him as such since he is more than a social correspondent, a thinker, or an evaluator.

The fact seems to be that he is all these combined in a unique and further unanalyzable unity. Living, feeling, willing, and thinking are merely so many *functions* of man, so many *aspects* of his being. His being or essence lies under and beyond. The central thing in man is neither body nor spirit as such, nor any specific function of either, but that deeper something of which the functions are the functions. It may be called the "core" or the "heart" of man, but the name we give it is relatively unimportant. The important thing is not to confuse it with any of its expressions or activities. In any case, it is here, in his heart, at the point which sustains and underlies all his intra-cosmic relations, that God impinges on man. Here, at the deepest, all-determinative level of his existence, man's fundamental nature is constituted by the specific character of the relation he sustains to God. Here, at the core of his being, man is religious.

III.

The second thing to be said is that *man's religion determines his thought.* Man is not only "religious" in the sense explained above; his religion—i.e., his conscious or unconscious relationship to God in his heart—determines all his activities, practical and theoretical. It must do this because, as has been said, it is the central thing in man. It defines man's self-hood, the ever-present subject of all man's functions. As such it must determine all of life's expressions. It must therefore determine the direction of one's thinking; more particularly, it must determine the set and cast of one's philosophy.

That it *does* do this can be seen if we stop to consider the very first question a truly critical philosophy must raise. That question is this: What is the vantage point from which the universe can be surveyed? It must be observed that this is a question which cannot be answered by the trial and error method. Nor is it a problem that can be argued, for every argument already presupposes a solution. It is a question that must be settled before any philosophic discussion can begin.

Traditional philosophy has been almost unanimous in its answer. It assumed that the cosmos is self-interpretative, self-explanatory. It assumed that the philosophic task consisted in interviewing the cosmos, coaxing it to yield its secret, and inducing it to reveal what is eternal and unifying in it, thereby further assuming that the cosmos had something eternal to reveal. It supposed that one could take one's stand somewhere within the cosmos, and thence discover its structure and meaning.

One can, of course, make another assumption. One can assume that the cosmos is not self-interpreting, that every final question addressed to it is a misdirected question. One can hold that the cosmos is a creation, ontically distinct from its creator, and by that token dependent, unable in itself to account for even its existence, much less for its more specific qualities.

It is important to observe that both classes of assumptions are *assumptions*—i.e., pre-theoretical choices of position. Both, moreover, determine the character of the philosophy constructed upon them. The entire phenomenon reveals that philosophy—all philosophy—lies irrevocably in a moral and religious context. It substantiates the thesis that all philosophy is based upon a non-theroetical, a priori, religious commitment.

In conclusion: Christian philosophy posits the inadequacy of a merely immanentistic approach to an understanding of the cosmos, and assumes the necessity of a transcendent vantage point. This means that it deliberately proposes to interpret the created world in the light of the Christian Scriptures. In doing so it denies that it is sacrificing its claim to the name philosophy. The Christian philosopher repudiates the dogmatism that would make the human consciousness autonomous and philosophy a purely "intellectual" enterprise, carried on in abstraction from "faith." He insists, on the contrary, that the beginning of an adequate interpretation of the world can be made only when a thinker allows himself to be instructed by that world's maker and interpreter, only when a philosopher enrolls himself in the school of God.

Part V

CHURCH

19

The Mind of the Church

THIS ESSAY initiates an attempt to delineate the complex "mind" of the Christian church. I write, of course, out of an intimate acquaintance with only one corporate member of Christ's multiform body, but I have allowed myself to think that the universal church is at bottom one, and that it displays a common, though typically nuanced, "mind" whenever it contemplates the "world" in which it has been set. It is this shared mind, with its internal differentiations, that I wish to set forth in dialogue with fellow-members of the church.

What I propose is that we consider not, indeed, the whole range of our being as church, but only what may be called the theologico-ethical structure of our churchly existence, or, what is the same thing, the spirituo-moral complexion of our ecclesiastical life.

The church has its own complexion, character, personality, or "mind." As with all things in history, however, this mind is not fixed. It is an emerging mind, a mind in process. Like all things so situated it is as much an aggregate of several and diverse minds as it is a single integrated one. It is a mind in tension, embracing not indeed contradictions (which would make it schizophrenic), but yet contrarieties and polarities which impart to it its characteristically erratic movements. It is these movements, these oscillations of a growing mind in tension, that produce in the life of the church those "disturbances" that sometimes vex us, but that may signify nothing more

This essay first appeared in *The Reformed Journal,* March 1957.

than that we are alive and growing, that we are engaged in producing out of relatively heterogeneous elements a bigger and more significant mind and personality than at present we possess.

In what follows I shall try to isolate a few of the elements that are in the crucible. I shall try to define a few of the disparate minds whose diverse expressions ruffle the surface of our corporate life, but whose disparateness vanishes at a point below the surface where, as I believe, a basic identity exists in a common loyalty to a common Lord.

This common loyalty to Christ is presupposed. The church I am describing is the body of the faithful who in fidelity to the Scriptures and the classical creeds acknowledge Jesus as the Son of God and as the Lord and Savior of the world.

It is evident, however, that the church's faithfulness to its Head, and its adherence to its confessions, is diversified by different slants or accents. There are different ways in which we "hold" our shared beliefs. There are in the church, I dare say, at least three distinguishable "minds," "mentalities," or "perspectives," all of them embracing a common fund of truth, but each of them distributing the emphasis upon that truth in a different way, thus creating those polarities and tensions within our common life which are open to the observation of us all.

These three "minds," rising up out of the body of the church and seeking to express its life and nature, are not to be thought of as allocated to three distinct groups or "parties," each of which is the patron and custodian of a single mind and each of which is engaged in an all-out war with the patrons of the other two. These three "minds" are in us all. Each of us, in so far as we are living members of the church and therefore genuine exponents of its developing life, exhibits in his own person the three minds which are struggling for articulation within the confines of our relatively heterogeneous fellowship.

It is true, of course, that in each of us one or the other of these minds is "dominant," but from none of us is any one of them completely absent. In this fact lies the secret both of the hold we have on one another and of the differences that sometimes arise between us. None of us is completely foreign to the "mind" or "perspective" of any of our fellows, and this, together with our common commitment to the Christ, cements agreement both at the depth and upon the surface of our communal life. On the other hand, none of us is really able in the long run to endorse all three of these minds. As "minds"— i.e., as "total outlooks" or "governing perspectives"—they exclude each other, and one of them must eventually be chosen and seated as king. Personal wholeness and integrity demands this choice.

When the choice is made, however, or when, as sometimes happens, the choice is made for us, we will naturally seek to make dominant in the church the single mind that dominates our person, the mind in terms of which we believe the Christian truth we share with our fellows can best be viewed and construed. It is at this point that we will be put into great temptation. We will be tempted, in the course of our effort, to make our "mind" and "outlook" prevail, to assemble the "like-minded" and organize them into a party. We will then be tempted to prepare a program that, by concerted action and with full use of the available power-techniques, we will seek to actualize, and thus chart the church's course. Sincerely believing that the mind we have chosen should govern the church we will be tempted to impose it through the machinery of force.

It goes without saying that this temptation must be resisted. There is no room in the church for parties, sects, or cliques resplendent in the panoply of power. It is not by organization and propaganda, but by discussion and persuasion that a single mind is made to prevail in the church. That one should seek to have his outlook prevail is natural and proper, and that he should welcome the assistance of all those who share his outlook is equally so, but he must always be testing whether his "mind" is the mind of Christ, and whether his "methods" are those that God can bless. The methods he employs should, indeed, be chosen for their efficacy in eliciting the singleness of mind he believes the church should possess, but their nature and employment should be such that they tend to preserve the fellowship while integrating and maturing it.

Meanwhile three minds exist in the church, modifying each other while they press their claims against each other and strive for the hegemony. What are these "minds," and how are they defined?

These minds or "mentalities" can best be discerned in their variety by contemplating them as giving answers to the questions "What is the relation of the Christian to the world?" or better: "How can we be Christian in the world?" or again: "How does a Christian act relative to the world?" or finally: "How do we maintain truth and piety within the world?" This is, you see, the age-old question, which every generation of Christians must face anew because it lies at the very center of the Christian ethic: How can I, not being *of* the world, yet live *in* the world?

Deep down there are only two, not three, answers to this question, because deep down there are only two attitudes we can assume toward the world: a positive and a negative attitude. Those two attitudes, it will be observed, do not absolutely exclude each other, for there is that in the world which must be affirmed and there is that which must be denied. These two attitudes can therefore, and indeed should, coexist in one person and, by that token, in one church. But, from the nature of the case, one or the other of these attitudes must take the "lead," and whichever does this qualifies and determines the other, and gives to the person assuming these attitudes his characteristic and defining "mind" or "bent." He in whom the positive attitude toward the world takes the lead comes to possess a different "mind" than he in whom the negative attitude dominates. What is important here is the matter of priority. What counts is emphasis or accent. The "mind" formed by a negative accent differs importantly from the "mind" formed by the alternate emphasis. They are two very distinct minds.

These two minds exist in the church. What I shall henceforth call the positive mind, from which negative responses are not excluded, stands toward the world in the token of love; whereas the negative mind, from which affirmative responses are not excluded, stands toward the world in the token of fear. Love (not without fear) forms one mind; fear (not without love) forms the other.

But because of the ambivalence of the negative attitude, because of the duality of the fear-response, there are really three, and not merely two, minds in the church. A predominantly negative or fearful attitude toward the world requires the adoption of a defensive stance. But defense can take two forms. It can take the form of withdrawal or the form of aggression. One may flee the world one fears, or one may launch an attack upon it. One may play "safe," or one may become "militant." In either case it is security that is primarily sought, and not positive outreach and redemptive action.

Three minds then—the safe, the militant, and the positive—operate out of and upon the church and shape her complex personality. Is this permissible? May a single church assume three different attitudes toward the world and enjoin three very different courses of action with respect to it? No doubt it may, but only on one condition: that the attitudes assumed are properly adjusted to one another, which means specifically that the negative actions are subordinated to the positive. World-flight on the one hand, and world-combat on the other, can have no independent status in the church. They depend for their status on the absolute command to love, and they have a right to exist only because and in so far as they subserve the ends of love. They are mere means, permissible only when used as instruments, not of self-preservation, but of world-redemption. Security, whether sought by retirement or aggression, may never be taken as an end in itself. The cry for safety and militancy should never be heard above the cry for positive outreach. When it is so heard, and when it is heeded, an imbalance ensues that cannot but hurt the church.

In various branches of the one church such an imbalance does, unfortunately, exist. In some orthodox churches a desire for safety and an inclination to oppose and attack, both good in their proper place and degree, have grown so strong and independent that they have taken on the status and proportions of veritable minds, and in their negativity are challenging the priority and governorship of the positive mind, whose purposes they were meant to subserve.

In the following essay I shall try to draw the lineaments of the first of these three minds—the mind of safety.

20

The Mind of Safety

I AM BOUND to comment at the outset on the use of the term "world," for it is in its relation to the world that the mind of safety is defined. The term world is notoriously ambiguous. It sometimes means a space, the earth, or the created universe as a whole; sometimes a time, the age; sometimes an inclusive society, the earth's inhabitants; sometimes a restricted society, the unredeemed; and sometimes a moral or spiritual quality, sin. Since we are engaged in a religious discussion we may ignore the first three of these meanings and attend only to the remaining two.

I am, of course, not using the term in the latter of these two senses. There can be no quarrel among Christians about the attitude to be taken toward sin. Sin is always and everywhere to be negated. The world, defined as flesh and devil, deserves nothing but an unqualified and everlasting no. The Christian is bound to flee it or destroy it. An affirmative attitude toward it would be an embracement of darkness and chaos, a repudiation of God. On this all Christians are agreed.

When, therefore, I refer in this discussion to the "world" I shall be referring not to a spiritual quality (sin), but to a concrete entity, the society of the unredeemed. The word in this usage refers to that group of men and women who—together with their thoughts, acts, institutions, and achievements—exist, untouched by saving grace, outside the Christian church. It refers to that complex historical magnitude into the constitution of

This essay first appeared in *The Reformed Journal*, April 1957.

which sin has entered, but also God's creative and providential action. It designates the people whose existence and culture stands in the token of depravity, guilt, and unbelief, but who are surrounded nevertheless by God's general revelation and are the recipients of his common grace and the beneficiaries of the general operation of his Spirit. It points to what Augustine called the City of the World as it stands in contrast to the City of God. It includes Nineveh and Babylon, Athens and Rome, Hollywood and Reno, Buchenwald and Belsen. It embraces pagans, heathen, and apostates, and all their works and ways: unregenerate philosophy, science, art, and morals—in short, the whole of unredeemed society, civilization, and culture.

*   *   *   *   *

In the middle of this world the church is set down. Itself not of the world, it is situated in the world and, because it touches that world at a thousand points, the question concerning its relation to that world must inevitably arise. The question may, and indeed should, take many forms, for only when our question is plural will our response to it be adequate. We should ask: How can we protect from the ravages of the world the divine gift we have received? We should also ask: How can we unmask and destroy the world's evil works and ways? And we should ask: What is there in the world to be thankful for, and how can we serve that world in Christian love? When all these questions are asked, and each receives its due and proper accent, and only when this is done, will we be in position to frame a single comprehensive answer in the embracement of which we ourselves will be integrated and made whole.

The safe mind, which we are now considering, puts the emphasis on the first of these three questions. In so far as it asks the other questions it does so in subordination to the first. Its central question is: How can the church maintain itself in the world, how can we preserve the truth and piety we possess, how can we remain unspotted from the world? Its fault does not lie in its asking this question. Its fault lies in making this question central, in according it a governing role, in giving it an accent it does not deserve. The question, it will be observed, does not turn the church outward toward the world, but inward toward itself. In it the church inquires not about its mission but about its safety. The question expresses the church's self-concern. And when, as here, the question stands insufficiently qualified by the others that could and should be asked, it expresses a self-concern which stands on the verge of anxiety and selfishness. Signs of this appear in the answer that is given to it.

*   *   *   *   *

The answer given to this question by the mind of safety, although it is certainly not the only answer available to the church, is this: We preserve our truth and piety by walling the world out; we remain unspotted from the world by immuring ourselves against it; the church maintains itself by playing safe. This answer, evoked in part by an improperly accented question, limits, if it does not preclude, the possibility of reaching out into the world either to destroy or save it. In the repetition of the answer a mind is developed that wants nothing so much as security, and that seeks it by nothing so much as separation and withdrawal. This mind is fond of saying: We must be distinctive above all else; in our isolation lies our strength. Its injunctions are: Be on your guard, don't lower the bars, avoid the dangerous thing. Its dominant mood is conservative and protective. And it is born of fear. It is born of a timid fear of the world and of a worldly fear of God, a fear like that of the man who said: "Lord, behold, here is thy pound, which I kept laid up in a napkin, for I feared thee, because thou art an austere man: thou takest up that which thou layedst not down, and reapest that which thou didst not sow" (Lk. 19:20, 21).

It should be observed that I am here delineating a mind and not any individual or any group of individuals. I do not wish to be understood as declaring that any person in the church adopts towards the world the simplistic attitude I have just described. I do not believe that there is a man anywhere for whom safety is life's alpha and omega. I do believe, however, that there is abroad in the church a spirit which, affecting each of us to a greater or lesser degree, sponsors the answer I have set down and generates the type of mind which feeds upon and discloses itself in this answer. This mind and spirit comes to expression in those extremely cautious policies and overly-protective measures that one sometimes hears advocated in the church and that, one suspects, are dictated less by biblical faith than by secular prudence.

I think I know, and I can certainly appreciate, the good intentions from which such advocacy springs. The intention is to preserve the purity of the church, to safeguard Christian truth and virtue. This good intention rests on sound perceptions. It is recognized that the church and all it stands for is under attack from every quarter of the world; it is recognized that "the devils and evil spirits are so depraved that they are enemies of God and every good thing: to the utmost of their power as murderers watching to ruin the church and every member thereof, and by their wicked stratagems to destroy all" (Belgic Confession, Art. XII). It is also recognized that the church is obliged by no one less than its ascended King to keep the faith, cost what it may: "I come quickly," the Lord said. "Hold fast that which thou hast, that no man take thy crown" (Rev. 3:11). The mind of safety has a lively awareness of these things and it has a true perception of what they centrally entail. Every Christian assents when it declares that Satan and the flesh are dire threats to truth and holiness and must be held off, that piety and purity are delicate things and must be carefully tended, that the biblical faith is a precious possession and must be strictly preserved. Its concern for rectitude of life and doctrine is a legitimate—indeed, an indispensable concern—and I could wish that we had more of it than we do.

*   *   *   *   *

But, of course, any concern to be legitimate must be biblically conceived and exercised. This means that the concern for doctrinal soundness and moral rectitude must not be allowed to lure us into monastic retreat where, through excessive preoccupation with ourselves, we become introspective, myopic, and domesticated, and thus unable to venture out with poise into a sinful world that needs nothing so much as the service of Christian hands and hearts. A biblical concern, furthermore, may not exclude respect for theological advance. Our doctrinal inheritance is not a mere deposit that can be kept as one keeps money; it is a living faith that, because it lives, must be always maturing and always carrying us forward toward new horizons.

A biblical concern for truth and virtue may not be conceived of as excluding concern for growth and outreach, and it should not be exercised against what in the world is good and proper. When it is so conceived and exercised it becomes a narrow and constricting thing which chokes and stifles what it would protect, and which resists and walls out much that should be claimed for Christ and appropriated in his name. Then the cry for safety becomes the voice of fear, and the protective embrace becomes a strangulation. Then Calvinism degenerates into Puritanism, and the Christian faith ossifies into "Standpattism." From this negativism and "Standpattism" no church that knows the value of distinctiveness is entirely free, and the mind that I am now discussing is the exponent of it.

For this mind all issues and practices in the church tend to be weighed and judged from the point of view of safety. Let a question be raised or a proposal made concerning something which cannot be settled out of hand by a direct appeal to Scripture, and this mind is ready with its protective veto. In matters of this kind, even though there are prospects of great gain, no risks are to be taken. It is better to walk the center line of safety, through territory already familiar, than to venture off into unmapped territory where who knows what lies in wait to destroy.

*   *   *   *   *

The mind of safety affects the life of the church in many and subtle ways.

Traceable to it is the nervousness we feel when we stand at the boundary of church and world. When, under the influence of this mind, we look out upon the world and observe its power to harm, we become frightened and anxious about our safety. When we look back upon our church establishment and observe its elaborate security arrangements, a sense of satisfaction takes possession of us and we grow complacent. But a periodic awareness of new

threats periodically punctures our complacency, and thus we oscillate between fear and satisfaction. Through it all we become nervous and lose our
poise; we grow deadly serious about everything and are unable anymore to
laugh, particularly at ourselves. The reason for this is that by the constraint
of a well-known psychological law a man who lives by fear becomes so
thoroughly occupied with himself that things get out of focus and he loses
his sense of proportion, and with it his sense of humor. The reason is further,
and more basically, that by a well-known spiritual law a church which defines itself negatively in opposition to the world, rather than positively in
affinity to Christ, will be victimized by the world it negatively honors.

The remedy for all this, the way to break out of the imprisoning polar-
ity, is to look first of all neither to ourselves nor to the world but to Jesus
Christ. After we have done so we will be more forgetful of self and more
thoughtful of the world, of the world not as a thing to be feared but as a thing
to be redeemed and enjoyed, and in its redemption and enjoyment the Lord
will return us to ourselves. Isn't it strange that we are so fearful of the world?
Why are we not more amused than we are by the vain antics and the hollow
threats of the demons and their subjects? He that sitteth in the heavens
laughs; the Lord holds them in derision. Are we not children of the Lord?
And why are we not more concerned to redeem these wildly flailing children
of the world and to make them citizens of the kingdom of peace and sanity? Is
not the Lord ever calling them to repentance, and are we not his children?
When we have gotten our Lord in view, and in self-forgetfulness have managed both to laugh at and to pity the people of the world, we will have lost
our nervousness and regained our poise. But then we will also have sloughed
off the mind of safety.

The mind of safety tends to put everything in wrong perspective. Under
its influence the church tends to be conceived of as a static thing without real
dynamic; a place, not an agent; a walled city, not a moving force; a reposi-
tory, not a creative energy. Speaking generally, and in respect of accent, the
church is, in the perspective of this mind, a vault in which the divinely
communicated revelation and its fixed creedal and theological elaborations
are securely kept and carefully guarded. It is a refuge and shelter for men and
women who, being taught to pray "Lead us not into temptation," are counseled to venture nothing. It is a walled city with gates whose bars are up to a
predetermined height, a city whose gates are tended by men whose faithfulness to the divine commission is measured by nothing so much as their fixed
determination never to lower the bars.

*   *   *   *   *

There are two things a Christian must be concerned about: doctrine and
life, faith and practice, truth and love. What does the mind of safety do for
the establishment and growth of these?

By throwing up walls this mind tends, for a while at least, to preserve the church's theological inheritance. It serves to prevent the existing doctrinal deposit from being squandered by its wardens within the church or corrupted by its enemies without. It favors the cause of orthodoxy and conservatism. How long it is able to maintain right doctrine, and what price it exacts for doing so, are questions I shall not now attempt to answer. I only observe that the mind of safety is, from the nature of the case, able to contribute little toward the growth and development, as distinct from the perservation, of theology. But since theology is or ought to be a systematic presentation of the living Word, a dynamic statement through which a living faith can find expression, it must itself be alive, and if alive, then subject to change and growth. It should not change its basic structure, it may not change its identity, but it should be kept relevant and responsive to the changing expressions of basic human needs. It must also grow fuller, richer, deeper. The alternative to such growth is atrophy and death.

The mind of safety, by tending to stifle the old questions which each generation must ask anew and the new questions which historical existence continually poses, stifles theological growth and blocks the way of theological advance. A theology grows only when questions are seriously asked. A theology grows not by adding anything to the Word once and for all delivered, but by coming to that Word with new questions and hearing it give answers which we had not heard before because we had not previously put the questions. The questions a theologian can put arise in part out of the Word itself, but many of them arise out of the ever-changing historical situation in which he finds himself, and to which he must, in the interest of his calling, be sharply sensitive. It is only as he is thus sensitive both to the Word and to existence that he has any questions to ask, and without questions he cannot theologize; he can only repeat answers to questions others have asked before him, questions the force of which he may not feel and the answers to which he is likely to carry about as a mere dead weight. Theology remains alive and grows only where there is a continuing curiosity and an insatiable desire to hear all that God has to say not only on what is our ancient and continuing concern but also on what history may for the first time call to our attention.

*   *   *   *   *

The mind of safety is concerned to protect not only the doctrine, but also the morals of the church. What it fears as much as heresy is worldliness. Worldliness is indeed its chief preoccupation: the mind of safety virtually defines itself in its relation to this moral quality. Unfortunately, however, it does not always treat worldliness as a quality. It tends to externalize it and to treat it as a thing. It is led to do this by its whole perspective, which is expressed in terms of walls, and bars, and shelters. You can wall out a thing, you can't wall out a quality. Worldliness therefore becomes associated in this perspective with certain specific activities or institutions which one can name and number—such as the theater, dancing, and card-playing. Worldliness is, indeed, practically identified with these and other entities, and when the identification is made it is natural both to take any sort of indulgence in these things as proof of unspirituality and to suppose that by proscribing these things one is actually banishing worldliness itself.

Of course one is doing nothing of the sort. Worldliness is not a thing, but a spirit. It is an affection and movement of the soul. It is a love of self and of the world to the exclusion of God. It lives and grows inside a man, in the depths of the human spirit. Because this is so the way to overcome it is not by first moralizing, then externalizing, and then proscribing it, but by attacking it with spiritual weapons upon the only ground it ever occupies, the human heart. It is not by decrees and edicts that it can be ostracized, but only by grace and a new obedience. In them alone lies the hope of uprooting and mortifying those evil affections in which the essence of worldliness consists. It is only as one recognizes this that one can escape the legalism to which externalism leads.

The mind of safety naturally tends toward legalism. Perhaps legalism is already implicit in the very conception of the church as a walled city with gates. Whatever passes from the world into the church must come through these gates, and at the gates, by duly authorized officials, it must be decided what comes in and what stays out, what passes muster and what does not, what is contraband and what is not. Whatever the case may be, the mind of safety as it has come to expression in the church has not hesitated to sponsor ecclesiastical decrees to keep out the world, and to interpret as legal decrees what were in reality spiritual exhortations. The mind of safety tends toward the publishing of bans, not realizing that in matters of this kind the Christian, made free in Christ, may not be put under the constraint of ecclesiastical law but must be thrown back upon inner spiritual resources for appraisal and decision.

Because the mind of safety encourages the church to look away from the world and toward itself, the church, under its influence, tends to lack the wide social concern which it ought to possess. The church has a God-given responsibility toward the whole of society. It has this responsibility not only because none of its members remain unaffected by existing social conditions, but also because the people outside the church should receive the church's verdict upon its social arrangements and the church's help in improving them. In the isolation, however, which the mind of safety sponsors and encourages, we tend to ignore certain large social evils—such as prostitution, segregation, tenement housing, tyranny, and the like—and to take merely private and protective measures against others. There is no impetus in the mind of safety toward the elaboration of a vigorous social ethic.

Because in the field of morality this mind encourages externalism, legalism, and individualism, we cannot look to it for a definitive Christian ethics any more than we can look to it for a vigorous Christian dogmatics, or indeed for anything else that is whole and complete. The reason is, of course, that the mind of safety raises to a central and governing position what should occupy a subordinate place under the governance of the positive principle of Christianity—truth and love. Thereby all things are thrown out of focus and the whole life of the church comes to stand in a false perspective.

21

The Militant Mind

WHAT, we have been asking, must the church do about the world? There is a mind operating in and upon the church that, in answer, bids us flee the world. There is another mind that bids us fight the world. The demand of the first mind is for safety; that of the second is for militancy. Having previously discussed the one mind, I turn now to a consideration of the other.

The militant mind counsels attack upon the world. The "world" which this mind offers for attack is not a quality only; it is a concrete entity, the existing whole of men and cultures which, qualified by sin, lies unredeemed outside the Christian church. The "mind" which counsels attack upon this world is not a person or a group of persons; nor is it a principle; it is a spirit that, generated through an exclusive devotion to a non-inclusive principle, animates to a greater or lesser degree persons and groups whose outlook is shaped in part by the force of other minds operating within the church. The "attack" upon the world which the militant mind calls forth is not physical in nature; it is an intellectual and spiritual assault which employs as weapons, not blades of steel, but words, ideas, arguments, and attitudes. These weapons, however, though themselves not physical, are often given names that are borrowed from the vocabulary of physical war. Under the inspiration of the militant mind they are called guns, bombs, bayonets, flame-throwers, and the like. The assault made with these weapons, it should be added, is launched and carried forward in the name of the antithesis.

* * * * *

This essay first appeared in *The Reformed Journal,* June, July-August, and October 1957.

The militant mind is to be distinguished from the mind of safety. Although there is a deep-seated identity in the two, both being predominantly negative in their attitude toward the world, they express their common negativity in such different ways that they may be regarded as distinct and separate minds.

The first thing to be observed is that these minds are differently oriented. Unlike the mind of safety, the militant mind compels the believer to look outward. It does not encourage him to turn his back upon the world and to bend in meek solicitude over an imperiled church; it bids him face the world with unbending resolution. More than that, it moves him out into the world. In this basic disposition it distinguishes itself sharply from the mind of safety and reveals affinities to the positive mind, which I shall attempt to characterize in the sequel.

Because it is oriented to the world, the militant mind induces in those who come under its influence such an awareness of the world's thought and movements as the mind of safety does not, and perhaps cannot, provide. It thereby lays the groundwork for significant theological advance and helps free the church from the dogmatic sterility which is the legacy—doubtless unintended—of safety.

Because of its basic orientation the militant mind moves men away from the asceticism toward which the mind of safety inclines them. Involving men in war, and engaging them in urgent preparations for the battle, it does not encourage preoccupation with the niceties of personal morality or with the merely prudential aspects of Christian ethics. Nor does it engender reliance on formal rules of behavior; it induces the Christian to oppose to legalistic enactments the liberty that he has in Christ, the freedom he needs to carry on the fight.

Whereas the mind of safety is congenial to many typical aspects of American fundamentalism, the militant mind evokes no sympathy for the quiescent pietism that is a feature of it. The mind of militancy detests passivity, being nothing if not dynamic; and it is not easily blinded by mere sentiment.

What has been said may serve to indicate that the mind of safety and the mind of militancy differ in important ways. Because they differ they tend to drive the church in different directions, at least when matters of policy and practice are at issue. It may be said, indeed, that on almost every issue arising in the church these two minds encourage men to place the accent differently and to propose differing solutions to problems. The mind of safety and the mind of militancy are quite distinguishable and frequently in tension.

And yet they are related. They are related not merely as all three minds in the church are related: by a common bond to God in Christ through the Scriptures and the creeds in the power of the Holy Spirit. They are related at another level also. At this level they are united in a common cultural vision and commitment which they jointly recommend in distinction from another which finds its advocate in the mind I have called positive. The mind of safety and the mind of militancy are, in spite of marked differences on the surface, one in their attitude toward the world. Both are basically negative: in the view of both the world looms up as nothing so much as a threat to Christian truth and practice; both fear this threat and in the face of it recommend avertive action above all else; both define themselves in reaction to a world regarded primarily as a hazard and only secondarily as an opportunity.

The militant mind, unlike the mind of safety, moves men out into the world. Its movement, however, as is the safe mind's movement of withdrawal, is not so much *for* the world (in the world's behalf) as *against* the world (in behalf of the existing church). Its central concern, like that of the mind of safety, is for self-protection. The militant mind does not induce a man to wrap his pound up in a napkin; it stimulates him rather to enlarge his inheritance. But it does not move him to scatter and distribute his possessions: it stimulates him rather to exercise a jealous guardianship over them by moving out with weapons of destruction against a world which he has trained himself to contemplate as more dangerous than needy.

$$* \quad * \quad * \quad * \quad *$$

Does the Scripture generate and justify the mind of militancy? Is this mind the product and expression of Christian principle? In order to answer these questions some necessary distinctions must be made: one must observe the difference between person, mind, and principle.

The militant mind is not a person; it is a spirit or temper which to a greater or lesser degree influences and inspires persons. It is also not a principle; it is an attitude or perspective formed with reference to a principle. Lying between principle and person, and touching both, it is identifiable with neither. No Christian person incarnates the militant mind and no biblical principle dictates it. The militant mind impinges upon Christians and modifies them in varying measure; it also impinges upon Scripture and reflects it to some degree; but it is not to be confused with either. Praise of the militant mind is therefore not praise of persons or of Scripture, and criticism of it is not criticism of them. The militant mind could, in theory, stand regardless of the faults of those it animates; and it could fall regardless of the excellence of the principle it appeals to for validation.

Now the principle that the mind of militancy appeals to is an excellent one. It is the biblical principle of the antithesis and its pendant, the principle of Holy War.

The doctrine of the antithesis is a thoroughly biblical doctrine. It teaches that in the history of the sinful world two forces, powers, and persons—sin and grace, hate and love, Satan and Jesus Christ—are arrayed against each other. It teaches that through the operation of these agencies two peoples are created with two allegiances, and that these peoples, incorporated in two kingdoms with different lords, are in radical opposition to each other, are indeed at war. It teaches that this war is no mere incident in the life of men, no mere episode that only temporarily disturbs the peace and unity of mankind; it teaches that this war is radical and enduring, engaging men in an all-pervasive and all-demanding conflict which will be terminated only at the end of the age. It teaches that this war has cosmic proportions and significance, embracing not only every human being, but even the angels and the demons, and having consequences that reach into eternity. It is to this sound doctrine that the mind of militancy appeals for validation.

Believing that the church is at war and is called upon to fight as long as history lasts, the mind of militancy appeals for justification not only to the theological doctrine of the antithesis, but also to the specific injunctions to do battle that, articulating the antithesis, are spread in great numbers upon the pages of the Bible. Back of the militant mind lie the words of the Old Testament prophets: "Awake, awake, put on thy strength, O Zion" (Isa. 52:1); "Strengthen ye the weak hands, and confirm the feeble knees. Say to them that are of a fearful heart, be strong" (Isa. 35:3); "Keep the fortress, watch the way, make thy loins strong, fortify thy power mightily" (Nahum 2:1); "Prepare ye the buckler and shield and draw near to battle" (Jer. 46:3).

Back of this mind lie also the words of the New Testament apostles: "Contend earnestly for the faith" (Jude 3); "Put on the whole armor of God" (Eph. 6:11); "Guard that which is committed unto thee" (I Tim. 6:20); "Fight the good fight of faith" (I Tim. 6:12); "Cast down imaginations and every high thing that is exalted against the knowledge of God . . . being in readiness to avenge all disobedience" (II Cor. 10:4,5); "Wax not weary, fainting in your souls" (Heb. 12:3); "Resist the devil" (James 4:7).

This mind acknowledges Jehovah as a man of war (Exod. 15:3); it understands that it is Jehovah who puts enmity between Satan and the woman and between their seed (Gen. 3:15); it hears the Savior say, "Think not that I came to send peace on the earth; I came not to send peace, but a sword" (Matt. 10:34).

These are the biblical representations which lie behind the mind of militancy and from which it derives much of its character and worth. The injunctions it recognizes are normative and binding; a turning from them is a repudiation of biblical authority, a flight from active obedience. No one who honors the Word may deny or minimize the obligation Christians are under to be vigilant, dynamic, and intrepid fighters. Christians must resist with strength and alacrity every attack made upon whatever is true, and good, and beautiful, and right, and holy. And Christians must fight evil in all its forms, wherever it appears. They must fight error and falsehood, injustice and heartlessness, pride and bigotry, fear and cowardice, passion and lovelessness, distrust and suspicion, disloyalty and faithlessness, dishonesty and misrepresentation, and every other vice both within and without the church, both in their own lives and in the lives of others.

But, of course, the fight must be conducted with a Christian purpose, in a Christian manner, with Christian weapons, against the proper objects, and in the context of a larger Christian life. When it is not so conducted a mind is formed which stands in danger of exhibiting the very evils the Scripture enjoins us to attack, a mind that, though it appeals to Scripture, is not the purest reflection of its principles but a kind of veil upon them. The mind thus formed I have ventured to call militant.

* * * * *

The militant mind is not at fault in urging men to fight in behalf of the Kingdom of our Lord. Nor is it at fault in representing the Christian life as a continuous and all-engaging war against every kind of evil. It is at fault in suggesting that the Christian life is nothing but a war. It errs in making warfare the inclusive symbol of the Christian life. It thus obscures the fact that the Christian life may, and indeed must, be described in other terms as well if it is to be fairly represented and lived in its completeness.

The militant mind has its own vocabulary. Its character and presence is revealed in the language it induces men to use. When, under the governance of this mind, men speak of the world, or of the church in relation to the world, they almost invariably resort to martial symbols: the Christian is a soldier; the man of the world is an enemy; the church is a citadel; the Christian community is an armed camp; life is a battle; history is a war; God's people is an army; his ministers are warriors; his Word is a sword.

This language is remarkable and revealing. What is remarkable about it is not that it is made up of metaphors (figures of speech are unavoidable, especially in religious discourse); nor simply that military figures are employed (the Bible is full of them); but that the military figures are disassociated from other figures with which the Bible joins them, and that in this isolation they are employed to define the very essence of church and world in their relation to each other.

It is permissible to think of the Christian as a soldier standing at attention before the Supreme Commander, but only if one remembers that the Christian is also a suppliant on his knees before the Savior, and that he is a child with a small weak hand held firm and lovingly by the tenderest of Fathers. The man of the world is doubtless an enemy of God and of the church, although he may not always be conscious of the fact; but he is no less a drowning man clinging desperately to a straw and requiring not the thrust of a sword but the help of compassionate hands. The church may be described as a citadel, with ramparts manned by dedicated soldiers ready to repulse the foe; it is also a bride awaiting with eager expectancy the coming of the bridegroom. The Christian life may be described as a battle; it is also a pilgrimage on which the weary traveler, guarded by the great Keeper of the sheep, is led beside still waters. The Bible may be contemplated as a sword; it is also bread, and a fountain of living water, and a green pasture, and a glorious and redemptive disclosure of the living God. The people of God may be thought of as an army marching in serried ranks against the foe; it is also the joyous company of the redeemed publishing to all the world the good glad tidings of peace.

But the mind of militancy ignores this complexity. In the simplistic perspective that it furnishes everything takes on a martial hue, and under its influence men tend to think and speak of church and world in nothing so much as the fighting words of war.

*   *   *   *   *

This ignoring of complexity, this inclination toward the simplistic, is characteristic of the militant mind. Under its influence men tend, as has already been observed, to use a restricted and homogeneous vocabulary, and to reduce the complex Christian life to the single dimension of war. Once this reduction has been made, however, other reductions follow hard upon it, for warfare demands simple and clear-cut issues. The soldier functions well only when the battle lines are clearly drawn; he best sustains the fight when he ignores all affinity with the enemy. The militant mind, therefore, depreciates the shared and common, and accents difference. It does not encourage recognition of the relativities of historical existence; it develops no eye for greys. It induces men to think in terms of black and white, and to deal in absolutes. Its genius is abstract and reductionistic.

Under the inspiration of the militant mind the Christian apologist or polemicist will sometimes try to reduce a complex of propositions—a given theology or philosophy—to a single principle or set of principles from which it is supposed to be derived by logical consequence. The invariable result is that the theology or philosophy in view is misconceived or misrepresented. Theologies and philosophies, because they are never simple, do not lend themselves to the reductionist procedure. Authentic Christian theology, for example, is not to be thought of or proposed as a deductive system derived by logical inference from some governing principle, but as a theoretical restatement of the correlated scriptural givens in their fullness and with their paradoxes and mysteries left intact. By the same token no non-Christian theology or philosophy is reducible to its real or alleged presuppositions. The theology of some errant thinker one could name is no doubt influenced by extra-biblical assumptions, and whoever points this out serves the Christian cause. But not all that such a thinker says is dictated by these assumptions or even compatible with them. To suppose that such is the case is to yield to a kind of abstractionism. This abstractionism may serve to sharpen the antithesis by pitting one principle against another, but it is not calculated to do justice either to Christianity or to its rival. The views of men do not issue in their entirety from their presuppositions; something of what they say is a reflection of reality as revealed and apprehended. It is therefore not by uncovering some explanatory principle that one is put in a position to understand completely the teaching of a man; it is only when one adds to the conceptual analysis a consideration of the teaching in its existential concreteness that one truly comprehends it. Reductionism is, however, what the mind of militancy recommends, perhaps because men can ordinarily be expected to fight a rival doctrine without reserve only when it is reduced to something simple.

The Christian polemicist who stands under the influence of the militant mind will be tempted not only to reduce a complex body of opinion to a single principle, he will be tempted to perform another closely-related reduction: he will be tempted to reduce a person to the set of opinions that person entertains. It is in the nature of the militant mind to urge the performance of this operation, for under cover of the reduction hostility can be carried over to persons without awakening the conscience. If one first reduces a man to a set of impersonal ideas one can attack him without qualms, for ideas are fair game. It is obvious meanwhile that, though a man may be held accountable for his opinions, he may never be reduced to them. He may never be taken abstractly. But this is precisely what happens when a person is not distinguished from the idea we entertain of him, from the idea which may be thought to control him, or from the opinions that he himself holds. When a person is reduced to a doctrine there is nothing to prevent a man from going after him hammer and tongs, for one may beat and badger an insensible doctrine to one's heart's content, and if it is a bad doctrine one should do precisely that until it dies. But it goes without saying that one may never do this to a person: the law of love prohibits it. A person, therefore, must be carefully distinguished from his opinions. This will be the more readily conceded when it is recognized that the distinction protects us against spurious absolutisms. A principle or idea, at least if it is a simple idea, is either right or wrong, it is either white or black, and one can accept or reject it without qualification. This one cannot do with a person, for a person is in his concreteness always some shade of gray, with possibilities, not closed before the judgment day, of becoming white or black. It should be noted, finally, that the proper exercise of love and hate depends upon observing the distinction now before us. We must hate sin, which is a principle; we may not hate the sinner. We must be militant in the face of evil; we may not be militant in our behavior toward a person. The uncompromising severity that we are obliged to exhibit against evil principles and practices we may not exhibit in our relations to our fellowmen. We must destroy an evil thing; we must redeem an evil person.

* * * * *

The dogmatic theologian who allows himself to be influenced by the militant mind is almost certain to develop reductionist habits, and the several doctrines he formulates will quite naturally be weighted on the negative side. This may be observed by considering what happens in the perspective of militancy to the doctrine of God.

In the perspective of the militant mind, God is markedly a God of war. He is a terrible avenger who visits destruction on his enemies. He is the God of wrath, whose sword is in his hand and whose very breath destroys. It is immediately to be observed, however, that God is something like this also in the mirror of the Bible. He is a God that has indignation every day (Ps. 7:11). He has garments of vengeance for clothing and is clad with zeal as a mantle (Isa. 59:17). He will come to render his anger with fierceness and his rebuke with flames of fire (Isa. 66:15). Upon the wicked he will rain snares (Ps. 11:6). He will break them with a rod of iron, and dash them in pieces like a potter's vessel (Ps. 2:9). He will execute judgment by his sword, and the slain of Jehovah shall be many (Isa. 66:16).

But, of course, there is another side to God, and this, too, is illumined by the Scriptures. God appears in the Bible, as he does in the experience of the saints, as merciful and gracious, slow to anger, and abundant in lovingkindness (Ps. 103:8). Before men call he answers them, and while they are yet speaking he hears them (Isa. 65:24). He is full of pity (James 4:11), is ready to pardon (Neh. 9:17), his hand is not shortened that it cannot save (Isa. 59:1), and he extends peace like a river to Zion (Isa. 66:12).

It is evident from this that the God of Scripture is a God of double aspect. One side of him is light and cheering, the other is dark and forbidding. On the one side he enchants and captivates, on the other he evokes terror and consternation. This ambiguity presents the biblical theologian with a very real difficulty. He needs to present a unified picture of God, yet one in which both sides of him appear, and this is a delicate operation not easy for a theologian to perform. Everything depends here on the stance he takes and on his angle of vision. If he is under the influence of the militant mind he is apt to place and set himself in such a way that from where he stands the darker side of God either obscures the brighter side or appears coordinate with it. Since he is a Christian, and has had direct experience of God's saving power, he is not likely to allow the obscuration. He is likely, however, to acquiesce in the coordination; he is apt to keep God's grace and judgment, God's love and wrath, in the strictest equilibrium; he is apt to give equal status to God's redemptive and destructive work.

It is plain, meanwhile, that the Bible does not do this. In the representation of the Bible the two aspects of God do not stand in simple juxtaposition. They are not on a footing of equality. From the Bible's angle of vision God's grace stands in the foreground and his judgments in the background. What is brightly illumined is his love; his wrath lies in the shadows, real, unmistakable, and terrifying, but in the shadows nevertheless. According to the Scriptures God is essentially and primarily the savior, and only accidentally and derivatively the destroyer. There is a glorious disproportion in his nature and activity; his frown is not in balance with his smile. When, therefore, a man lays as strong an accent on God's destructive activities as he does on those that are redemptive, the biblical proportion is disturbed, the dark and negative side of God looms larger than it ought to loom, and his love and tenderness is relatively reduced.

That there is no warrant for this reduction is evident from the fact that even divine power is an instrument predominantly of salvation. It is as standing in the service of his love that God's imperial might is chiefly celebrated in the Scriptures. God is all-powerful; none can stay his hand or disturb his designs; what he wills, that he performs. But this will is asserted and this power is exercised chiefly in the winning and preservation of his own. It is as a loving Father of children that he is a refuge, a fortress, and a high tower. It is as a tender keeper of sheep that he stretches out a mighty arm and wields a flaming sword. There is an enemy abroad in the land and he will not allow the enemy to hurt or to destroy in all his holy hill. He will defend and protect his own. Let the enemy attempt to wrench God's little ones out of his strong hands, let him try to erase out of God's palms the names he has written there, let him try to pluck out the apple of God's eye, and God's power to preserve will come immediately into play. This power will keep his children safe. It will also slay the enemy who in madness hurls himself headlong against it. It will do this not because it is designed to kill, but because, being the instrument of an unshakable love, it both cannot bend or break, and must negate its opposite. The enemy who persists in his attempt to frustrate God's beneficent purposes will die in the attempt. He will die, not because God wishes him to die, but because God's purposes of love are sure, and because God will not yield to any onslaught.

The relation of God to sinners, and the effect of his power upon them, can be even more clearly seen when we contemplate not God's concern for his children, but his concern for himself, his infinite concern for his being and status as God. God is God, and there is none beside him. He is the Lord, the Holy One, who cannot and will not share his honor with another. Divinity belongs to him alone, he alone is glorious, he alone is pure, he alone is transcendent over all. No other being participates in the bright and burning glory of his Godhood; he dwells alone on the mount of splendor. And it is his will to maintain his status, to assert and defend his eternal uniqueness, to guard the flaming contours of his exclusive deity. He declares: "I am Jehovah, that is my name; and my glory will I not give to another" (Isa. 48:11). But sin, which he did not create, is such a force as moves the creature to challenge his uniqueness. It moves him impiously to ascend the holy hill in an attempt to rob God of his glory. But God will not be robbed; he is the jealous God who takes deity—that is, himself—with infinite seriousness, and will not permit it to be profaned, for "how should my name be profaned," he asks (Isa. 48:11). But the unrepentant sinner, in league with Satan the Supplanter, obstinately pursues his arrogant course, the Holy One meanwhile shouting down to him as he makes his perilous and vain ascent, "Woe unto him that striveth with his maker" (Isa. 45:9), and "look unto me and be ye saved . . . for I am God, and there is none else" (Isa. 45:22). But this warning and invitation goes unheeded: the sinner persists in storming the very throne of God. What happens then is terrible to relate: the sinner breaks himself to pieces on the immovable rock of God's holy determination to maintain himself, and he burns to death at the very feet of God, for "our God is a consuming fire" (Heb. 12:29).

But in this burning, in this death, God takes no delight. He has no joy in the destruction either of those who attempt to rob him of his children, or of those who attempt to rob him of his glory. "As I live, saith the Lord Jehovah, I have no pleasure in the death of the wicked, but that the wicked turn from his way and live" (Ezek. 33:11). The fact is that destruction is not his proper work. He is glorified in it, indeed, for in it he celebrates the triumph of his sovereignty and faithfulness, and vindicates his holiness. But still it is his strange work, for in his proper work he takes great delight. He loves to save.

The Scriptures do not carry us much beyond this point. They do not solve for us the mystery of iniquity and the mystery of judgment and perdition. In order to stifle all complacency and to drive men into the arms of the Redeemer they open the door upon the mystery, but they leave it in the shadow while illumining the face of Jesus. Obedience would seem to require the biblical theologian to do the same.

*　*　*　*　*

When a man views the Christian life in the perspective of war and defines the Christian's relation to the world in terms of conflict, he will sooner or later have to give serious attention to the love commandment, for love is at bottom a constructive and not a destructive force, and not at home in war. It is true, of course, that love does not commit one to pacifism. In a sinful world, where tyrannous and destructive forces are abroad, love is in the service of justice and conservation and necessarily in conflict with what imperils these. Yet it is not in conflict that it has its seat; it is not in destruction that its inner nature is revealed. Love is the bond of unity. It restores, heals, saves, and celebrates its triumph in fellowship and peace. In the measure, therefore, that love is taken seriously and given its rightful place as the comprehensive virtue and man's whole duty, the militant and the martial will be given a subordinate position.

But militancy cannot allow the subordination. Militancy lives by, is defined by, the priority of the martial. The militant man cannot, without ceasing to be himself, acknowledge the supremacy of love. This being the case, one would expect every Christian to abandon the attempt to construe existence in terms of conflict, for Christianity does not leave the status of love in doubt: love is the very fulfillment of the law. Yet there are Christians who continue to press the claims of militancy, and in the interest of their militancy they are forced to formulate a new, a militant doctrine of love, which in one or another way reduces love in scope and power.

1. The simplest and most direct way to do this is to deny that love is always and everywhere the Christian's duty in his relations with other men. One then asserts that Christians are permitted, if not obliged, to hate some men at certain times and under certain circumstances. I wish I could report that this position is merely a logically possible one, and that it is not actually occupied by any member of the church, but I cannot. So powerful is the influence of the militant mind even on those who bear Christ's name that some seek to evade in this most radical of all ways Jesus' unmistakable commandment to love all men, always, and under every circumstance.

Christ, meanwhile, does not leave us in doubt about our duty. Nor do the apostles (Matt. 5:43–45; 22:37–40; Luke 6:27; 23:34; Acts 7:60; Rom. 13:8,9; Gal. 5:14; etc.). Nor, indeed, do the great teachers in the church. In one of the earliest manuals of instruction, the *Didache*, one may read, "You shall not hate any man." Clement of Alexandria informs his readers that a Christian "hates none of God's creatures" (*Stromata*, VI, 9). Minucius Felix told the Romans of his day, ". . . we love one another . . . with a mutual love because we do not know how to hate" (*Octavius* 31). St. Augustine declared, ". . . he who lives according to God ought to cherish towards evil men a *perfect* hatred, so that he shall neither hate the man because of his vice, nor love the vice because of the man, but hate the vice and love the man" (*City of God*, XIV, 6). Calvin said, "Thus hatred and Christianity are things incompatible. I mean hatred towards persons—in opposition to the love that we owe them" (*Letter* DCLXIV to the Duchess of Ferrara). And in commenting on Psalm 139:21,22 Calvin remarked, "We are to observe . . . that the hatred of which the Psalmist speaks is directed to the sins rather than the persons of the wicked. We are, so far as lies in us, to study peace with all men; we are to seek the good of all, and, if possible, they are to be reclaimed by kindness and good offices" (*Commentary, in loco*).

2. When militancy does not seek to justify itself by positively legitimatizing hate, it may seek to do so by negatively immobilizing love. This is done

by developing a doctrine of stages and degrees of love, a doctrine in which the exercise of love is correlated with the historical process of differentiation within mankind. This doctrine requires that a Christian's love for an unbeliever be in proportion to the unbeliever's unbelief. According to this doctrine, we are not required to love the Anti-Christ, the fully differentiated and completely self-conscious sinner. If, however, we are confronted by a less fully differentiated sinner, him we must love—but only in the measure that he is undifferentiated. The more differentiated he is, the greater sinner he is, the less I am required to love him.

There can be no doubt that this ingenious doctrine, when believed, sustains and encourages militancy. But the doctrine is not taken from the Scripture; it flies into the face of it. I make no judgments now about the Anti-Christ, who is represented in the Bible as quite unique in any case, but I daresay that Christian love is meant in every other instance to be spent entire upon all who cross our path. Who can set bounds to love?

3. When militancy does not justify itself by making hate legitimate, or by relatively immobilizing love, it does so by adopting another expedient. It does so by subordinating love to truth. Here is a very interesting application of the reductionist technique. Love and truth, which in the Scriptures always stand together in mutual embrace, are separated and then shifted onto different levels. By this device the road is cleared for the free advance of hostility and strife. Truth is made loose from love, and she can now in perfect freedom pursue a loveless way. The claims of orthodoxy can now be pressed at morality's expense. Controversy can go on with no holds barred. When the theological issue is judged important, questions concerning polemical methods may be dismissed as being of no consequence. Ethics must give way to doctrine. What is important is the faith; love must beat a fast retreat in the face of truth's advance.

It would be possible to counter this quite unscriptural proposal by employing the reductionist technique in reverse and making love supreme and truth subordinate to it. A very plausible case could be made for this, seeing the apostle declares that prophesyings shall fail and that love is greater than either faith or hope. The fact is, however, that love is no more superior to truth than truth is to love. They are coordinate. Truth appears to be superior to love, for no one can love truly who does not stand within the truth. Yet love appears superior to truth in that truth cannot really be heard apart from love: only the sheep who love him can hear the master's voice. The fact is that love and truth mutually define each other. Because this is so, each may be looked at through the prism of the other; but this does not justify subordination. Calvin, for example, may on one occasion say, ". . . charity itself ought to be subservient to the purity of the faith" (*Institutes*, III, 19, 13), yet on another occasion he may say, "Faith by itself cannot please God, since it cannot even exist without love to our neighbor" (*Commentary* on Hosea 6:6). Truth seems to be prior, for God can hardly be loved if he is not known, yet as Herman Bavinck says, "God is known in proportion to the extent that he is loved" (*Reasonable Faith*, p. 30). Love without truth is sentimental and indulgent; it is not Christian love at all. Likewise, truth without love is impossible there where truth counts for the most; for as G. F. Thomas says, ". . . religious truth can come only to him who is pure in heart" (*Christian Ethics and Moral Philosophy*, p. 476).

The militant man, it is obvious, tries in most ingenious ways to circumvent the love commandment, but he doesn't succeed in doing so. Love blocks the way. It is not possible to construct a biblical theology able to validate militancy; biblical love will refuse forever to become part of its supporting structure.

* * * * *

A man who is concerned to encourage true belief and to establish and defend sound doctrine can hardly avoid giving some attention to the complex question of knowledge; and in seeking an answer to this question he will sooner or later develop a theory or doctrine of truth. It will surprise no one, therefore, to discover that the militant man, who is very much concerned with orthodoxy and right opinion, has developed such a doctrine. It is not in all who practice militancy a clearly defined or consciously held doctrine; it is often no more than an approach to the problem of truth and knowledge; yet it is substantial enough to impart to the outlook and practice of militancy a characteristic quality and direction.

1. One notable feature of militancy in the area of truth and knowledge is what might be called its dogmatism. Dogmatism is the habit of taking for truth what is only opinion, of regarding as sure what is still uncertain. The militant man tends to be dogmatic; he tends to accept as established what is actually in question. The reason is plain. What is still in process of being identified, apprehended, and defined cannot be fought over with maximum force and enthusiasm. When a man is still in search of truth, when an area of knowledge is still under investigation, when conviction is not yet formed, and when statements of belief are still tentative, a man fights, if at all, to only a limited extent, perhaps only to the extent necessary to safeguard his right to explore. He is both too occupied with his explorations and too uncertain about the value of his findings to do more. To fight continuously, doggedly, and effectually, he must already have settled his convictions; he must regard himself as in sure possession of indubitable truth.

Now, because the true Christian is in possession of some indubitable truth by virtue of an authoritative divine disclosure, he is a man of conviction and he fights for his convictions. If he has no convictions, or if he does not care to proclaim and defend them with all diligence, though in meekness and in fear (I Peter 3:15), then he is either no Christian or he is a Christian who grievously sins. But the Christian who stands sure in the faith takes care not to transfer the mood of unshakable conviction onto territory where it is not appropriate, into areas where he is only a learner. Considering the wide range of reality and truth, this territory is very large indeed: the areas in which he is still a relative stranger and in which the assertive and defensive mood ill befits him are vast.

Even within the restricted area of theology he will move with modesty and caution, for even here there is ample room for honest and blameless differences of opinion, differences which for their resolution require not a battle but a discussion, not a fight but a conversation. There will be truths, however, and they will not be few, upon which the Christian will be required to stand unmovably. But even as he settles himself to defend these and turns his will against the opponents and detractors of the truth, he will let ring in his ears the words of the apostles: ". . . the servant of the Lord must not strive; but be gentle unto all men, apt to teach, patient, in meekness instructing those that oppose themselves; if God peradventure will give them repentance to the acknowledging of truth" (II Tim. 2:24,25).

2. Closely related to the dogmatism of militancy is its inclination to depreciate the value of non-Christian insights into reality. This depreciation is, indeed, a necessary preliminary step to their rejection and opposition. One does not oppose and fight values. Convinced that he is obliged to fight the world, the militant man is under constant temptation, therefore, to deny that truth and goodness and beauty have any residence there. He is tempted by the ever-present spirit of reductionism to represent the world simplistically, as altogether evil, and therefore quite deserving of rejection.

He will find it hard, however, to make his representation and denials stick, for the ordinary person observes on all sides the contributions that the world has made to science, art, and general culture. The militant man will not be deterred by this fact. He will counter the objections of common sense with theological analysis. In order to reinforce his judgment of condemnation he will go beyond the surface aspects of things; he will go below appearances, and point to the evil source of worldly culture. He will point to the depraved heart of unregenerate man, and ask whether anything good, anything true, anything beautiful can come out of a fountain so totally corrupt. He will, in other words, refer whatever appears to be good in worldly culture to a single evil source, and thus justify his judgment of rejection. He will interpret the very complex phenomenon of worldly culture simplistically, and fail to see that it contains not only what rises up out of the depraved heart of man but also what comes down from the white throne of God. He will fail to see, or fail adequately to take into account, the fact that even unregenerate culture is a mixture, a product of grace as well as of sin.

The fact is that the Christian is not permitted simply to fight unregenerate culture. He must discriminate. He may not view the world only in the perspective of the absolute antithesis. There is an absolute antithesis, although I should prefer to call it radical. This antithesis is, deep down, between the regenerate and the unregenerate heart, and it makes its presence felt in culture. But there is more than sin in the culture of the unregenerate; there is the common grace of God and his mercy to men in flight from him. Because of this fact, obscured I fear in militancy, we may and indeed must take to ourselves many of the fruits of worldly effort. This will still leave us with much to oppose, for there is expressed in the worldling's work not only God's grace, but also the sinner's opposition to the person and purposes of God. However, while we should not make ourselves guilty of adopting what we should oppose, we should also not oppose what we are required to appreciate and adopt, for we should be guilty then of opposing God himself.

> Whenever, therefore, we meet with heathen writers, let us learn from that light of truth which is admirably displayed in their works, that the human mind, fallen as it is, and corrupted from its integrity, is yet invested and adorned by God with excellent talents. If we believe that the Spirit of God is the only fountain of truth, we shall neither reject nor despise the truth itself, wherever it shall appear, unless we wish to insult the Spirit of God; for the gifts of the Spirit cannot be undervalued without offering contempt and reproach to the Spirit himself (John Calvin, *Institutes*, II, 2, 15).

22

The Positive Mind

THE POSITIVE MIND is generated not by fear, but by love, which casts out fear. It is unlike the mind of safety in that it does not counsel hiding behind protective walls, but urges a forward movement into the open. It is unlike the militant mind in that it moves outward not with programs of destruction, but with stratagems of salvation. It differs from both in that it subordinates flight and combat to positive redemptive action.

This positive mind is the exclusive possession of no individual or group of individuals in the church. It is in fact the mind which more than any other animates the whole of the redeemed community, and which is entirely absent from no single part of it. But it is constantly under siege by alien forces, and it is sometimes compromised by the unwholesome fears emanating from the safe and militant mentalities attending it. This accounts for the ambiguities of conduct and witness which can occasionally be observed in the church's official and unofficial acts.

What this mind is, what perspectives it provides, what accents it lays, and wherein it differs from the other minds which challenge it, it is the purpose of this essay to inquire.

*   *   *   *   *

It should be observed at once that the positive mind embraces and includes all that is sound and biblical in the mentalities of militancy and

This essay first appeared in *The Reformed Journal*, March 1961.

safety. It does not stand to these in a relation of simple negativity, for it recognizes that these, too, have not been uninformed by an indispensable, though partial, good. It lays these minds under judgment not because it considers them to have by-passed the Scriptures altogether, but because it believes them to be unbiblically attenuated. What it challenges in these minds is not their appreciation for certain real, if limited, aspects of the Christian revelation, but the claim they make to have gotten that revelation into focus; it challenges their claim to wholeness. It deplores not their recognition of the need for security or offensive action, but their habit of regarding the church primarily as a shelter or the Christian life as primarily a fight. The positive mind disputes their implicit claim to absoluteness, but it does not refuse a proper and subordinate place to what in these mentalities is raised to an intolerable preeminence. Whatever hold these have on truth, it shares, though in a different way, and within a different structure.

* * * * *

With respect to considerations of safety and security, a man informed by the positive mind will have no quarrel with anyone who asserts that the Christian truth we possess must be carefully guarded, that Christian ways of behavior must be well-defined and circumspect, that the Christian institutions we have established must be preserved, and that all which is holy must be kept from profanation. No Christian can take issue with these statements rightly understood, and the positive mind does not encourage anyone to do so. It does, however, insist that they be biblically interpreted and christianly endorsed; it demands that they be placed and read in scriptural context. When this is done the massive richness of Christianity comes into view, and acknowledgment of important complementary truths becomes inescapable. It then becomes the part of Christian wisdom to declare that truth simply preserved serves no purpose beyond that of selfish contemplation, that circumspect behavior can by-pass all the areas where human need is greatest, that time alone modifies all human institutions and makes them candidates for reconstruction, that what is holy is meant to touch and sanctify what is profane, and that security, though acceptable as a means, can never be an end. It then becomes necessary to insist that safekeeping is in the interest of imparting, that purity must risk contamination in Christian service, that stewardship must be sensitive to change, and that sanctity must actively redeem. Because the mind of safety has no patience with these complementary and qualifying aspects of the "truth" it stands for, it is one-sided, articulating neither the Gospel in its fullness nor man's situation in its depth. It should therefore be abandoned and replaced by another which does fuller justice both to the richness of the Christian revelation and to the complexity of Christian existence in the world.

What is required is the adoption of the positive mind, which is generated by the many-faceted Gospel as it impinges on commissioned men residing in a temporal world full of ambiguities. This mind is not simplistic, and it has no ready answers for every problem that arises, but it apprehends two things clearly: that the Christian stance is outward, and that, in imitation of God in Christ, the Christian community must exercise toward all men the love which "seeketh not her own." By this token it is incapable of praising and seeking security above all else. When confronted by some proposal this mind does not ask whether its adoption would be safe, but only whether it would move the church outward in saving action. Of any program, policy, or venture it asks only this: Is it divinely enjoined, and is it calculated to further the aims of the world-wide Kingdom? If the answer is affirmative, then any consideration of personal or ecclesiastical safety is to it irrelevant; the project must in any case be undertaken.

The positive mind proclaims that we are called to obedience only, and that obedience often puts us in places where the going is rough and where the dangers are both real and frightening. But, it declares, no fearful anticipation of the hazards of the way may be permitted to deter us, nor may actual exposure to dire threats move us to seek asylum and retreat. It is in the world that the Christian has his task, and though he may and should in relative isolation commit to heart the divine directives and attend to the procurement of his other furnishings, he may never build walls which shut him out from where his duty lies, or raise gates which impede his service to a lost and needful world. Nor may he out of apprehension set up extra-biblical rules and regulations which deny grown men legitimate access to that world for purposes of enjoyment and appreciation, for grace is there as well as sin, and the gifts of grace are waiting to be thankfully accepted no less than the effects of sin are awaiting expiation and removal.

*   *   *   *   *

What has been said about the relation of the positive mind to that of safety holds, with variations, of its relation to the mind of militancy. Against this mind, as against its near kin, the positive mind directs no simple negation that leaves out of account the truth here apprehended. It acknowledges the partial insights militancy possesses and it itself includes these in the interest of wholeness. But the insights are merely partial nevertheless, and in their isolation they can fashion no acceptable perspective. Unattended as they are by complementary awarenesses, they impart to the mind of militancy an imbalance no less unfortunate than the one we have already had occasion to deplore. The eccentricity of militancy is different from that of safety— instead of flight it advocates attack; but the cause of the eccentricity is the same—the world is contemplated as primarily a threat. When the world appears in this guise, flight or attack is reasonable, of course, and of the two, attack would appear to be the more manly and courageous; but that the world is only, or even chiefly, a peril, requiring nothing so much as assault, is hardly a Christian affirmation, and the positive mind cannot bring itself to make it. "Attack" is something to which it can not give a central place.

What the mind of militancy correctly apprehends is that evil exists and that evil needs uprooting. If it proclaimed no more than this no one could quarrel with it, least of all a Christian whose canon and whose creed makes the knowledge of sin a first requirement and its extirpation a continuing duty. The positive mind, accordingly, does not here demur. On the contrary, it is most deeply conscious of the fact that sin is not of God, that it has no title to existence, that it deserves nothing but annihilation, and that Christians must ferret it out of every hiding place and summarily destroy it. The positive mind, therefore, is far from disparaging all negativity; in a fallen world it is necessary to say "No!," and no one has ever said it more awesomely than the Holy God himself when at Calvary he delivered his well-beloved Son to death and hell. In imitation of him the positive mind is properly iconoclastic. It legitimatizes wrath, authorizes war, mounts offensives, utters condemnations, makes rejections, delivers judgments, sanctions debate, sponsors polemics, and in general encourages every Christian effort to rid the world of ignorance and perversity. By the same token it repudiates the spurious irenicism which cries peace when there is no peace, which appears incapable of indignation, and which is disposed to tolerate error, injustice, oppression, vice, and every other evil. Such an irenicism has no place in the Kingdom of Peace; there is no love in it, neither love of God nor love of man.

It was necessary to say this with maximum force and clarity, for there appears to be a feeling in some quarters that the advocacy of love and positivity and the repudiation of a militant mentality commits one to spiritual pacifism and is consonant with nothing but callous indifference to evil and easy indulgence of wrong. Nothing is, of course, farther from the truth. Love has in it a flaming jealousy not unlike that by which God maintains his deity, and love brooks no profanation of the holy, no subversion of the good, no violation of the right.

But all this adds up to something less than the militancy that would attack the world and deliver it to destruction. However obligatory it may be to declare total war on abstract evil, there is no call to declare such a war on the concrete evil world. To that world no unqualified "No!" can be addressed; a completely negative stance in relation to it is christianly impossible. There are at least three reasons for this—reasons philosophical, theological, and religious.

The philosophical reason is that the world, simply because it is a creature, has its own inherent and inalienable goodness. No fall, however radical, can dispossess it of this divine conferment; no evil that infects it can destroy

its God-determined structure. Evil, in fact, presupposes this good endow-
ment and could not exist without it. Since evil is not referable to the Author
of all being, it has no proper being of its own. It is no more than adjectival,
modifying while never becoming part of the substance of the world. It never
appears in isolation, but always in conjunction with some good, upon which
it feeds, and without which it would simply cease to be. It is parasitic. It
depends for whatever reality it has upon that which God has made and
which, because he made it, he continues to affirm. This world-directed
affirmation, uncanceled by sin and the very ground of sin's possibility, no
Christian may fail to echo, lest he be guilty of disparaging God's handiwork. Philosophical considerations alone, therefore, make impossible an attitude of unqualified negativity; they encourage positivity by pointing unmis-
takably to a worldly goodness which needs recognition, restoration, and
embracement.

So, too, do the well-known theological doctrines of general revelation,
common grace, and the universal operation of the Holy Spirit. These are
distinguishable doctrines and have severally their own peculiar bearing on
our problem, but all alike enforce the need for complementing the bare "No!"
of simplistic militancy with the "Yes!" and "No?" of the positive Christian
mind. Alongside the worthwhileness and stability that creation and providence gives to cosmic being are the many good gifts that common grace
bestows. It will not do to disparage this grace, however short it falls of
effecting inner renewal, for it is God's, and it fills the earth with many things
to appreciate and enjoy. Its presence and operation keeps the world from
being burdened with the extremest outworkings of man's radical perversity;
it enables society to establish a tolerably just order in which men of every
faith can live their common life; and it preserves that solidarity of mankind
that makes possible the association of Christian and non-Christian in all sorts
of cultural enterprises. The undoubted truth and vast importance of the
antithesis must not be allowed to obscure these facts and entice the Christian
to go out and wage undiscriminating war upon the world. The doctrine of the
antithesis needs always to be complemented by that of common grace,
and—to silence all cavil let it be said with utmost clarity—the doctrine of
common grace needs always to be attended by that of the antithesis. Neither
one in isolation can fashion a Christian perspective on the world; each must
internally qualify the other. It is the merit of the positive mind that it holds
these two in tension and tolerates, on that account, no absolutisms either of
the right or of the left. In the present context this means that the absolutism
of militancy is quite uncongenial to it.

But the chief reason for the stance of positivity is religious. There is one
all-determining fact—a fact central to the Bible, definitive of Christianity,
and regulative of all approved behavior in and toward the world: the fact that
God is in Christ reconciling the world unto himself. This fact the positive

mind takes with utmost seriousness, allowing it, together with the supporting truths already mentioned, to shape its whole perspective upon mankind. It apprehends not only that the world as God's creation is well and permanently structured and thus never beyond salvaging; not only that it is illumined and enriched by the gifts of universal grace betokening God's general favor; but also and especially that it is so much the object of God's love that for its redemption he gave his only begotten Son. It is this love, which gives and heals, and disdains assault, that is set as a pattern to be followed by all who call upon the name of the Lord. No appeal to the reprobative acts of God, or to the reality of hell, or to the divine sovereignty and justice that mysteriously underlie these things can avail to obscure the centrality of love in God or to compromise the moral necessity we are under to govern our lives by charity to all. Whatever be the prerogative of God it is since Calvary no prerogative of man to waste or destroy anything that God has made, not even under the piously false pretension that we are thereby furthering the plans dictated by the inviolable righteousness of God. Whatever judgment shall be finally passed upon the world, it will be God's judgment and not ours (except by sanctified consent), and it will be in view of man's recalcitrance in the face of overtures to peace; it will be because man spurned the proffered love of God. Love, meanwhile, is the all-controlling word, and it precludes all assaults upon men with a view to their destruction or with intent to hurt or damage their true humanity. Sin and evil as abstract entities remain fair game throughout all time; but since God struck at himself on Golgotha all blows struck by men at other men are irrelevant and proscribed. The battle joined in Christ precludes all further battles, except such as may be permitted by special authorization to the ministers of state. In the sphere of morals and religion there is for sinners one message only: that God is appeased and at war no more. What is therefore proper to God's messengers are beckonings, invitations, overtures to fellowship; and what they are called to are acts of healing, restoration, and reconstruction. It is this that the positive mind affirms in the face of militancy, and, in affirming it, it believes itself fixed at the center of the Gospel.

*   *   *   *   *

When fear of the world is replaced by love for it, when flight and attack are arrested by the impulses of helpfulness and service, when, in short, a stance is taken at the center of the Gospel, then a position is achieved from which the partial insights and relative worths of safety and militancy can be duly appreciated and thankfully embraced. It would seem, accordingly, that it is from this center that all of us in the church should proceed in our effort to attain the wholeness and unity we seek. If we are in any measure separated by differences of emphasis and outlook, there are available in biblical positiv-

ity all the elements required for a fruitful rapprochement, for in its healing
outreach toward a dying world there is both a sword-thrust against whatever
may impede the process of redemption and a protective guardianship of the
Gospel remedies to be administered. To recognize this is to take the first step
toward that oneness which, when achieved, would infuse our fellowship with
such powers as could well revolutionize the world.

Let it be observed, then, that however mistaken the mentality of safety
may be in isolation from the redemptive activity which is the church's central
task, the redemptive activity itself cannot be carried on without due concern
for the offices of piety, the soundness of the redemptive message, the personal purity of its bearers, and the security of the base from whence they go
out to exemplify and bear witness to Christ's healing ministry. This means
concretely that the positive mind, while discouraging all merely mystical
flights to spiritual ivory towers, imposes upon every Christian the obligation
to sometimes turn his back upon the world in order in solitude to face God in
acts of pure devotion. It also means that the positive mind, while encouraging
periodical critical reappraisals of our theological formulas, can give comfort
neither to those who in their enthusiasms to reach out lose their grasp of the
very Christian truth which alone justifies their outreach, nor to those who in
their effort to make the bitter medicine of the Gospel palatable to the taste of
sinful men dilute it to the point where it soothes without restoring. It also
means that the positive mind, while judging no one in respect of meat or
drink and authorizing all to sit with publicans and sinner in the interest of
their redemption, can look only with disfavor on those who conform in heart
and walk to the moral pattern of unredeemed society, thus losing all their
Christian savor. It means, too, that while the gates of the church must always
be open *on the side* of the world, they must never be open *to* the world in such
a way that through the intrusion of a debilitating worldliness the church loses
all power to exert *upon* the world the redemptive influence it was appointed
to exercise. Meanwhile, of course, none of us should be so conservative as to
disallow a valid Christian freedom in relation to inherited ethnic conventions,
nor so fearful of new proposals as to discourage original attempts to make
Christianity relevant to the new and puzzling problems that face the world in
which we live. Yet this latitude, in its turn, should not be taken as allowing
any want of soundness, rectitude, and certainty in the essentials of our faith,
for without these we have nothing at all to say to the world and cannot share
at all in the Christian program of redemption.

Something similar must be said in relation to militancy. However little
justification there may be for making "war" the controlling idea in Christian
morals, and however mistaken and ruinous the militant disposition is when
divorced from redemptive purposes, these purposes themselves can hardly be
pursued without employing tools, techniques, and tactics which in some
sense do "destroy." The stratagems of salvation do require the application of

a knife to the diseased parts of the world; and they do require the overthrow-
ing of every stronghold raised against the Lord. We shall have to be prepared,
therefore, to make incisions that may hurt, and to conduct assaults which
may discomfit. No mistakenly romantic notion of what love is and no sentimental squeamishness may here deter us. The world being what it is, the
healing ministry cannot dispense with surgery and the goals of peace cannot
be reached without deflating pride, pricking pretension, and wearing down
the stubborn will in ways which do not usually "please" the object of our
solicitude and care. But this cannot be helped; the job must be undertaken.
Of course, it is unchristian to *like* the job. Christians do not want to hurt.
They detest war and conduct it with great reluctance. If, therefore, they see a
fellow Christian who delights to stand in the panoply of battle, who relishes
the fight and daily sallies forth to see with whom he may cross swords, they
will know that this is a deluded Christian wanting in the meekness and
humility of the Master. Yet, when all is said and done, there is ample room in
Christian positivity for unpleasant and regrettable surgical operations serviceable to health and restoration.

23

On Church Leadership

A FEATURE of the times is the call for leadership that is heard on every side. The citizen is calling for leadership in the affairs of state, the parent is calling for it in the schools, and the believer is calling for it in the church.

The mere fact that the call is issued is not in itself a commentary on the uniqueness of the times. The call has been issued before. The demand for leadership is perennial. Our fathers called for it in their generation, and our children will call for it in theirs. This is because genuine leadership is hard to come by, and therefore rare, and because new times always require new instances of it. Being the thing it is, no one is likely at any time to think there is enough of it. The call for it will therefore continue to be made so long as time goes on.

Of course, the call for leadership is not equally urgent in every age. Sometimes the call is extraordinarily loud and insistent. Ours seems to be such a time. There is a widespread feeling that in certain important areas of our corporate life—in politics, for example—leadership is either entirely lacking or dangerously misdirected. In other areas, such as education, it is held to be either confused or wanting in vigor and militancy. And because such a state of affairs is rightly held to be intolerable, the call for leadership goes out.

It goes out not only in the state and school, but also in the church. Our people have been heard to issue such a call. You and I have joined them on occasion. It is true, our call was much less critical than plaintive. But the

This essay first appeared in *The Reformed Journal*, March 1951.

point is that we called. We felt, no doubt, and still feel, that since there are exceptionally great dangers threatening us today, and since there are exceptionally important goals to be achieved before our opportunities run out, the need for wise and vigorous leadership is at present exceptionally acute. And so we called.

For this we deserve no blame, but praise—provided, that is, that we understood what it was we were calling for. The fact is that people who call for leadership are by no means agreed as to what it is they want; and I suggest that you and I owe it to ourselves and to our God to inquire what it is we understand by leadership before we issue our call again.

* * * * *

When the Christian calls for leadership he certainly does not wish to be understood as calling for dictatorship. He wants to be led, but it is not in chains that he wants to be led. He wants no halter on his neck, no blinkers on his mind, no muzzle on his mouth. He wants no leadership by constraint and fear, none that lies beyond the reach of his criticism and amendment. He does not want this because he is a man, and because as a man he stands upon his dignity. He does not want this because he is a Christian, and because as a Christian he cannot put his heart in pawn to any man.

The fact is that the dictator has no rightful place anywhere, least of all in the Christian community. He has no place there not merely because considerations of comfort and self-esteem rule him out, but because Christianity itself has no place in its scheme for such a man. The Christian community is a committed community. It is made up of men and women who have surrendered their wills to Christ, and have no will remaining to yield to any other. They have their Master, and can own no other. They must therefore proclaim their freedom and independence from any man who would lay an absolute claim upon their allegiance. They cannot recognize among their fellows any lords and masters. It is an axiom to them that no man or group of men may be allowed to tyrannize Christ's body.

When the Christian calls for leadership, therefore, he does not want a Hitler to respond, nor a Mussolini or a Stalin, nor indeed a Pope. He is not asking for a Führer. A Führer is a man whose will supplants and negates our own. To acknowledge him is to empty ourselves of our humanity. But more than that, it is to forget that our wills are already captive to the Lord.

The only leader a Christian can acknowledge is one who recognizes that Christians, by virtue of their Christianity, have a momentum and direction of their own, and are unwilling to be deflected from their course. The only leader a Christian can follow in the deepest things of life is one who travels with him in the Way. In important things the Christian will defer to no man who does not stand committed with him to a common Master, who does not kneel as low as he before a common Maker. When we Christians ask for leadership, therefore, we are asking first of all for a fellow servant of the Christ, and then, since all are one in Christ, for a man who on that account is sensitive to the massive and historic will of the Christian community he leads. We are asking, too, for one who is not above consulting us as brothers in one communion, who recognizes and respects the range of private judgment, and who is always prepared to submit his thoughts and programs for our scrutiny and critical evaluation.

* * * * *

We do not want a leader who imposes his will upon us from without. But neither do we want a leader who recognizes no will but our own. We do not want a leader who tyrannizes us. But neither do we want a leader who is merely concerned to obey us.

This may appear obvious, yet in practice the call for leadership is often nothing more than the call for obedience and submission. People choose a political leader and then demand of him that he do nothing but reflect the variegated and often conflicting opinions and interests of his constituency. They ask that he be in all particulars subservient to their wishes, that he entertain and express no ideas they do not fully share, that he be a kind of puppet who has no mind and will that can be called his own. The call for such a man is not a call for a leader, but for a follower.

When we call for leadership in church and school, it is surely not for this we call. We are not asking, when we ask for leaders, for men concerned only to confirm us in our prejudices. Perhaps a teacher does not share your racial attitudes. You may like to discuss the matter with him but you do not question his leadership on that account alone. It is not the function of a leader to find new and better grounds for the private or provincial view we hold. His function is to discover the truth, and in the process he may well uncover grounds for discrediting our views. It will not do for us to call for leadership and then demand that our leaders merely echo our own frequently untutored sentiments. No man is our leader if, merely in deference to us, he reinforces the status quo, avoids saying anything that may discomfit us, or leaves us in undisturbed possession of our sinful smugness.

The leader we want is one who represents not our narrower but our bigger self. We want one who, because he is united with us in Christ, knows the elemental impulses of our heart, and who dares, in order to give them scope, to disabuse us of whatever obstructs their wholesome exercise. We want a man who has the courage to shift at some points our wonted perspectives. We want a man who will voice our ideals and not our actualities, who will represent our better self and not our worse. We want, in short, a man who knows better than ourselves what we should want, who will exhibit for us the implications of our most basic faith, who will lead us by the bright attractiveness of the high goals he delineates away from our merely common and familiar attachments. And we want a man who will not hesitate in the process to burst the bubbles of our pride and to reveal the emptiness of our conventional formulas and clichés. With such a man we can go forward.

* * * * *

It may be said then that when we call for leadership what we want is neither a dictator nor a follower. The former stands superior and detached, and in his detachment cannot win our inner confidence and loyalty. The latter sinks into subservience and on that account can effect no improvement. When we call for leadership what we want is men who are able to draw us to a point beyond the one we now occupy, and yet never loose their grip upon our hand or their hold upon our heart.

A leader is no leader unless, turning his back upon the actual, he strikes out for and delineates the ideal. He is no leader unless he has courage to move into uncharted paths and venture into unmapped areas. He is no leader unless he is in the van, in advance of those who have called him and singled him out for leadership. To deny this—to deny a leader the privilege of having visions, to deny him the right to criticize the status quo, to insist that he do nothing and say nothing that has not always been said and done—is not to have a leader, but at best a propagandist, and is not to advance but to stultify.

On the other hand, a leader is no leader if he does not remain in the closest possible touch with those it is his privilege to guide. He must share their deepest convictions, stand with them within the framework of their most basic commitments. That means, if he is to be a leader of the Christian community, that he must stand with all who look to him for guidance upon the single foundation of the Christ. If he is to lead, and not mislead, he must tie himself to God, and to the sense of God that resides in the Spirit-filled community of Christ. From this he may never wander; it is only in this that he may advance.

* * * * *

We will get the kind of leadership we are worthy of, the kind of leadership we are willing to pay the price for. The call for leadership, when we issue it, is a call and challenge to a man bigger and better than ourselves, but it also lays upon us an obligation to recognize him when he appears. The sign of him will be that he will not always leave us in our comfortable conceits. But if we are wise we will look more closely before we take offense at him. We will look to discover whether he speaks not in his own name, but in that of his Master and our own. We will seek to discover in what he says the accents of the Lord. And when we discover it we will follow him in the growing realization that it is not really this man we follow but Him who is the Way.

24

Tradition and the Church

I MET A LADY the other day who told me she was a Daughter of the American Revolution. One of her ancestors, she said, had fought at Bunker Hill and wintered with Washington at Valley Forge.

I distinctly remember her words, but it was not these that impressed me at the time: it was her manner. She spoke with feeling and animation, and with considerable pride. She wasn't arrogant. She did not boast or patronize. She merely reported. But it was plain that the thing she reported made a difference in her life. When she spoke of it she held her head erect. It seemed to give her strength, and poise, and presence.

I thought about this as I drove home, and wondered whether a sense of the past and of one's rootage in it always made a difference of this kind. I concluded that it did.

It is from the past, I reflected, that we get important knowledge about ourselves. From it we discover something of our identity and meaning. It was by consulting the past that the lady of my acquaintance discovered her lineage. She thereby found her place in the succession of generations; she thereby located, identified herself. And in and with that identification she acquired meaning. It is true that the identification was made in narrow genealogical rather than in broad historical terms, but at least an identification was made, and that for her was gain. She had found her "place."

But more than that, she had entered into an association. You could tell:

This essay first appeared in *The Reformed Journal,* December 1951.

she knew she "belonged." She belonged to something bigger and more important than herself. She belonged to a family. She had identified herself with a group, and in thus transcending her own individuality she had grown in significance. This happens whenever an individual reaches back into the past and appropriates a tradition. He becomes a member of an historical community whose larger life increases his stature. He finds his context. He takes his place in an environing whole, by which he is defined, sustained, and disciplined. He enters into a fellowship that strengthens and inspires.

* * * * *

The Jew is a case in point. Into him as into few others the past has entered as a defining element. And it has made him formidable.

The Jew finds his roots not in a family merely, but in a race. The pride of race is strong in him, and the strength of race has gone into him. This is why he has been able to stand up under the fearful bludgeonings of the last two thousand years. He has been ghettoed, beaten, and burned, but he has not died. This is because in the critical hour he has been able to remind himself that he is Abraham's child and of the prophets' lineage.

In many countries, particularly those of Eastern Europe, the Jew does not "belong": he is without rank or privilege. But, of course, he does "belong": he belongs to his own. And he is not only supported, he is constituted, by that to which he belongs. He is a Jew by virtue of it. What makes him what he is is his anchorage in the past, his rootage in his tradition, his oneness with his fathers. This gives him identity. This gives him meaning and significance. This makes him a person to be reckoned with.

* * * * *

If we are to be strong we must do what the Jew does, and what the lady did of whom I spoke: we must find our context and take our place within it; we must discover and appropriate our past; we must establish ourselves in our tradition.

Everything depends, of course, on what we regard as our context, our past, our tradition. If we conceive these narrowly, we will not expand; if we fail to understand ourselves, we will conceive these narrowly.

We conceive our past too narrowly when, like the lady I mentioned, we restrict it to a family. There is no harm in tracing one's pedigree, and it may have its advantages, but we are a great deal more than members of a clan, and we will never find our whole self by looking into our ancestry. It is not family history that constitutes and defines us. We are more than Vandermas and Murphys, and we need more to feed on than genealogies.

The Jew knows that. He doesn't pride himself on being a Finkelstein; he prides himself on being a Jew. It is not a family he roots in; it is a race. And he is stronger for it. But even he is narrow, for a man is more than a member of a race or nation. It is not as a Hollander or as a Pole, nor as a Caucasian, Negro, or Jew that a man is ultimately significant.

I am far from disparaging either race or state. You are an American. America produced you. Its ideals inspire you, its institutions form you, its fortunes affect you. Without the whole context which is America, without the tradition which is America, you would not be the man you are. But yet the term "American" does not define you. You are more than an American, just as you are more than a Vanderma. You are a Christian. That is your name. It defines you.

* * * * *

To be a Christian means to belong to a group, to be a member of a community. The name of that group is church, the community of believers.

I know; the Christian has two dimensions. He moves on a vertical as well as a horizontal plane, and the vertical is first. In that reference he is pointed to heaven and the supernatural. In view of it he is defined as a man in touch with God. But he also moves on the horizontal plane, and in this reference he embraces the historical. In view of it he holds communion with a people recruited from all times and places. To be a Christian is to be in fellowship with God; but also, it is to be in fellowship with those in every age who have fellowship with God; it is to be in relation to that vast fraternity, the church.

The church, then, is the historical context in which we Christians stand. It gives us our identity, our name, our meaning. I am speaking, of course, of the one church as it is spread out gloriously through all space and time. I am speaking of that company which includes Seth and Noah, Abraham and Moses, David and Jeremiah, Peter and Paul, Tertullian and Luther, and those many millions more to whom the grace of God has come. Of this company we who call ourselves Christians are members. To this company we belong. This is our milieu. To this our entire life is oriented. From this we draw strength and inspiration. In view of this we are proud and hold our head erect.—Or is this not so?

* * * * *

Are we perhaps not proud? Do we perhaps go with head hung low, with apologetic gait and abject demeanor? Do we perhaps live in this world as if we had no past, no history, no tradition? Do we perhaps live as aliens in the world, as though we did not "belong"?

If so, we had better recollect that the church we are members of is in the world. It is on earth. It is a fraternity existing in time; it is an historical magnitude moving on the horizontal plane. It is as actual and concrete as a family, a race, or a nation.

Having reminded ourselves of this we may observe that it is more important, more illustrious, older, and stronger than any of the other communities, groups, or associations that exist on earth. This community rode out the flood, despoiled the Egyptians, penned the psalms, stopped the mouths of lions, raised up the gothic cathedrals, laid the foundations of modern states, abolished slavery, wrote the world's best lyrics... "and what shall I say more? for the time will fail me if I tell of Gideon, Barak, Samson, Jephthah; of David and Samuel and the prophets"; of Athanasius and Constantine and Cyprian; of Augustine, Charlemagne, and Gregory; of Bernard and Thomas and Dante; of Calvin and Milton and Cromwell. . . .

This is no little thing. This is no petty tradition. We have no hollow past. The context we stand in is not narrow and bare. And since this is what we belong to, we dare not be timid. Surely no man who has gotten into this can cower. Does the lady say her ancestor fought at Bunker Hill? Mine climbed the broken walls of Jericho. Does the Jew call Abraham his father? I claim him first: it is not as a Jew that Abraham is significant, but as a believer: and I am Abraham's child.

As Christians, then, we can be done with the abject and servile attitude. One is our Lord, and before him we bow; but for our faith, for our church, we make no apologies to men. We are a kingly race, a royal priesthood, a chosen people. God made us this, and there can be no boasting; but there can be recognition and gratitude. And there can be the uplifted head, and the steady hands, and the unwavering knees, and the bold and forthright witness.

*   *   *   *   *

It is one thing to be proud of that to which we belong; it is another to be disciplined by it; and the last is what is required. It is in this history, this tradition, that we stand; it is the context of our lives. This being so, we must let it define and form us. We must allow it to pour its strength into us. It is only so that we shall acquire depth and scope, stability and direction. It is only so that we shall become mature. It is only so that we shall become Christians in the fullest sense of the word.

Part VI

EDUCATION

25

Note to a College Freshman

YOU HAVE COME to college and you have taken a mind with you. Notice that I said mind, and not brain or intellect. Mind is as different from brain as soul is from body, and it is as different from intellect as whole is from part. Mind is intellect, will, and feeling fused into one. Mind is what you are on the deeper level of your being. It is the spiritual measure and size of you, the conscious center and core of you. It is you at the point where you most centrally confront the world. Mind sets your perspectives, determines your judgments, dictates your loyalties. It defines you.

The mind that is in you as you enter college is the product of many historical forces and influences. Not all of these, when they played on you, were under your direction and control. Yet many of them operated with your consent and under your active governance. This means that you have been an agent in the making of the mind you have. For its present set and temper you must, in consequence, accept the responsibility. And you must accept the same responsibility for its future form and texture.

It is, I suppose, because you realize this that you have come to college. You have come, I like to believe, because you want deliberately to expose your mind to the liberalizing and formative influences that a college is meant to generate and release. You want, with the assistance of others, to shape your mind after the best and most enduring pattern that exists. And you

This essay first appeared in *The Reformed Journal,* September 1952; the response to its criticism appeared in the April 1953 issue.

want to know the size and contours of that pattern. You want to know the character and dimensions of the ideal mind.

I must say that for the attainment of your purpose you could not have come to a better place than college. It is the business of a college to acquaint you with the ideal mind and to shape you into its likeness. It is the business, that is, of a good college, a liberal arts college, a Christian college. If you have enrolled in one of that sort you have set your foot on the way to your goal. What progress you make will depend, of course, on how well you travel.

*   *   *   *   *

The first thing you will be asked to do is to abandon whatever you have retained of the sophistic mind. The sophistic mind is the mind that is no broader or deeper than the individual self. It is the mind of sheer subjectivity. The Sophists of ancient Greece believed this to be the only kind of mind a man could desire or achieve. They thought of man as a mere particular. In consequence, the mind they sought to cultivate was one able to express no more than the provincialisms, the idiosyncrasies, the incommunicable and unshared tastes of the isolated self. Insulated against all contact with other selves, confined within the narrow limits of the private individual, utterly without range and scope, this wizened and constricted mind was barren, its only knowledge being information about its own petty and passing moods.

The ancient Sophists have long since died, but their spirit lives on in raw and undisciplined persons. It comes to expression whenever a man sets up his private opinion as the standard of truth or allows whim and impulse to determine action. It is found in every man who thinks of his particular self as the center of the world and regards his own opinions as the measure of the real.

If this mind, or any part of it, is in you, it must be eradicated. It must be replaced by that broader mind that lifts you out of your privacy and identifies you with mankind.

*   *   *   *   *

This more acceptable kind of mind was in ancient times delineated and recommended by Plato, the arch opponent of the Sophists. It has since been celebrated by every humanist who succeeded him. The mind I am speaking of is the universal, the shared, the common, the human mind. You have it potentially within you, for you are in fact more than this or that particular individual strictly as such; you are a human being, sharing with your fellows a common nature, and residing with them under an objective and universally binding law of righteousness and truth.

In consequence your cultural and formative task consists, in part at least, in transcending the merely particular and attaining the universal. Being what you are, you are obliged to negate the individuality defined as ultimate in order from the vantage point of a more inclusive humanity to rediscover it as relative. You must leave behind the subjectivity of your narrow self and reach out for the broader mind of man. It is the purpose of a liberal—that is, a liberalizing—education to form this mind in you, to enlarge the cramped perspective of your cabined self, and make you kin to the large-minded men who have created our art and science and become the teachers of the race. With this mind in you, you can enter appreciatively into the thought and labors of the Platos, the Goethes, the Shakespeares, the Michelangelos, and the Beethovens of our rich cultural tradition, and attain in some measure to the dignity and freedom of disciplined man.

*   *   *   *   *

But there is a higher level of education still, and another mind to be attained. It is not your own mind in its sheer particularity that you want. You want your own mind indeed, but only as it somehow shares in the common human mind. But also, it is not merely the mind of man you want. It, too, must be transcended if you are to achieve your ultimate range and scope. You must attain the mind of Christ.

Just as the movement from the first mind to the second was not a mere negation of the first, but an enrichment and enlargement of it (a finding of it through losing it), so the movement from the second to the third does not involve the abandonment of the second, but the inclusion of it within a larger perspective, a subordination of it to a higher, indeed, the highest, the ultimate rationality. To be truly educated, to be completely liberated, to be wholly enlightened, is to share in Christ the thoughts of God and thus to transcend the relativity not only of the subjective but also of the merely human. To understand ourselves, to understand the world, to truly and fundamentally understand anything at all, we must take up position neither in the individual nor in the race, neither in sophistic intelligence nor in human rationality, but in the Truth himself, which is what is meant by taking on the mind of Christ.

It is with difficulty that a person shakes off the confining chains of his own discrete individuality. Also it is only after years of discipline and training that he sustains over any considerable period that objectivity and universality which is the mark of the educated man. It is even more difficult to attain the mind of Christ. Indeed, strictly speaking, one cannot attain to it at all. It is in the first instance a miracle and a gift, and only secondarily an achievement and possession. But without it no man is educated, just as without it no man is saved.

Here, then, is the goal of education: to be shaped by the Word and Spirit and the whole of God's creation into conformity with the mind of

Christ, to be fashioned anew in the image and likeness of God. Unless this goal is reached nothing is reached but failure, and nothing lies ahead but judgment. Let then this mind be in you which was also in Christ Jesus.

APPENDIX

Toward Better Understanding: A Reply to my Critics

Some time ago I wrote a note to a college freshman. I expected no comment on it—good or bad. It was a little thing, occupying scarcely a page and a half in the Journal. And it was a simple thing, expressing a commonplace idea. It had passed, I thought, like most transient pieces, into oblivion.

But five months after its publication you wrote in your magazine a *Note to a Seminary Professor* recalling my piece. It was a long note, like an extended letter. It was a public note, like an open letter. And it was critical of what I had written to the freshman. This is my reply.

*　*　*　*　*

Analysis reveals that you are occupied in your letter with two related but distinguishable things. The first, and most obvious, is my *Note*. The second, and most important, is my *philosophy*.

Though they are related, these two are not the same. The *Note* is a writing; the philosophy is a view of things. The *Note* is a single utterance; the philosophy, in its articulated form, is the sum of many utterances. The *Note* is a surface expression; the philosophy is an underlying creed.

There is some evidence in your letter that you recognize this difference and that you wish to honor it. There is some evidence that you wish to distinguish between my particular and transient *Note* and my general and enduring philosophy. There is some indication that you wish to attack my writing and not my creed. "We hope," you say, "that our readers will not interpret our discussion as an attack on Dr. Stob's orthodoxy. We are simply debating the merits of one piece of writing in which Dr. Stob has given what we regard as a very faulty presentation of a highly important matter." Elsewhere you put rhetorical questions which enforce this statement of limited intent. "Does not such writing call for... ?" you ask. "Why then is the argument not constructed so that... ?" It would appear from this that the Christian character of my philosophy is not at issue. It would appear that the only thing you are concerned to challenge is the adequacy of my expression.

Yet one need not go very far into your letter to discover that the *phrasing* of my *Note* is not your chief concern. Your main complaint is against my views. You wish to "debate" with me. It is not questions of terminology and structure that you wish to debate. It is not the limitations of my composition that offend you. You hold "high respect" for me as a writer. You believe that in my *Note* I "have set up a line of thought that is fairly clear and definitive, even though briefly done." What offends you is my ideas. You think there is a "basic difference of opinion" that divides us. It is "matters of principle" that you wish to debate with me. You are "jealous for the accuracy" of my "opinions" and feel yourself under solemn compulsion to "take issue" with them. As against the views I hold you wish to present "a sounder point of view in Christian higher education."

This leaves me in something of a quandary. It leaves me wondering what complaint it is I am expected to reply to. I am puzzled to know whether you wish to acknowledge or to dispute the structural adequacy of my *Note*; whether you wish to affirm or deny the basic soundness of my philosophy. In two statements of intent you say two different things. You say that my writing is inept, and yet that it is definitive. You say that I am orthodox, but indicate that I am on the wrong side of the most important question facing the church today. You suggest that I am guilty of misstating the sound conceptions I possess—and that my conceptions are unsound. You suggest that my *Note* is a misleading presentation of the truth I own, and that, on the contrary, it is a clear account of a basic error I embrace.

This circumstance compels me to do not merely the one thing that might otherwise be required. It compels me to do two things. It compels me to exegete my *Note*, and also to state once more the basic elements in my view of education. I shall try in what follows to do both as plainly as I can. It will be done, of course, against the background of your expressed critique.

* * * * *

First, then, my view of education:

1. I hold that the natural man has not the mind of Christ (cf. I Cor. 2), and that between the natural man and the Christian there exists a basic and inexpungible *antithesis* that divides them at the root, and separates them into two fundamentally incompatible, radically different, and mutually hostile kingdoms, the Kingdom of God and the kingdom of the world.

2. I hold that entrance into God's Kingdom is solely by a miracle of *grace*, and that it is effected by a divine regenerative act apart from education, in accordance with the redemptive love of God revealed in Jesus Christ.

3. I hold that a person, of whatever age or education, upon whom this miracle of grace has been performed, is Christ's, and that he has in principle the *mind of Christ*; that he has this mind in a moral and religious, not in a metaphysical sense involving identity with God; and that this mind is both a gift conferred and an ideal to be attained, according to the apostle's teaching:

"So then, my beloved, . . . work out your own salvation with fear and trembling; for it is God who worketh in you both to will and to work. . . ."

4. I hold that the believer stands in a *covenantal* relationship to God, in accordance with which both he and his children are "received unto grace in Christ," God the Father in holy baptism witnessing and sealing unto them that he adopts them "for his children and heirs."

5. I hold that a Christian college exists to educate *these covenant children* and to establish them in their commitment to the Christ.

6. I hold that education is a *process* in which the student's potentialities are progressively actualized, a process in which a student increasingly becomes what he essentially is; and that, accordingly, the aim of all instruction at a Christian college is to bring to fullest flower the mind of Christ that the student both in principle possesses and through God's sanctifying Spirit must achieve.

7. I hold that the process of education in a Christian college must be *governed from start to finish* by Christian principles; that all things must be seen and known with and by the mind of Christ; and that neither teacher nor student, in giving or receiving instruction, may ever at any juncture betray this mind by forsaking the Christian foundations upon which by grace they are established.

8. I hold that the process of education and sanctification is *never complete*, and that since sin remains in us until we die, the new heart is never *in actuality* the sole determinant of our thought and action.

9. I hold that God, through his general revelation, the general witness of his Spirit, and the restraining influences of his common grace, enables the non-Christian to discover and disclose *facts* and complexes of fact which the Christian may and must use as constitutive elements in a Christian science of reality.

10. I hold that the Christian educator, in his effort to fashion the student's mind, must utilize the materials provided by *both special and general* revelation; and that the Christian student should be formed and informed not only by the Word and Spirit, but also by the funded wisdom and experience of the race, the two operating always in indissoluble *union*, a union in which the Word is the sovereign norm and corrective.

11. I hold that Christian education, in the process of forming in the Christian student the Christian mind he already in principle possesses, does not destroy but redeems his manhood and, by making him a man in Christ, *humanizes* him as no non-Christian education can.

12. I hold that Christian education must be both education and Christian. To be *Christian* it must be based upon the Christ and be in its whole extent pervaded by his Spirit. To be *education* it must fashion a student into a whole man completely furnished for every good work.

These principles have governed whatever I have written on Christian education. They governed the addresses to which you make favorable reference. They governed no less my *Note* to a college freshman. It was squarely upon the basis formed by them that the *Note* was laid.

*   *   *   *   *

My *Note* was addressed to a freshman—to a Christian freshman on his way into a Christian college. It was concerned with education—with the process of forming and shaping students. And it focused attention on the entity which undergoes the educational process—the self, or mind.

Since "mind" is prominent in the *Note,* and the subject of some misunderstanding, I perhaps should indicate again how I employ the term. I employ it to designate that which lies neither on the surface nor on the deepest level of our being.

On the surface of our being lie our bodies, our feelings, our manners, and our overt judgments. At the root of our being lies our heart. Neither the one nor the other of these do I consider the proper object of educational forming. An education concerned merely to modify the surface aspects of our life—to give health to our bodies, dexterity to our hands, form to our manners, precision to our speech—would be a shallow education. An education concerned to modify the root of our being—to alter, form, and shape the heart—would be an impious and impossible undertaking.

The direct or proper "object" of education is the mind. It lies, not indeed on the deepest, but yet on the deeper level of our existence. Itself subject to the direction of the heart, it, in its turn, directs our judgments and volitions. Less basic than the heart, from which it derives its fundamental cast and direction, it is fuller and more basic than the intellect, since intellect, will, and feeling are included in it.

I find you representing me as using the term mind "very much as the Bible uses the term heart," and, what is even more strange, commending me for such usage. I don't use "mind" as a synonym for "heart." Mind and heart are, in my judgment, two distinct things, which ought not to be confused.

The heart is the religious ground of our being; it lies below the threshold of our consciousness; it functions on a transcendental level of our existence; it cannot be altered by an activity of man, and it undergoes no process of development as such; it cannot be educated; when changed it is changed in an instant through the miracle of regeneration; it determines but is not determined by our choice and decisions.—About the heart no man may say what I said about the freshman's mind—that it is the product of many historical forces and influences, that he has been an agent in the making of it, that he must expose it to the formative influences that a college is meant to generate and release.

The mind, unlike the heart, can be altered or improved by taking care.

The mind is, as I told the freshman, the *actual you*, in distinction from what you are in principle and promise. It is you in your concrete existence. It is you in your empirical totality. It is you with all your modifiable thoughts, imaginings, attitudes, and desires. It is you as you stand in history, affecting and being affected by the various influences that operate there. It is the variable size and measure of you. It is you where you centrally confront the world. It is the conscious center of you. It is you as you reveal yourself in specific judgments, evaluations, choices. It is what you now or at any time *concretely are*. It is you as educable, alterable, sanctifiable. It is you as made and still unmade, as being and still becoming. It is quite simply you, in your full concrete actuality, and including all your contradictions and consistencies.

* * * * *

The distinction between mind and heart may be seen in the relations they sustain to one another.

The heart, regenerate or apostate, gives the mind its basic "set," but it does not, in this life, completely control the mind. The unregenerate heart, because of common grace, does not come to full expression in the unbeliever's mind. The regenerate heart, because of sin, does not come to full expression in the Christian's mind.

There is an unqualified and absolute antithesis between the regenerate and unregenerate heart. There is not an absolute antithesis between the Christian and the non-Christian "mind." He who is in his heart a Christian, in principle Christ's, may have a mind that embraces egregious error and breathes a reprehensible spirit. He who is in his heart a non-Christian, in principle Satan's, may have a mind that embraces much of truth and breathes a temperate spirit. In the case of both the Christian and non-Christian, the mind, though for different reasons, can be false to the heart.

To avoid all misunderstanding a terminological remark must here be appended. The Christian, whose heart is regenerated by God's Spirit, may be said to have a Christian mind—in principle. He who has a new heart has a new mind—in germ. Sometimes in speech and writing these qualifications are dropped, and we speak of any and all Christians as having a Christian mind. There is no objection to this, provided we remember the elliptical nature of the expression. I myself have used such expressions both in my *Note* and in the twelve-point credo that I set down above. When the expression is used in this way, however, one is compelled to atone for the ellipsis by speaking in paradox. One is compelled to say that the Christian both has and has not the mind of Christ. In speaking of the heart one may not use an expression of this kind. One may never say that a Christian both has and has not a new heart.

* * * * *

My note, as I said, was written to a Christian student. The note concerned the student's education. He had just come to a Christian college. I commended him for this. His choice of schools, I thought, was excellent.

He might have gone to some technical school of secular vintage. I should have regretted that, for technical schools do not educate. They train, they develop skills and techniques, but they do not reach the deeper levels of the student's life. They do not form the mind.

The student might have gone to a secular college of liberal arts. This would have been better, for a college of this kind does educate. It confronts the student, if it is a college of the better sort, with the best that has been thought and said, lifts him out of his narrow conceits, and exposes him to universal knowledge. Had the student applied himself he might have acquired there a broad and disciplined mind. Even so I should have regretted his going, for a secular college does not ordinarily help a student acquire a Christian mind.

It is only at a Christian college that a systematic effort is made to form in the student a Christian mind. And what other mind would a Christian student want? A Christian student, as I reminded the freshman, wants "to shape his mind after the best and most enduring pattern that exists." He wants to acquire the ideal mind. But there is only one way of acquiring that—by being shaped through "the Word and Spirit and the whole of God's creation into conformity with the mind of Christ," by being fashioned anew in the image and likeness of God." It is this kind of forming, this kind of education, that a Christian college, and only a Christian college, undertakes to do.

But it requires doing. The college has to work on the student—and hard. One of the first things it has to teach him is that there is no room in the Christian mind for sophistry. You cannot ever have a Christian mind if, like the ancient Sophists, you lock yourself up in your own little world and indulge your private fancies. Some Christians do that to an alarming degree. We all do that, I fear, more frequently than we should. We "set up our private opinion as the standard of truth and allow whim and impulse to determine action." This is reprehensible. It is the mark of an uneducated man. It is the mark of a frail and immature Christian.

The Christian student must get beyond, transcend his private self. He must enlarge his perspectives. He must become a man. He must become a man because he is one. Each one of us is "more than this or that particular individual strictly as such; we are human beings, sharing with our fellows a common nature (in virtue of which we bear the common name, Man), and residing with them under an objective and universally binding law of righteousness and truth." Even Plato saw this. He saw that man was bigger than the Sophists supposed, and he urged each in his generation and in every generation since, to be a man rather than an isolated self, to be human rather than merely individual, to acquire a universal rather than a private mind. And he was right.

This doesn't mean that we must have Plato's mind. But we can and must adopt Plato's suggestion that the narrow mind of the Sophists "be replaced by that broader mind which lifts us out of our privacy and identifies us with mankind."

We are already identified with mankind, for we are men, but we must enter into our heritage. The Christian college seeks to lead the Christian student into that heritage by acquainting him with those laws—of logic, mathematics, and the like—that hold and operate for every man, and by pouring into him the knowledge concerning the cosmos that the human race has through millenniums acquired and stored up, and that is the common property of all educated men.

There is no one who has better title to that knowledge than the Christian. It is his by right. The non-Christian has this knowledge, combined with much that is false, but not by a law of right. It is borrowed or poached, poached from the Christian universe whose Christian character he is concerned to deny but cannot destroy. Were he correct in his assumption that God is not, or that God is not sovereign, there would be no knowledge at all, least of all for him. But he is not correct in his assumption, and there is knowledge, also for him. In God's great goodness to his people he so directs affairs that unbelieving men are found pouring treasures of knowledge into a coffer, accessible to all, but really owned by Christians only.

I told the freshman to raid that coffer and thus "enlarge the cramped perspective of his cabined self," become "kin to the large minded men who have created our art and science," and attain "in some measure to the dignity and freedom of disciplined man."

But I had more to tell him. He was not to forget that he was a Christian. He was not to spend his time at college becoming human merely; he was to become Christian man. It was not that he should become human first and then Christian. That would be preposterous. He couldn't manage that in any case; and no Christian could possibly propose it. The student should be doing both at once. He should be growing as man and Christian simultaneously—as Christian man. His appropriation and assimilation of knowledge should be Christian assimilation, an assimilation in which facts are shorn of the spurious interpretation put upon them by the non-Christian, and set in a framework differing at the root from that employed by those who are not in Christ. The knowledge and experience he acquires should go to form a Christian mind, a mind governed in all its range by the new heart born of grace. Without that mind, I said, "no man is educated, just as without it no man is saved."

It is possible to look at the world through the narrow aperture of the isolated self, and to find a little bit of truth; the Sophists are there to prove it. It is possible also to look at the world through the broader mind of man, and to see more truth; Plato is there to prove it. But it is only as one is in Christ and it is only in the measure that one looks at the world through the mind his Spirit gives that one attains the whole and steady look and sees things as they truly are. "To understand ourselves, to understand the world, to truly and fundamentally understand anything at all, we must take up position neither in the individual nor in the race, neither in sophistic intelligence nor in human rationality, but in the Truth himself, which is what is meant by taking on the mind of Christ."

This is what I said in my *Note to a College Freshman*. This is what you could have read in it.

26

Academic Freedom at a Christian College

THE QUESTION of academic freedom is currently a very live issue in American university circles. Educators are discussing it avidly. Many of them feel that under the pressures of the times this freedom is being lost or seriously curtailed. The forces of reaction, they think, are hampering free inquiry and action. Whether this is actually so depends, of course, upon what one understands by academic freedom, and I propose to make an elementary analysis of that concept.

We may begin by recalling that there are at least two things that an academic institution is concerned to do. It is concerned to disclose truth, and it is concerned to publish truth. A college must be engaged in research, and it must teach. It must both investigate and disseminate. These two functions are sometimes separated. The one is then assigned to the university, and the other to the college. Expediency seems to require this. In reality, however, the two functions belong together, and they ought to be kept in the closest possible contact. A college, even though it offers no advanced degrees and therefore cannot in strictness be called a university, must perform the university function of research as well as the college function of teaching. And if both are to be real there must be academic freedom: freedom of inquiry for the scholar and freedom of expression for the teacher.—But what are we to understand by freedom?

*   *   *   *   *

This essay first appeared in *The Reformed Journal*, August 1952.

In the Christian view, freedom is at bottom positive in nature; it is freedom *for* something—freedom to obey the norms that structure human existence, freedom to do one's duty, freedom to bow before the imperious claims of God the Lord. This does not mean that the freedom sponsored by the Christian is without a negative element. Precisely because man's freedom is essentially a freedom for something, it is also a freedom from something—a freedom, not indeed from all restraints, but yet a freedom from undue restraints. Just because he is a creature residing under law and ordered to a destiny, man may claim a relative independence. Because he bows before the Lord, he may claim exemption from every kind of worldly enslavement. It is this nice balance between liberty and restraint, freedom and subjection, that is the essence of the Christian conception of liberty.

In modernity this nice balance is not always preserved. In the secular mind freedom tends, indeed, to be thought of almost exclusively in terms of exemption from restraint, absence of commitment, emancipation from presuppositions, and detachment from the a priori. Freedom is generally viewed as freedom *from* something. This negative view dominates public discussions and is the bond of agreement even between disputants. Most pride themselves on being liberated, liberated especially from the domination of religious faith, the dictations of a sacred book, and the bonds of a dogmatic creed.

That this is so could be amply evidenced from the literature. Practical illustration of it is afforded by the events that transpired at the University of Washington some years ago. The president of that institution dismissed a number of prominent professors on the ground that they had Communist Party affiliations. When the news of the dismissals reached the campuses of the land, a great hue and cry went up. The action of the president was loudly denounced as a violation of academic freedom. A university, it was maintained, is a place where every voice must be heard. Education as such is uncommitted to any specific theory or position. It must remain free of entanglements with any economic, social, or religious view, and be hospitable to all. The truth is at no point finally made out. To suppose that it is, is to hamper and restrict free critical inquiry. One must maintain the open, indeterminate mind, and by that token keep a completely open door at college and university. Academic freedom demands this.

The president had to reply to his detractors, and it is interesting to note that though he differed from them in practice, he agreed with them in theory. "True," he said in effect, "a free scholar is an uncommitted scholar, a free school is one that owns no basic faith, a good teacher is one that has an open and undetermined mind on all fundamental questions. The great enemy of freedom is faith, dogma, conviction, commitment. That is why I fired the communists. They are dogmatists, they are doctrinaire, and there is no room for such in an academic institution."

That the president and his critics differed in practical policy is at this juncture of little concern. What is of concern is that they shared a common assumption and adhered to a common philosophy of freedom. Both parties would for that reason be critical of the educational effort carried on at a Christian college. Were they to measure such a college against their definition they would be able to find on all the campus not a wisp of academic freedom. What they would find is scholars and teachers thinking out of a living faith. They would find men and women conducting research and educating students in the light of a divine disclosure set forth in an inspired book. They would find an institution based upon a religious commitment and operating out of a set of basic assumptions. They would discover there a settled mind oriented to an established principle, set upon a firm foundation, and directed toward a fixed end. And they would repudiate the whole business as quite unacademic.

*   *   *   *   *

Well then, that raises the whole question once more: Is there academic freedom at a Christian college? The answer to that question is twofold.

At the level on which the so-called liberal asks it, the answer is yes. There is at such a college not that attenuated and impoverished thing that the secular man mistakes for liberty. Scholars there are not tempted by the spirit of the eighteenth-century Enlightenment to cut themselves loose from their moorings or to remove the ground from under their feet. They claim a liberty that is anchored in the bedrock of the universe, the liberty that sets them free to survey the world *sub specie aeternitatis*. They experience themselves as endowed with the only kind of freedom a human being can possess—the creaturely freedom that is rooted in obedience and which subserves ends posited by One who transcends them infinitely. By this freedom they know themselves to have been released from the subjectivism, the relativism, and the nihilism of the age, and set upon the only course in which true humanness can be achieved.

But, unfortunately, this divinely-conferred freedom is sometimes compromised by members of the church. It happens more often than it should that fellow Christians impose undue restraints upon the college community, and involve it in a spurious heteronomy. Accordingly, when at this level and in this context the question is asked, Is there academic freedom in a Christian college? the answer is, Yes, but it is sometimes unduly taxed by outside forces.

No doubt such an answer can always be given. There is no perfection in this world. There are and always will be accidental and arbitrary restrictions on liberty, even in the best societies. But this is no excuse for their presence. Despite their actuality, arbitrary restrictions are always undesirable, and they are most undesirable in a Christian community, where freedom is held as a sacred possession. Let no one misunderstand. There must be restraint. There must be the quite academic restraint of the truth; not the restraint of some merely amorphous, undefined truth always in process, but the restraint of the truth authoritatively disclosed in the sacred Scriptures. By this the scholars and teachers at a Christian college are bound. And they are bound by another thing. They are bound by the law of love, by the obligation to walk humbly with their God and considerately and self-sacrificially with their fellows. But by nothing else are they bound, and with no other yoke should they be burdened.

They must not be compelled to establish anyone in his private conceits, nor to further the ambitions of any party. They must be free, within the framework of a shared commitment, to come to a conclusion that contravenes the majority opinion, or perchance the opinion of an articulate and militant minority. They must be at liberty to explore new areas of truth, and to do so in their own responsible way. And they must have the same liberty to hold at arm's length new ways of thought, however impatiently presented for adoption. They should, moreover, not have men breathing on their necks and constantly peering over their shoulders. They can't work that way. What they need is trust. They must be free to attack knotty and complex problems in the knowledge that they have the confidence of the church, and they must have the freedom to express and expose to public criticism tentative ideas that may require revision or abandonment. They also need freedom from the weight of custom and from the tyranny of venerable names. What they need, too, is freedom from fear and reprisals. And what they need most of all is freedom from the sting of uninformed prejudice, freedom from name-calling, and freedom from silent but enervating suspicion.

Christian teachers and scholars have together undertaken a great and delicate task. They have undertaken to construe the world in the categories of eternity. It is a terrifyingly responsible task. To discharge it they need the utmost degree of consecration and competence. Doubtless they need watchfulness, too, but it must be the watchfulness of the friend who cares, the watchfulness of the brother that is quick to help. What they need is the loyalty and charity of the like-minded, who are able to provide them with a suitable climate, and to give them elbow room. It is only as they have this room that Christian scholars will be able to perform their demanding tasks.

27

Moral Education

I

EDUCATION is not creative, but cultural. It does not cause anything to be, but only to be in a certain way. God, who creates, calls something into being from nothing; the teacher, who educates, merely modifies already existing being. The stuff of his task is provided. He operates with *givens*.

These givens are never completely indeterminate. They are not merely there, they are there already partly formed—or deformed; and they are there with their characteristic and increated structures, within the limits of which all further forming must take place. They are also there with their own inherent dynamic, to which education can attach, but which it cannot supply. The teacher operates not only with givens, but with *determinate givens*.

Given to the trainer engaged in physical education is the *body*. It is given to him, moreover, not as a congeries of atoms, nor as a lump of protoplasm, but as a living organism. It is with this highly determinate entity that he begins. He takes as a datum the complex thing called body, together with the structure of its parts, the laws of its operation, its characteristic drives, its natural tendency towards maturation, the pattern of its muscular and nervous systems, and the like; and in terms of these and within the boundaries set by these he undertakes to bring it to a peak of efficiency.

In a similar way there is presented for forming to the teacher of truth the

This essay first appeared in *The Reformed Journal*, September 1962.

thing called *intellect*. No teacher of truth has ever had to call an intellect into being. The child is rational at the outset. Given to all instruction is the intellect, together with its native powers of conceiving, judging, and reasoning, and with its immanent though imperfect apprehension of the laws of logic, to which it is inseparably bound. The teacher of truth can impart knowledge because he finds before him a mind prepared beforehand to receive and understand it.

The teacher of morality is similarly favored. He is required to make no one *moral*. The pupil he must teach is already moral, and he is this just as irrevocably as he is physical and rational. Morality is given, and this givenness provides the teacher with both the possibility and the opportunity to develop Christian character in the child.

II

The moral givens are fundamentally two: (1) moral sense or moral reason, sometimes called *conscience;* and (2) *will* or freedom, in the exercise of which a person commits himself to what he apprehends or regards as good.

Moral sensibility or *conscience* is given in and with humanness. By conscience a child distinguishes between good and evil; knows that he is obliged to do what is good and to avoid what is evil; and understands that the doing of evil renders him guilty. These several apprehensions constitute the contact points towards which moral instruction may and should be directed. The teacher of morals should understand that when he speaks to a child of good and evil, obligation and guilt, he is not speaking to him in a language with which the child is unfamiliar. God has been beforehand with the child; he has endowed him with a living sense of all these things; and this sense can never truly die. Through conscience, which can never be blacked out, man is and remains a moral being, amenable until the end to moral education.

The possession of a *will* distinguishes man from members of the lower creation, and his will represents his capacity to commit himself to values, to posit goals in accordance with these values, and to initiate courses of action calculated to achieve these goals.

The will that a child possesses is bound closely to his *conscience*. The two affect each other. The "good" apprehended by conscience appeals to the will for endorsement, and the ends set by the will significantly influence the perceptions of conscience. They also depend upon each other. The will can act only in reference to apprehended "good," and a consciousness of guilt can arise only in a being endowed with will.

Will implies freedom. It is in the freedom of man that responsibility is rooted, and it is man's inexpungible sense of freedom that accounts for his equally inexpungible sense of *responsibility*. The child the teacher must educate does not need to be made responsible. He is responsible, and he knows that he is responsible. His every thought, word, and deed, when not forced out of or upon him by irresistible external constraint, is his *response* to the challenges, the opportunities, and the demands of life as he apprehends and interprets them; and although he may not have the vocabulary to express it, or the wit by analysis to exhibit it, he will nevertheless in the depth of his being know that it was *freely*—i.e., with the consent of his will—that he did and said and thought what he did do and say and think; that he is accountable; and that he is therefore rightly subject to praise or blame, approval or disapproval.

A will therefore is given, and in and with it freedom and responsibility. And conscience is also given. It is on these two givens that the teacher of morality must focus his attention, for only out of them, and by the application to them of appropriate measures, can Christian character emerge.

III

Although the moral givens are positive qualities, constituting man moral and making him susceptible of moral improvement, yet they are *defective*.

There are perhaps three reasons why things are, or are considered to be, defective. Things are considered to be defective either because they are finite, or because they are undeveloped and immature, or because they are sinful.

Finite things, merely because of their finiteness, cannot be really said to be defective. Yet, when compared to the Infinite, a certain kind of imperfection seems to attach to all that is finite. So, for example, man, for no other reason than that he is a creature, cannot comprehend the God who made him. This limitation is native to him, apart from sin, and may, in some relative sense, be regarded as a defect in his being, although strictly speaking it cannot be a defect for a man not to be a God.

A more familiar and a more truly authentic form of imperfection is immaturity. In this sense a child may be said to be a defective man, an acorn a defective oak, and the child's first pencil scrawl a defective writing.

The third form of imperfection—sinfulness—is neither ontological, nor merely tempero-historical, but spiritual and moral. It is radical imperfection and the root of every evil. Although not every kind of relative defect can be referred to it (finitude is certainly possible without sin; and immaturity, it would seem, as well), yet its blight lies over all, and there is nothing in the world of fallen creatures, whether mature or immature, that it has not defaced and made defective.

Among the things it has infected are the conscience and the will, which besides being sinful are, as they appear in children, also finite and unde-veloped. If there are three reasons why things are defective, all three of these apply to the things with which, as givens, the teacher of morality is chiefly concerned—the conscience and the will.

Although the will is directly implicated in whatever good there is in human life and character, yet the will as it appears in the natural man is radically defective, and in God's children it is very far from being what it ought to be.

Nothing save the heart of man, his ego itself, is so determinative of morality as the will. Through the will man commits himself religiously to what he takes as ultimate. This "ultimate," of whatever sort it be—whether it be the true God or some false god like Baal or his modern counterparts—lays hold through the will on the entire life of man and qualifies it in every part, including, of course, the moral.

The most important moral question, then, that any man can ask himself is this: to whom or what am I basically committed, by what ultimate is my will engaged? It is permitted to the will to be engaged by only one ultimate, the only true ultimate—the living God. When thus engaged, the will is fundamentally good, however many and however deep the marks of sin still left upon it. If, however, it is not engaged by the living God, but by some other and spurious god, then it is fundamentally bad, however productive it may seem of human virtue. Apart from regeneration, man's will is in this radical sense simply bad.

This fundamental defect of the will is, of course, a defect that no amount of moral training can remove. The radically disoriented will marks the point at which ethics must surrender to religion, and human efforts must make way for supernatural grace. The most that moral education can do for a man whose will is radically defective in the sense here contemplated is to urge upon him the adoption of those subsidiary values which, available even within his perspective, conduce to what is known as "civic good."

It is quite otherwise with the man or child who, touched by grace, has his will engaged by God in Christ. Here the radical defect of the natural will has been removed, not by himself but by his Savior, and, in the new heart given him, the groundwork has been laid for a veritable Christian character. But only the groundwork has been laid. Defects, deep and disturbing even though not of the radical sort, remain to mar the will. From these defects flow the secret lusts, the wayward affections, and the vaulting pride that belie our profession, stain our lives, and cast reproach upon our Lord. And these defects are basically intolerable.

Like the will, the conscience, too, is full of imperfections. Although it is a precondition of morality, the starting point of moral education, and implicated in everything that can be called good in human life, the conscience, through its deep connection with the fallen heart, and by its direct dependence upon the will, is radically defective.

Although conscience was meant to be the voice of God in man and therefore to speak in all men uniformly, it does not as a matter of fact echo God's words alone but also those of foreign gods, and so its deliverances within any individual are ambiguous and within the community of men self-contradictory. Also, it gives no clue, or at least provides no certain answer to the question: What is the ground and source of my obligation? Finally, the conscience has no power to enforce its demands. Its dictates can be and often are disobeyed.

Because conscience yields to opposition and submits to its own violation, there exists in the very center of our moral life, and of course in that of the child, a point of very considerable weakness, a point at which moral disintegration can set in. It is at this point that moral disintegration did set in on a wide social scale in the Hellenistic age. And it is here that it sets in with every one of us.

IV

Because of their defects, conscience and will, and indeed all of man's faculties and powers, should be amended and developed—i.e., *perfected*—and someone should undertake the job of perfecting them.

These statements assert a very great deal, and though on their face they appear incontrovertible, they cannot fairly be said to be mere truisms.

It is certainly not self-evident that the defective as such imposes obligations. It cannot easily be maintained that every defective thing should be mended or amended. It would seem that some things—like broken dishes— should rather be discarded and forgotten.

If to counter this a distinction is made between valuable things and worthless things, and it is argued that valuable things should always be salvaged and repaired, it could be replied that the use of the word "valuable" begs the whole question. It is of defective things we are talking, and defective things, to the degree that they are defective, are by definition not valuable.

If to counter this a distinction is made between things and persons, and it is argued that persons, whatever their defects, should always be perfected, it could be pointed out that such a statement involves one in several difficulties, not the least of them a difficulty in theology. Are we prepared to maintain that God is obliged to perfect every sinner and to leave none residing under his wrath?

One could go on in this fashion for a very long time, but enough has been said to indicate that the obligation to work at the moral improvement of imperfect and therefore immoral people is not a self-evident obligation. There have been those, indeed, who have refused to engage in the business, and they have come both from the left and from the right. Some cynics have with high indifference abandoned care and delivered everyone to his fate; and some who wished to be considered pious have delegated all the work to God.

What is one to say to these things?

It must be said at once that things that are absolutely defective do not require our solicitude. The absolutely bad cannot be meaningfully enjoined to perfect itself or to be perfected. Defects do not deserve and cannot bear improvement. They can only bear negation. But it is of the utmost importance to observe that defects never *are* just by themselves. They are dependent for their actuality and power upon some good, in which they inhere, and by whose sufferance they exist.

The *good*, without which evil and sin, defect and badness, cannot and do not exist, is of two sorts—created and uncreated. Both are opposed to evil, yet in some mysterious sense involved with it.

There is first the Uncreated Good, or God. He is in his nature the very antithesis of evil. No evil exists in him and no evil, wherever it exists, escapes his condemnation. Besides being opposed to evil in his essence, God is distinguished from it in the mode of his existence. He is concrete and personal, whereas evil is abstract and impersonal (even Satan is not evilness; he is a good angel gone incorrigibly bad). And God is absolute, existing eternally in and through himself, whereas evil is relative, existing inexplicably, not indeed by God's creative will, but nevertheless by his sufferance, in his plan, and under his control.

God did not create evil or evil things. But he did create. And the things he created were good. Among these things was man. And man was good in a twofold sense, corresponding to the twofold relation he sustained to God, the Ground and Source of all good. He was good as creature and he was good as son. He was good in his existence and he was good in his acknowledgments. He was ontologically good and he was morally good. He was good because he was tied to God by the tie of creation, and he was good because he clung to God by the adhesion of his will and affections.

Now when man fell it was not his entire goodness that he lost. He lost only his moral goodness, and this he lost centrally. His affections were transferred radically and completely to something else than God, and he became totally depraved, morally and spiritually, in such a way that none of his works was acceptable to God.

But he did not lose the value of his existence. This other sort of goodness, existing in his being and possessed by virtue of the creation, he could not lose, for it exists independently of his wickedness and regardless of his moral estate. It is indeed crippled, since it lacks the support of the other good with which it was once associated; it is impeded in its operations by its present association with moral depravity. But it is not in and of itself bad, but good.

Now that good thing in man which, though associated with radical evil and affected by it, retains its goodness, is a thing which God loves, which he created for himself, and which he wants to possess. He wants man to dedi-- cate it to him. Man is putting this good thing now into the service of false gods. He exercises his strong intelligence, his potent energies, all his excellent increased powers, in pursuing phantoms. God wants him not to do that, but to return to him those valuable assets with which he was originally and inalienably endowed. And so God *commands* him to return, and this command is what the whole of morality is about. This command is the call to be *perfected*.

There are two existences which cannot be perfected. One of these is God, who *is* perfect and above amendment. The other is sin, which, residing under an everlasting No, is delivered to condemnation, and for this reason is beyond amendment. The only kind of being that can be perfected is one which is both good and bad. Man is such a being. It is because he is *not* perfect that he can be urged to *become* perfect. On the other hand, it is only because he is *worth* perfecting, and because there is that in him which can *bear* perfecting, that he is addressed at all. Being imperfect he is yet perfectible.

We have thus arrived by a circuitous route at an answer to the objection raised against our thesis that conscience and will should be amended, developed, perfected. It had been objected that since they were defective they should perhaps be simply ignored or condemned. The answer to the objection is that they are *goods*—valuable, worthy, precious—to be retrieved for God who gave them.

V

If we concede that defective people should be perfected, we have to fix upon the agent of this perfecting. Who perfects whom? Could it not be that each is responsible for himself, and for none other? If this be thought intolerable, and it be maintained that every individual, and certainly every child, needs the assistance of another, does it follow that it is the assistance of a school teacher that he needs? Might not his parents suffice, and wouldn't they surely suffice if they were Christians, the kind of people who maintain Christian schools? What have the schools to do with moral education anyhow? Is this not the function of the home, as spiritual education is the function of the church? And aren't the schools sufficiently engaged with the training of the intellect, the culture of the mind? In answer to all these questions it must be said that moral education is a co-operative affair.

Moral perfecting waits, in the first instance, upon *God's grace and Spirit*. Only a saved man can be a truly good man, for only such a man has his will detached from the false values which in their variety break up his integrity, in their non-existence leave him without anchorage, and in their falsity vitiate all his natural powers.

But it waits, too, upon the unceasing efforts at self-improvement of the *individual* who, redeemed by grace, is called upon to work out his salvation with fear and trembling. The chief human agent of moral perfecting is no doubt the individual himself. His, and not some other man's, is the chief responsibility for his own perfecting. He can here as elsewhere be his own best friend or his own worst enemy. Unceasing efforts at self-improvement are enjoined upon every individual.

And yet it must be observed that *society* has not only a considerable stake in the goodness of the individuals who compose it, but an obligation to the individuals in this matter. Society owes us assistance in our efforts to be good. We have—and the child has a fortiori—a right to society's help. This right, like all rights, rests upon duties, in this instance the duty to be good. This duty implicates society, for how can a man articulate his goodness except among, in relation to, and by the corrections of his fellows? This fact is generally recognized by moralists, but no ethic has emphasized it as strongly as the Christian ethic. It is at the heart of Christianity's teaching that goodness is possible only in and by community—specifically, the redeemed community, the Kingdom of God.

Since the *church* lies at the very center of that Kingdom, is the agent for proclaiming the law of the Kingdom, and is the appointed medium for the communication of grace (in the economy of God the preached Word is the vehicle of his Spirit), the church plays a very important role in the development of Christian character.

And next to the church is the *home*. It is in the social unit called the family that morality finds its most natural and most intimate area of exercise. Here in the presence of father, mother, brother, and sister the child learns concretely what it means to be good. Here he learns, less by formal instruction than by example and by the exigencies of corporate existence, what Christian character and Christian behavior can and must be like.

But there is also the *school*. The school's responsibility in the training is plain the moment one recalls that the school is but the long arm of the family. It builds on, carries forward what was begun in the home, specifically the home established with the sanction and under the instruction of the church. But of course the school is neither the church nor the home, but a distinct agency with duties and responsibilities of its own. The peculiar function of the school is to *teach*. This means that in the area of morality its main job is *clarification*. This is not its only job. The teacher, like the minister on the one hand, and the father on the other, should set forth both by precept and example the pattern of the Christian life. Unless he does this he will alienate himself from church and home, as well as fail to maintain his moral authority. But his main job still is to clarify for the child the moral situation in which he finds himself, along with every human being.

What I have said above is an attempt, within a necessarily limited space, to help clarify that situation.

28

Catechesis:
On Using and Revising the Compendium

A.

IT HAS BEEN REPORTED that in teaching doctrine to catechumens only one half of the ministers of my church use the authorized compendium as a basic text. The others use either the old and superseded compendium or one or another of the numerous manuals of independent authorship available in the book shops. This is regrettable for a number of reasons.

In the first place, the existing state of affairs obscures the fact that catechesis is properly the work of the church. Catechesis is an ecclesiastical and not a personal undertaking. The minister functions in it not as a private individual but as an official of the church. This limits his prerogatives. Although he commands a wide area of freedom in which to express his individuality, he is hardly free to consult his own wishes in the selection of a statement of faith; and a catechetical manual is or ought to be a statement of faith, proceeding from the only body able to sanction one, the church.

Consider the rationale of this. Catechesis is the church in the process of teaching the young. When the church teaches, it teaches dogma, and when it teaches dogma it teaches the creeds. Catechesis, by that token, is the ecclesiastical communication to the young of the content of the creeds.

In the abstract there is no better way to teach the creeds than to place them directly before the student. This has many advantages, not the least of

---

This essay first appeared in *The Reformed Journal,* January and May 1952.

them being that the student learns at first hand the official position of the
church. But in catechesis the direct presentation of the creeds is hardly
feasible. The language of the creeds is in general too involved for the young,
and the matter is frequently too technical and discursive to be wholly intelligible. It is necessary, in consequence, to put some other, simpler text into
the student's hands. What text? None other, surely, than one prepared by
the church as a pedagogical substitute for the creeds. The creeds constitute
the church's statement of the truth; if this complex statement cannot be used
in catechesis, the church must make another that can be used. In the absence
of the creeds the church must provide a text that will adequately reflect and
safeguard the meaning of the creeds.

This is but to say that there must be an officially sanctioned "shorter
catechism," or compendium. Its content and its language should be ecclesiastically determined and controlled, and its employment ecclesiastically enjoined. In the pulpit the minister is required to comment on the Bible and the
catechism; in the classroom he should be required to comment on the compendium. There should be in his hands, and in those of his students, a basic,
shared, and official statement of Christian truth. Only in this way can the
church honor the fact that it, and not the individual minister, is the ultimate
agent of catechetical training.

$$* \quad * \quad * \quad * \quad *$$

It is to be observed, in the second place, that the use of variant texts
restricts the power of catechesis to form a single mind within the church. It
has been said that "an enlightened and intellectually homogeneous church
membership can be preserved only when fixed and uniform standards are
maintained." This is true. The creation of a common mind and a common
idiom in the church will be furthered by nothing so much as a common
manual of instruction. Let such a manual be everywhere employed and new
energies making for unity will immediately be released.

Consider the power the English Bible possessed to fashion the thought
and diction of the English people. Recall how the Dutch Psalter shaped in
our fathers a single heart and tongue. Think of how McGuffey's Readers,
because so widely used, created a common fund of ideas and expressions for
generations of Americans. With these examples before us, it is not romantic
to suppose that something similar could happen in the church were a classi-
cally formulated compendium to be taught in every classroom.

A culture, in the secular sense, is a homogeneous whole inspired by a
common spirit. Within that culture, in so far as it is not in process of disintegration, there reigns a common set of ideas and ideals expressible in a common
language and fed from a common source. I should like to think that our
Reformed community is such a homogeneous whole, and that we are all
concerned to keep it that. One way of doing so is by nurturing every
catechumen on a single text, a text by which each is raised to a common level
of spiritual and theological self-consciousness, a text to which in later years

each can refer in any company with every expectation of being understood, and around which popular discussions of religious questions can always profitably gather.

*   *   *   *   *

In view of all these considerations the failure of the authorized compendium to win its way to general acceptance is in every way regrettable. As a result of this failure there is a veritable welter of catechetical texts in use, a state of affairs which is quite unwholesome.

Fortunately, my church is doing something about it. Synod has instructed its permanent Committee on Education to take another look at the compendium and to improve it at the points where it is weak. It appears that weaknesses showed up in it when it was put to classroom use, and that it was these weaknesses, and nothing more sinister, that induced scores of ministers to lay the book aside.

According to the testimony gathered by the Committee on Education, the compendium is formally defective. Ministers allege that the answers are too long and involved to be readily apprehended by the young. The formulations suffer, they think, from too many adjectival and adverbial modifiers, and there is, they believe, too wide a use of archaic words and technical terms. As far as the evidence goes there is no complaint concerning the weight of the questions, the accuracy of the answers, or the arrangement of the material. The objections are all linguistic.

As already indicated, Synod took note of these objections, and finding them shared by its Committee on Education, instructed that committee to effect a revision. Unwilling to freeze the compendium at its present level of perfection, it is submitting it to a new critical scrutiny in order to get, in the end, a truly classical text capable by itself of winning the approval of all who are able to recognize excellence in the statement of Christian truth.

That the existing compendium does not always achieve maximum felicity in expression, and that it can stand improvement in pedagogical force and relevancy, is beyond all doubt. There is truth in what its critics say of it. The revision committee is therefore bound to take quite seriously all the objections raised against it. But it must take the objections critically, too, for problems lurk in them, and the way these are settled will determine to a great extent what kind of compendium emerges.

1. It is objected, for example, that there are too many complex sentences, too many modifiers, and too many technical terms in the compendium. Now if there are in fact too many of these, then there are too many, and some must be removed. But what is too many? and how is this determined?

Determinative here, I think, is what we wish a compendium to be. If we wish its formulations to be simple approximations to Christian truth designed for easy learning, we can cut a wide swath through the existing compendium. If, on the other hand, we wish its formulations to be full and exact *definitions*, we shall have to learn to live with a not inconsiderable number of technical terms, adverbial modifiers, and complex sentences. This is in the nature of the case. Truth is elusive, and to be held exactly it must be fenced in on every side by linguistic devices of the kind under consideration.

The compendium says, "Regeneration is that gracious and irresistible work of the Spirit by which. . . ." We can drop the "gracious and irresistible" and facilitate memorization, but we shall have to impoverish the truth to do so. Shall we say that the purity of the church is maintained through the preaching of the Word, the administration of the sacraments, and the exercise of discipline? or shall we say that it is maintained through the *pure* preaching, the *proper* administration, and the *faithful* exercise? Choices of this sort will have to be made at every turn.

The choice, I think, should always be for the richer and completer statement. The answer to each question should be the entire truth so far as it is known, but in its concentrated essence, from which through the years new insights can continue to be distilled. Every facet of the truth should be tied down with an appropriate word or phrase, so that every answer is big with possibilities for further theological reflection and development. The answers should be scientific formulae in which in briefest compass the whole truth is packed and folded.

2. It is objected that the existing compendium, probably because it attempts to be definitive, is hard to memorize. This may be conceded. Memorization is always hard, as is learning in general. The reason is, I suppose, that truth itself is hard to come by. But then, the catechism class is a school, and the significant question is: How insistent shall we be in that school on rigorous intellectual discipline; or, conversely, how willing are we to yield to contemporary pressures for lower standards of achievements?

The existing compendium is designed "for the instruction of those desiring to partake of the Lord's Supper." It is the book on which a young man rides into full membership in the church and by which he is qualified for such membership. He is eighteen years of age at the earliest when he lays it down. He began its study presumably when he was twelve. Is it now being contended that during the six years he was being drilled in it, and receiving explanations of it, he was able neither to memorize nor to understand it?

In its report to the Synod the Committee on Education declared, "The criticisms of the Revised Compendium which we have encountered all have to do with pedagogical difficulties in the *memorizing* and *understanding* of the lessons by the catechumens." Let the existence of the difficulties be granted. The question is: Are the difficulties greater than those demanded by the enterprise, and are they, in the long run, beyond the growing capacities of the average catechumen?

It is possible that a boy of twelve, just entering junior high school, has trouble memorizing certain of the propositions in the compendium, and it is possible that his understanding of none of them is complete. But education is a *process*, and given time he will learn his lessons, provided he is both incited and required to learn them. The present compendium was not meant to be communicated in a day, nor even in a year. It is the sort of thing that a catechumen matures in, and that, when he is mature, he rests in. And this, I should think, is the way it ought to be.

At eighteen nowadays a young man is practically committed to college or to a job. With what knowledge of Christian truth in their possession will the church project her young men into the world: with thin slices of information readily picked up, or with richer portions of knowledge, acquired only by effort and discipline, but able to occupy and satisfy a mind grown to maturity? The way we answer this question will affect the way we revise the compendium.

B.

The word "truth" has a number of meanings.

Taken absolutely, truth is predicable only of *God*. This is so both because God is the only completely self-conscious person, and because his mind and thought constitute the ultimate standard of all truth.

In a secondary and derivative sense *created things* are true. Because God created things in accordance with his eternal thought of them, they possess and embody truth. A stone, for example, is true in that it exhibits in its being and structure the divine idea entertained of it even before it entered into existence.

In a third and still more derivative sense, *human thoughts and judgments* are true. I have an adequate idea of a stone when my thought conforms to the structure of the stone as that is guaranteed by the will and intellect of God. My judgments concerning a stone are true when they are validated by the stone and by God who stands behind it.

It is only at a fourth remove that *language* is true. Words are meaningful when they convey an intelligible idea. Statements are true when they give adequate expression to a correct mental judgment about an objectively existing fact embraced in the mind of God.

Truth, therefore, has God as its source and things as its embodiment. Truth requires mind to apprehend it and language to express it. God is truth itself. A thing is truth in creaturely existence. A thought, when sound, is truth apprehended. Language, when adequate, is truth expressed.

*   *   *   *   *

Error and falsity are the enemies of truth, but these can enter at only two points. There can be no error in God, for he is absolute truth. Neither can there be error in things, for these are truly, though derivatively, what they are. Error can enter only on the levels of thought and speech. The mind can err, and language can err; God and things cannot.

The mind errs when it conceives, judges, or reasons falsely. When this occurs language can do nothing but perpetuate the error, for language is subordinate to thought and cannot purify and correct it. It can only follow it, adequately or inadequately. Mind, however, is under no compulsion to err. By taking care it can apprehend and discern correctly. It cannot do this without divine illumination, and it cannot do this comprehensively, but it can do this genuinely. Knowledge, though partial, is possible.

And knowledge, when secured, can be expressed. It can be translated into speech. Thought can take on the form of words. The idea can be bodied forth in symbols. Through a wise disposition of God an adequate correspondence can be set up between truth and language. This correspondence cannot be established, of course, without effort. To reveal truth, language must be carefully fitted to the chastened thought. It must be painstakingly fashioned and selectively applied. This takes doing. Words must be chosen that are supple enough to follow the sinuousness of truth and exact enough to contain it. And they must be properly arranged in due order. To do all this is not easy, but the job can be done, and when it is done we have every right to call our formulae true—not absolutely true indeed, but nevertheless genuinely and adequately true.

Of course, our formulae are not always true even in the limited way proper to man. Sometimes they fall short of what they could and ought to be. Even when our thought is true and our understanding sound, we may, and sometimes do, fail to bridge the gap between comprehension and expression. We sometimes fail to fit the word to the idea. With inept language we falsify the truth we know. Through the employment of bad words we corrupt good notions.

Whenever this happens someone who shares our conception of the truth will sooner or later press for a revision of our language. He will urge that we bring our language into accord with truth. And we are bound to comply. Responsible calls for such linguistic revisions cannot be ignored. Because truth is precious no man in our communion who suggests "It would be truer to say . . ." may be dismissed without a hearing. Honest proposals to increase the truth-content of our formulae are always in order.

*　　*　　*　　*　　*

Now it is possible for a person to take exception to language not because it is thought to be in error, but for quite another reason. While freely acknowledging that a given text is in complete accord with truth a man may object to its style and manner. He will then complain not that the language is untrue but that it is uncouth. Granting the material soundness of the diction he will consider it to be formally defective. Accordingly, he will wish to see it purged, not of errors, which it has not, but of certain rhetorical impurities which it allegedly does have. He will wish, for example, to see all archaisms, barbarisms, and jargon removed, and the whole made more modern, simple, uniform, and mellifluous. Such a man would not be far from representing what Synod desired when it charged its Committee on Education to revise the compendium.

The position just outlined assumes that language can be at once both materially sound and formally defective. The assumption is correct. Language can be true yet uncouth, exact yet styleless. The reason for this is that language moves simultaneously on two different planes. It has both a vertical and a horizontal reference. In its vertical reference language is oriented to idea. In its horizontal reference it is oriented to its own immanent canons of excellence. To be completely successful, therefore, it must attend to two things at once. While accommodating itself on one plane to truth it must on another be fashioning itself into a thing of beauty. This double action is difficult and the thing doesn't always come off. Sometimes language achieves style and beauty but fails to be true; at other times it reaches truth but comes out rough hewn. In either case it has to be revised.

If now we assume that the language of the compendium is of the latter sort—true but formally defective—then not material alteration but only verbal modification is required to render it acceptable. The committee, I think, realized this. It set out, therefore, merely to polish the language in its formal sense.

But there are hazards in this kind of work, as in every other. The job which the committee undertook moves on the horizontal plane, and persons at work at it are apt to slight the vertical even though it touches the horizontal at every point and thus cannot but be modified by operations on the latter plane. Polishers of language are apt to forget that every word and phrase has two dimensions and that an adjustment of language to the canons of style may put it out of relation to the truth. I think the framers of the new revision forgot this. I think that when they made certain formal alterations they unwittingly introduced material error. The committee has completed only nineteen questions and yet of this small total a great many effect what I cannot but regard as an *unwanted* change in the truth content of the compendium. Let me illustrate what I mean.

1. The old compendium answers the first question of the catechism by saying, "My only comfort is that I, with body and soul, both in life and death, am not my own, but belong to my faithful Savior Jesus Christ."

It is not difficult to see what in that answer would strike the attention of revisers concerned to polish and streamline. What would strike them is, first, the "I" standing at such distance from the "am," and, then, the two juxtaposed prepositional phrases. It was precisely these elements, it appears, which offended the committee, for they were purged. In the draft of the revisers the first question is answered in this way: "My only comfort in life and death is that, with body and soul, I am not my own, but belong to my faithful Savior Jesus Christ."

This is an obvious attempt to modify the language in accordance with the canons of simplicity. But observe what has happened meanwhile to the theology of the catechism. The catechism is here made to say that *in death* I have the comfort that I belong to my savior. Now the catechism says something quite other than this. This, it says, is my *present* comfort, that whether I live or whether I die I am the Lord's. According to the revisers my only comfort *now* is that with body and soul I am the Lord's. This is great comfort indeed. But not so great a comfort as that described by the catechism or the old compendium.

2. As its third question the old compendium asked: "Whence do you know your sin and misery?" Notice that word "whence." It's an old word, no longer in popular usage. Put it in a room with a committee of revisers and it has no chance of survival. It is accordingly gone from the question framed by the committee. The proposed question asks: "What teaches you your sin and misery?"

On this I should like to remark that I have no prejudices in favor of obsolete words. But until a better word is offered in exchange I will keep "whence." Surely we cannot pluck this little mote and put that beam in our eye which the committee offers. Let the reader decide who sins more against the English language, the man who says "whence" or he who says "what teaches"?

Furthermore, the substitute question goes counter both to the spirit of the catechism and the realities of the spiritual life. What man or child, concerned about his soul, goes about asking, "What teaches me my sin?" What he asks is "How can I get to know myself as I truly am; where am I revealed in all my nakedness?" And this is in effect the question that the catechism and the old compendium ask and answer.

3. The fourth question that the old compendium asks is this: "Where are the principles of God's law laid down?" Notice that phrase "laid down." A reviser is bound to stumble over that. For one thing it is two words, and for another it is uncommon. It is accordingly deleted from the version of the committee. The revisers frame the question in this way: "Where are the principles of God's law expressed?" This is presumably better language.

But observe what happens on the vertical plane. Consider the truth that has been lost. The old compendium had declared that "the principles of God's law are laid down in the Ten Commandments." To understand the full import of this statement one must ask oneself what sort of "being" or "existence" principles enjoy. Principles obviously in some sense "are." But in what sense? The answer is that principles are "put" or "posited" or "laid down" by a mind, just as laws are "enacted" by a lawgiver. Only thereafter are they "expressed," and they can be "expressed" by anybody at all. When God wrote the Tables of the Law with his own fingers, this was more than a mere "expression" of the principles of morality. It was a "putting" of them, a "laying down" of them. To regard the ten commandments as the "expression" of God's law is to derogate from their high dignity and authority. Moreover, the ten commandments do not "express" the principles of God's law; they *are* or *constitute* the principles of God's law.

4. In the seventh question the old compendium asks, "Did God create man wicked and perverse?" The revisers ask, "Was man created wicked and perverse?" At some other time I may wish to comment, among many other things, upon that shift to the passive voice, but now I am concerned only with the answer to this question.

In answer to its question the old compendium says, "God created man good and in his own image, endowed with true knowledge, righteousness, and holiness." Notice that word "endowed." It's a good word, but it's old, and it must go. Accordingly the revisers answer, "Man was created good and in God's own image, which means that man had true knowledge, righteousness, and holiness." Notice that phrase "which means." It is preferred to "endowed." And then notice what it does to doctrine and to truth. Reflect on what the substitution does to theology. It is here declared that to say that "Man was created good and in God's own image" is equivalent to saying that "Man had true knowledge, righteousness, and holiness." The members of the committee know better, but they were staring at that word "endowed," and they lost sight of truth.

5. In the eleventh question the old compendium asks, "What are the results of Adam's disobedience?" This same query is made by the revisers in their question thirteen.

To this question the old compendium answers, "The guilt of Adam as our covenant head is imputed to all men, and our nature is become totally corrupt, so that we are all conceived and born in sin." As in the other instances already noted, the key to the committee's mind is found in the uncommon word. In the present instance it is the word "imputed." Being uncommon, it must go. The revisers accordingly delete it. The compendium is a book on theology, the only book on theology that the vast majority of catechumens will ever read, but the word "imputed" must not appear in it. It must not appear in it even though Reformed theology is unthinkable without it. See what happens in its absence.

The old compendium had said, "The guilt of Adam as our covenant head is imputed to all men." The revisers say, "Adam's disobedience brought guilt upon us all." Compare these theologies. In the first formulation Adam's guilt is "laid upon us" by *someone*, namely God. In the second, an impersonal *act*, "Adam's disobedience," is thought of as an *agent* bringing guilt upon us.

But more. The old compendium said, "Our nature is become totally corrupt. . . ." The revisers say, "Adam's disobedience brought . . . total depravity into our nature." Consider what is here said. It was bad enough to ascribe agency to disobedience; it is worse to hypostatize total depravity and represent it as a substance "brought" into us. With this kind of language we can't teach doctrine. This language is calculated only to confuse the mind and obscure the truth. These words do not reveal; they hide.

29

The Shape of Excellence

IN WHAT FOLLOWS I have undertaken to make some comments upon "The Shape of Excellence." This is a somewhat hazardous undertaking, for it appears to be self-involving. I do not mean it to be so, however, and I hope no one will so regard it. I have a vision of the shape of excellence, I admit, but the vision, such as it is, is a gift conferred, or perhaps a reading taken off the lives of distinguished men, but it is in no way self-involving or biographical. Just as a delicate physician in fragile health is himself no example of what he sponsors, so I am not a model of that shape which from a distance I admire. If I serve it at all it is by pointing to and recommending it.

When the word "excellence" is uttered the word "excel" obtrudes, and I should like to caution against licensing that obtrusion. It is no doubt good in some sense to excel. But in most contexts the word carries noxious overtones. It is obviously a relative term, and it makes comparisons—usually odious. It involves other people, and it involves them negatively—by putting them down. To excel means to surpass, outdo, outstrip, and eclipse someone else, and the will to excel is the will to visit defeat, failure, or, at best, second-rank upon the other. This, in most areas of life, is not good, for in these, including academia, we are called not to rivalry, but to unity, cooperation, and helpfulness.—I am aware, of course, that there are contexts in which one is enjoined to excel. The realm of competitive sports is one of these. Here a carefully structured adversary relationship is set up, and rule-regulated

---

This speech was presented at the honors convocation at Calvin College on May 8, 1975.

rivalry is playfully enacted. Under these conditions one should try to excel; here cooperation is contraband. If something is billed as rivalry, let it be serious, even though controlled, rivalry; seize every advantage, give the opponent no quarter, and strive to come in first. In contests one should be out to win. But life as a whole is not a contest; it is a social venture. And in life one should try not to excel, but rather to put on excellence.

"Excellence" is hard to define, and I shall not even try to formulate a definition of it. I must attempt a characterization of it, however, and I shall accordingly suggest that excellence can be viewed from both an ontological and an ethico-religious point of view—both descriptively and evaluationally. I start with the first.

The word "excellence" is clearly not a socially relative term; it does not, like the word "excel," compare people and establish a distance between them. It seems rather to name something in people, but then not this quality or that in them, but the fullest and most harmonious development of all qualities resident within them.—If this be so the word has ontological overtones; it suggests the actualization and integration of potentialities. From this point of view God, understood as Being itself, possesses the highest excellence, and excellence is in fact what Scripture repeatedly ascribes to him. But excellence of this ontic sort can also be found in human beings, though of course in finite measure and in diverse forms. Because all of us are temporal creatures in process of development, no one of us is truly excellent; and because all of us are individuals with unique gifts and callings, such excellence as we have or can acquire is fully shared by no other. Both because we are in process and because we are individuals we occupy different points upon the moving and unending line of life.

Descriptively speaking, then, the general shape of excellence is harmonious actualization. The particular shape and size of it, however, vary with time, place, circumstance, and function. There is the excellence of the child and of the adult, of the philosopher and of the musician, of the farmer and of the carpenter, of the boxer and of the runner—and so on ad infinitum. There is no need, or even warrant, for entering upon a discussion of all these, but perhaps a word could be said about excellence in students.

Excellence in students is normally measured by grades, sometimes evoked by prizes and the promises of degrees and titles, and almost always induced and established by structures and processes of education. What then does it mean to educate? There are at least two ways of conceiving of the process.

From one point of view, to educate a person is to lead him out. It is to make him blossom forth, to unfold his wings. It is to give him his native dimensions, to evoke his essential humanness. In this view education adds nothing to the student: it simply elicits what he already has.—What he has are his potentialities. In school, with the cooperation of teachers and fellow students, his potentialities are actualized. By pedagogic art the involuted personality of the student unfolds and emerges. In this view of education the student is recognized as himself a tiny world—a microcosm—in which the whole of created reality is contained and able to be exhibited. The whole school is there to help make the exhibition, to let the whole cosmos come into focus at this point.

From another point of view, education is not a process of leading a student out, but a process of impressing something upon him. In this view the student is relatively unshaped and malleable stuff in need of patterning. The student in this view requires structuring, and education is the process of providing it. It is the process of giving form to his mind and spirit, and also to his movement.—The important question here concerns the nature and the source of the form employed in the structuring. One school may wish to form the student according to the pattern of a particular society. Another may wish to bring him into conformity with a particular tradition of thought and action. Neither is quite satisfactory. What students must be patterned by is nothing but reality itself. Reality has an increated structure. The world—the macrocosmos—is patterned being. It has its order and configurations, its laws and uniformities. It is within these orders and structures that the student exists. They constitute his environment, being the context and matrix of his life. It is to them that he must conform. And the only real way in which he can conform to them is by being informed by them. Education is this process of in-forming students, of patterning them according to the structure of reality, of imprinting on them the face of being. The means employed in this process are the generic sciences, man's transcripts of the patterns that structure the cosmos. Through them the student is brought into contact with every basic aspect of reality and, these aspects entering into him, he acquires, when education is perfect, all the various dimensions of the cosmos, and he recapitulates the world.

In either view of education, what the good school attempts to achieve is humanness. To be educated is to have received an inner structuring of mind and life, in accordance with our nature and the nature of the cosmos. It is not to have acquired information merely: education and erudition are not the same. Nor is it to have acquired a manual skill; mastery of a technique is, in itself, no sign of being educated. Education is the transformation of one's person, the structuring of one's being. It is not something one puts on as a cloak; it is what enters creatively onto the deeper levels of our being, and fashions us. Through education, properly conceived, a student is enlarged from within. He acquires the dimensions of a man and achieves a clearer vision, a new sensitiveness, a larger reach, a firmer grasp, and greater poise.—The student who can be thus characterized will have achieved a certain excellence, for he will have been filled out and integrated by the larger reality which lies in, around, and beyond him.

But excellence of this sort is not enough. An acute intelligence, a well-stocked mind, a focused eye, a disciplined taste, a dexterous hand, an integrated personality, an affable manner, and whatever other things of this sort could be mentioned, are not enough. They are not enough because they are, as such, morally and spiritually neutral—i.e., they can be set upon evil ends as well as upon good, and serve the kingdom of darkness as well as the kingdom of light. True excellence requires not only the full and harmonious actualization of our resident powers, but their proper orientation.

Christian education, in distinction from education in general, seeks to foster this orientation and to support and strengthen it when and where it exists, but it cannot, alas, engender it. For its engendering there is needed a gracious incursion into this world of a God who lays our erstwhile values and native orientations under judgment, and beckons us to enter into a new and better existence. It is the thesis of Christianity that such an incursion has been made, and that through it a Kingdom is in the making which will truly humanize mankind, because it is able to make men partakers of the divine nature, in which paradigmatic excellence consists. Entrance into that kingdom is by repentance—i.e., by a repudiation of our erstwhile orientations and values—and by faith—i.e., by adhesion to and trust in him through whom God dwelt savingly among us, and in whom we are perfected, made truly excellent.

As to the shape of this excellence, there are many passages of Scripture which delineate it, two of which I now commend to you. In the first chapter of his second letter to the churches, Peter tells his readers that the divine power of Christ

> ... has granted to us all things that pertain to life and godliness, through the knowledge of him who called us to his own glory and excellence, by which he has granted to us his precious and very great promises, that through these you may ... become partakers of the divine nature.
>   For this very reason, make every effort to supplement your faith with virtue, and virtue with knowledge, and knowledge with self-control, and self-control with steadfastness, and steadfastness with godliness, and godliness with brotherly affection, and brotherly affection with love. For if these things are yours and abound, they keep you from being ineffective or unfruitful in the knowledge of our Lord Jesus Christ.

The Petrine formula for excellence seems, accordingly, to be this:

Have *faith* in Christ: put your trust in him and commit yourself to his cause;
To Christian faith add *virtue*, or moral goodness;
That virtue may be rightly formed, add *knowledge*, prudence, wisdom;
That knowledge and wisdom may be gained, add *temperance*, or self-control;
That temperance may continue, add *patience*, endurance, fortitude, perseverance, *hope*;

That hope and patience may be retained, add *godliness* and piety;

That godliness may not be alone, add *brotherly kindness* (*philadelphia*) as this shines forth in the Holy Community, the church;

That brotherly affection may be enlarged and function redemptively, add *love* (*agape*) to all mankind.

And then there is this word of St. Paul:

Finally, brethren, whatever is true, whatever is honorable, whatever is just, whatever is pure, whatever is lovely, whatever is gracious, if there is any *excellence*, if there is anything worthy of praise, think about these things—and do them; and the God of peace be with you.